Sally J. Stevens, PhD
Andrew R. Morral, PhD
Editors

Adolescent Substance Abuse Treatment in the United States
Exemplary Models from a National Evaluation Study

Pre-publication
REVIEWS,
COMMENTARIES,
EVALUATIONS . . .

"Contributors to *Adolescent Substance Abuse Treatment in the United States* have done an excellent job of providing summaries for ten different substance abuse treatment programs for adolescents. All treatment programs were funded by the Substance Abuse and Mental Health Services Administration (SAMHSA) and are being evaluated using the Global Appraisal of Individual Needs (GAIN).

Several aspects of this book make it a useful reference for practitioners, applied researchers, and educators. The book begins with a chapter that provides a foundation for the following chapters, each of which presents a summary of a different treatment model.

Readers will find that this first chapter provides a concise background and history of adolescent substance abuse and evaluation of treatment programs. The descriptions of GAIN, the evaluation used by the SAMHSA-funded treatments is easy to read and will be useful for applied researchers and evaluators. The remaining ten chapters summarize the various treatment models. Especially useful is the grouping of treatments by type including outpatient, family-oriented outpatient, residential, and modified therapeutic community. Educators and practitioners will find this organization useful in comparing and contrasting treatments."

Mari S. Wilhelm, PhD
Director, Institute for Children,
Youth, and Families,
University of Arizona

More pre-publication
REVIEWS, COMMENTARIES, EVALUATIONS . . .

"*Adolescent Substance Abuse Treatment in the United States* is the result of a unique and successful collaboration among scientists, drug treatment programs, and the federal government. Each chapter is a pleasure to read because of the attention to detail and sensitivity to the scientific-practitioner audience. All the major treatment models are addressed—from clinical and developmental perspectives—giving the reader a clear understanding as to how the model logically addresses the addictive process and related problems for young people. This book will be a valuable resource for professionals who serve and study drug-abusing youth."

Ken C. Winters, PhD
Director, Center for Adolescent Substance Abuse Research, University of Minnesota

"The field of adolescent substance abuse treatment comes of age with this impressive new volume. A wide range of state-of-the-art models of treatment for substance-abusing youth are provided. Of particular note is the broad overview of historical context and overall system characteristics of treatment for substance-abusing adolescents that is provided. Each program model is thoroughly described, including its theoretical underpinnings as well as the unique geographic and cultural context in which the program model has been developed and implemented. A broad range of issues are described for each model, including typical client characteristics, therapeutic components and treatment curricula, staffing patterns, hands-on issues with implementation, assessment, and patient placement protocols, development of treatment plans, and evaluation designs. Areas that differentiate substance abuse treatment for adolescents from that of adult-oriented treatment have been emphasized, such as the need to address identity formation and developmental issues within treatment, involvement of family members in the treatment process, integration of academic issues within a therapeutic context, approaches to delinquency and conduct problems, the role of the peer group in treatment and recovery, age-appropriate skill development, and flexible and individualized treatment responses.

Treatment practitioners will turn to this book to learn about therapeutic interventions that have been modified or developed specifically for substance-abusing adolescents, including family therapy and family systems treatment, therapeutic communities, cognitive behavioral approaches, culturally competent treatment for members of ethnic groups, milieu therapy, linkages and cross-system interventions, behavioral therapies, motivational interviewing, twelve-step participation, and 'step-down' and continuing care models. Special topics pertaining to substance-abusing youth are highlighted, such as exposure to trauma, psychiatric comorbidity, involvement in the juvenile justice or social services systems, and gender differences. Researchers and evaluators will find a range of study designs, assessment tools and schedules, quantitative and qualitative data-collection protocols, and study hypotheses that can guide the development of future studies. In all, this new volume sets a new standard for future program development in the field of adolescent substance abuse treatment."

Christine Grella, PhD
Associate Research Psychologist, UCLA Integrated Substance Abuse Programs/Neuropsychiatric Institute

More pre-publication
REVIEWS, COMMENTARIES, EVALUATIONS . . .

"*Adolescent Substance Abuse Treatment in the United States* provides a profile of the range of treatment programs that participated in the Adolescent Treatment Models project, funded by the Substance Abuse and Mental Health Service Administration's Center for Substance Abuse Treatment (CSAT). There are relatively few publications that have presented a compendium of treatment programs addressing adolescent substance use and abuse; this volume is a contribution to the field."

Nancy Jainchill, PhD
Deputy Director,
Center for Therapeutic Community Research,
National Development & Research Institutes,
New York City

The Haworth Press®
New York • London • Oxford

Adolescent Substance Abuse Treatment in the United States

Exemplary Models from a National Evaluation Study

THE HAWORTH PRESS
Drugs and Society
Bernard Segal
Mario De la Rosa
Senior Editors

Adolescent Substance Abuse Treatment in the United States:
Exemplary Models from a National Evaluation Study
edited by Sally J. Stevens and Andrew R. Morral

Adolescent Substance Abuse Treatment in the United States

Exemplary Models from a National Evaluation Study

Sally J. Stevens, PhD
Andrew R. Morral, PhD
Editors

The Haworth Press®
New York • London • Oxford

The Haworth Press, Inc., 10 Alice Street, Binghamton, NY 13904-1580.

Cover design by Lora Wiggins.

Library of Congress Cataloging-in-Publication Data

Adolescent substance abuse treatment in the United States : exemplary models from a national evaluation study / Sally J. Stevens, Andrew R. Morral, editors.
    p. cm.
  Includes bibliographical references and index.
  ISBN 0-7890-1606-0 (alk. paper) — ISBN 0-7890-1607-9 (soft)
  1. Teenagers—Substance use—United States. 2. Substance abuse—Treatment—United States—Evaluation. I. Stevens, Sally J. II. Morral, Andrew R.

RJ506.D78 A3645 2002
362.29'0835—dc21

2002068758

CONTENTS

SECTION IV: RESIDENTIAL TREATMENT MODELS

Chapter 6. Mountain Manor Treatment Center: Residential Adolescent Addictions Treatment Program   135

Marc Fishman
Philip Clemmey
Hoover Adger

Chapter 7. Culturally Competent Substance Abuse Treatment for American Indian and Alaska Native Youths   155

Candice Stewart-Sabin
Mark Chaffin

Chapter 11. Thunder Road Adolescent Substance Abuse Treatment Program 257

Patricia Shane
Linda Cherry
Tom Gerstel

ABOUT THE EDITORS

Sally J. Stevens, PhD, is a research professor with the Southwest Institute for Research on Women at the University of Arizona. Dr. Stevens has worked in the field of substance abuse and specifically on the negative health consequences of substance abuse for over fifteen years as both a clinician and a researcher. She has received numerous large-scale federal grants to administer and research innovative drug treatment programs for women and their children as well as for adolescent populations. Dr. Stevens is widely published in the area of women and adolescent health, particularly on issues that encompass the concerns of underserved, disenfranchised minority populations. She is the editor of *Women, Drug Use, and HIV Infection; Women and Substance Abuse: Gender Transparency;* and *HIV Risk, Prevention Strategies, and AIDS Care for American Indians and Alaska Natives.*

Andrew R. Morral, PhD, is Associate Director of RAND's criminal justice program and a behavioral scientist in its Drug Policy Research Center. His research examines behavioral treatments for adolescent and adult substance abusers. He has worked closely with criminal justice agencies and community treatment providers to develop program evaluation strategies and treatment planning instruments.

CONTRIBUTORS

Loree Adams, MSW, LCSW, is affiliated with Chestnut Health Systems, Bloomington, Illinois.

Hoover Adger, MD, is affiliated with Mountain Manor Treatment Center; and Johns Hopkins University School of Medicine, Department of Pediatrics, Adolescent Medicine Program, Baltimore, Maryland.

Martha Barron, BS, is Senior Survey Interviewer, Southwest Institute for Research on Women, University of Arizona, Tucson, Arizona.

Robert J. Battjes, DSW, is affiliated with the Social Research Center, Friends Research Institute, Inc., Baltimore, Maryland.

Kirsten Becker, MA, is affiliated with the Drug Policy Research Center, RAND, Santa Monica, California.

Douglas Carl, BA, is Assistant Research Scientist, Services Research, Research Foundation for Mental Hygiene, New York State Office of Alcoholism and Substance Abuse Services, Albany, New York.

Karen Carlini, CASAC, is Associate Director, Dynamic Youth Community, Inc., Brooklyn, New York.

Theodora Carter, MC, MA, is affiliated with EMPACT-SPC, Tempe, Arizona.

Mark Chaffin, PhD, is affiliated with the Center for Child Abuse and Neglect and is co-investigator and Associate Professor, Pediatrics, University of Oklahoma Health Sciences Center, Oklahoma City, Oklahoma.

Linda Cherry, MA, is an independent consultant in Albany, California.

Philip Clemmey, PhD, is a research director, Potomac Healthcare Foundation, Baltimore, Maryland.

Samia Dawud-Noursi, PhD, is Deputy Project Director for Research and Evaluation, Knowledge Development and Application, Logicon, ROW Sciences, Inc., Rockville, Maryland.

Michael L. Dennis, PhD, is Senior Research Psychologist, Chestnut Health Systems, Lighthouse Institute, Bloomington, Illinois.

Patricia Ebener, MA, is affiliated with the Drug Policy Research Center, RAND, Santa Monica, California.

Barbara D. Estrada, MS, is affiliated with the Southwest Institute for Research on Women, University of Arizona, Tucson, Arizona.

Marc Fishman, MD, is Assistant Professor, Department of Psychiatry and Behavioral Sciences, Johns Hopkins University School of Medicine, Baltimore, Maryland; and Mountain Manor Treatment Center, Baltimore, Maryland.

William Fusco, CASAC, is Executive Director, Dynamic Youth Community, Inc., Brooklyn, New York.

Patricia Garcia, BS, is Research Technician, Southwest Institute for Research on Women, University of Arizona, Tucson, Arizona.

Tom Gerstel, BA, is Administrative Director, Adolescent Treatment Centers, Inc., d.b.a. Thunder Road, Oakland, California.

Susan Harrington Godley, RhD, is affiliated with Chestnut Health Systems, Bloomington, Illinois.

Michael Gordon, MA, is affiliated with the Social Research Center, Friends Research Institute, Inc., Baltimore, Maryland.

Joseph Hasler, PhD, is Clinical Psychologist, CODAC Behavioral Health Services, Inc., Tucson, Arizona.

Tanya L. Hedges, MA, is Research Scientist, Services Research, Research Foundation for Mental Hygiene, New York State Office of Alcoholism and Substance Abuse Services, Albany, New York.

Lisa H. Jaycox, PhD, is affiliated with the Drug Policy Research Center, RAND, Santa Monica, California.

Elizabeth C. Katz, PhD, is affiliated with the Social Research Center, Friends Research Institute, Inc., Baltimore, Maryland.

Timothy W. Kinlock, PhD, is affiliated with the Social Research Center, Friends Research Institute, Inc., Baltimore, Maryland.

Howard Liddle, EdD, is Professor and Director, Center for Treatment Research on Adolescent Drug Abuse, Department of Epidemiology and Public Health, University of Miami School of Medicine, Miami, Florida.

Melissa McDermeit, MSW, is Research Associate, Chestnut Health Systems, Bloomington, Illinois.

Randolph D. Muck, MEd, is Project Officer and Public Health Advisor, Systems Development and Integration Branch, Center for Substance Abuse Treatment, Substance Abuse and Mental Health Services Administration, Rockville, Maryland.

Bridget S. Murphy is Research Specialist, Southwest Institute for Research on Women, University of Arizona, Tucson, Arizona.

Elizabeth Parker-Sloat, MA, is Research Assistant, Center for Treatment Research on Adolescent Drug Abuse, Department of Epidemiology and Public Health, University of Miami School of Medicine, Miami, Florida.

Patricia D. Perry, PhD, is Principal Investigator and Research Scientist, Services Research, Research Foundation for Mental Hygiene, New York State Office of Alcoholism and Substance Abuse Services, Albany, New York.

Zöe Powis, BS, is Senior Survey Interviewer, Southwest Institute for Research on Women, University of Arizona, Tucson, Arizona.

Lynn Reinardy, MC, CPC, is affiliated with EMPACT-SPC, Tempe, Arizona.

Richard Risberg, MA, CRADC, LCPC, is affiliated with Chestnut Health Systems, Bloomington, Illinois.

Cynthia Rowe, PhD, is Research Assistant Professor, Center for Treatment Research on Adolescent Drug Abuse, Department of Epidemiology and Public Health, University of Miami School of Medicine, Miami, Florida.

Nicholas Salerno, CASAC, is Program Director, Fallsburg Facility, Dynamic Youth Community, Inc., Fallsburg, New York.

James Schneider is Program Director, Dynamic Youth Community, Inc., Brooklyn, New York.

Seth Schwartz, PhD, is Postdoctoral Fellow, Center for Treatment Research on Adolescent Drug Abuse, Department of Epidemiology and Public Health, University of Miami School of Medicine, Miami, Florida.

Emily A. Sears, MS, is affiliated with Epoch Counseling Center, Catonsville, Maryland, Friends Research Institute, Inc., Baltimore, Maryland.

Valerie Seitz, BS, is affiliated with the Southwest Institute for Research on Women, University of Arizona, Tucson, Arizona.

Mark Senior, MC, is Program Coordinator, Southwest Institute for Research on Women, University of Arizona, Tucson, Arizona.

Patricia Shane, PhD, MPH, is Senior Research Scientist, Public Health Institute, Berkeley, California.

William Smith, MA, is affiliated with the Phoenix Academy of Lake View Terrace, Lake View Terrace, California.

Alan Sodetz, PhD, is affiliated with Chestnut Health Systems, Bloomington, Illinois.

Candice Stewart-Sabin, PhD, is affiliated with Our Youth Our Future, Inc., Farmington, New Mexico; and Principal Investigator and Clinical Director, Four Corners Regional Adolescent Treatment Center, Shiprock, New Mexico.

Tara Swartz, BS, is a Survey Interviewer Senior with the Southwest Institute for Research on Women, University of Arizona, Tucson, Arizona.

Rebekah Taylor, MS, is Project Director, Arizona's Children Association, Tucson, Arizona.

Preface

Substance abuse disorders among adolescents are a serious public health concern. As the number of adolescents presenting for treatment to the nation's public treatment systems continues to increase, the urgency for effective substance abuse treatment models also continues to increase. Few evaluation studies on the effectiveness of adolescent substance abuse treatment have been conducted. Those that have been conducted are limited by the variety of different programs and undefined approaches evaluated, along with problems related to small samples and marginal follow-up rates. Moreover, the field lacks manualized treatment approaches that can be easily disseminated to treatment providers who work with our nation's substance involved youth (see Dennis et al., Chapter 1).

To address the need for evaluating, documenting, and disseminating effective adolescent substance abuse treatment models, the Substance Abuse and Mental Health Service Administration's Center for Substance Abuse Treatment funded the Adolescent Treatment Models program in which ten exemplary adolescent treatment programs in the United States are being evaluated. Adolescents enrolled in these exemplary programs participated in a baseline (intake) assessment and follow-up assessments at some or all of the three, six, nine, and twelve-month postbaseline follow-up points. With follow-up rates averaging over 90 percent for all ten sites, treatment outcomes can be compared not only within each program (i.e., early drop outs compared to treatment completers) but across the ten exemplary treatment programs. Each site also participated in a cost analysis so that treatment outcomes can be compared against the cost of treatment. Perhaps most important to the field is the dissemination of information about the ten exemplary adolescent treatment programs, including a detailed description of the treatment model, age-specific treatment issues pertaining to adolescent substance users, and a description of client characteristics. To this end, program directors for each program have not only agreed to manualize their program approach but have also contributed a chapter to this edited collection describing the treatment model along with treatment issues and client characteristics.

This edited collection begins with an overview by Dennis and colleagues, which examines trends in adolescent substance use and treatment approaches along with the need for developing and evaluating adolescent substance abuse treatment programs. Specifics on the Adolescent Treatment Models (ATM) program are detailed including the assessments used in this national evaluation study.

In the second section, three exemplary outpatient treatment programs are described. The first chapter in this section by Stevens and colleagues describes the teen substance abuse treatment program including the program design, treatment issues, and client characteristics. This chapter is followed by the Harrington Godley and colleagues chapter which describes an outpatient and an intensive outpatient treatment model implemented at Chestnut Health Systems. The final chapter in Section II, authored by Battjes and colleagues, describes a group-based outpatient adolescent treatment program.

Section III includes one chapter which focuses on a family-oriented outpatient treatment model. Rowe and colleagues describe the multidimensional family therapy approach (MDFT) used to intervene with younger adolescents.

In the fourth section, three exemplary residential treatment models are examined. The first chapter in this section authored by Fishman, Clemmey, and Adger describes a thirty- to sixty-day residential treatment program which is primarily based on a medical model but incorporates treatment approaches from the therapeutic community model. This chapter is followed by that of Stewart-Sabin and Chaffin which illuminates special treatment issues of American Indian youth and details a bicultural approach that takes into account the treatment needs of substance-involved American Indian adolescents. The final chapter in this section by Stevens and colleagues describes a residential step-down approach to treatment which includes a one-month residential component followed by a two-month intensive aftercare component and a two-month nonintensive aftercare component. Issues of gender differences in drug use and experiences of trauma are also examined.

The fifth section includes three chapters on modified therapeutic community treatment models. Morral and colleagues describe the adolescent therapeutic community model employed by Phoenix House along with baseline client descriptions of both the exemplary program and a comparison treatment group. Next, Perry and colleagues describe a multiphase, step-down approach to treatment embedded within the therapeutic community model. In the final chapter Shane, Cherry, and Gerstal examine Thunder Road's hybrid residential approach which is primarily based upon a therapeutic community approach incorporating elements of the medical model.

SECTION I:
OVERVIEW

Chapter 1

The Need for Developing and Evaluating Adolescent Treatment Models

Michael L. Dennis
Samia Dawud-Noursi
Randolph D. Muck
Melissa McDermeit

The growing number of adolescents presenting for treatment to the nation's public treatment system pose many challenges. Rather than personally seeking treatment, many of these adolescents are being mandated to attend treatment by the criminal justice system or their parents. Most providers in the system use treatment approaches geared toward adults and their patterns of substance use, and evaluations of these approaches when used with adolescents have produced mixed results. Few formal adolescent treatment models exist that have demonstrated effectiveness and affordability in community-based programs. Furthermore, even fewer exist that have been manualized sufficiently for replication by other programs.

The Center for Substance Abuse Treatment (CSAT) has responded to this gap with a three-prong effort:

The presentation and chapter were supported by funds from the Center for Substance Abuse Treatment (CSAT) of the Substance Abuse and Mental Health Services Administration, Department of Health and Human Services. The opinions stated here are those of the authors and do not reflect official positions of the government or any other agency. The authors would like to thank Rod Funk, Kristin Zempolich, Joan Unsicker, Bill White, and Michelle White for assistance in preparing the manuscript. Contact Information: Michael Dennis, PhD, Senior Research Psychologist, Chestnut Health Systems, Lighthouse Institute, 720 W. Chestnut, Bloomington, IL 61701; Phone: 309-829-1058, x3409; Fax: 309-829-4661; <e-mail: mdennis@chestnut.org>.

3

1. Collaborating with the National Institute on Alcohol Abuse and Alcoholism (NIAAA) to fund fourteen research studies on adolescent treatment (personal communications from Cherry Lowman on March 28, 2001)
2. Funding a multisite randomized field experiment of five of the most promising approaches to adolescent outpatient treatment based on research and expert opinion (see Dennis, Babor, et al., 2000; Dennis et al., in press)
3. Setting up the Adolescent Treatment Model (ATM) program to fund the manualization and empirical evaluation of existing exemplary adolescent programs (described in this book)

This chapter provides background on the problem, the public treatment system for adolescents in the United States of America (USA), evaluations of existing practice, and CSAT's efforts to identify and develop evidence-based models of effective treatment based on exemplary programs under ATM.

ADOLESCENT SUBSTANCE USE AND PROBLEMS

After declining from the early 1980s until 1992, illicit drug use among adolescents has begun to increase (Monitoring the Future [MTF], 1999). Between 1991 and 1999, past-year illicit drug use rose from 29 to 42 percent among twelfth graders and from 11 to 21 percent among eighth graders. Although the rate of increase has leveled off in the past three years, the current rates are almost 1.5 to 2 times the 1992 low. More than twice as much past-month marijuana use exists as all other drugs combined among adolescents in eighth grade (10 percent versus 5 percent) and twelfth grade (23 percent versus 10 percent); marijuana is also more likely to be used daily than even alcohol by both eighth graders (1.4 percent versus 1.0 percent) and twelfth graders (6.0 versus 3.4 percent). Moreover, among twelfth graders the perceived risk of using marijuana, which is inversely related to use, is as low as it has been since 1982. Unfortunately, these perceptions do not match the facts.

A common progression of adolescent substance users includes some experimentation followed by opportunistic (e.g., parties with friends) use of tobacco and alcohol (often to intoxication), followed by regular (weekly or more) use of marijuana (with continued use of tobacco and alcohol and increasing experimentation with other substances) (Golub and Johnson, 1994; Johnson and Gerstein, 1998; Kandel and Yamaguchi, 1985, 1993; Kandel, Yamaguchi, and Chen, 1992; Newcomb and Bentler, 1986, 1990). Compared to nonusers, adolescents in this latter group were three to forty-seven times more likely to have a host of other problems including symptoms of dependence, emergency room admissions, dropping out of school, behavioral problems, fighting, nondrug related legal problems, any legal problems, and being arrested. Unfortunately, fewer than 10 percent of adolescents with past-year symptoms of dependence have ever received treatment (Dennis and McGeary, 1999). While alcohol use continues to be a problem with this generation of adolescents, for the first time another illicit drug, marijuana, has become the leading substance mentioned in adolescent emergency room admissions and autopsy reports (Office of Applied Studies [OAS], 1995a). Part of the reason for this is that from 1980 to 1997 marijuana became significantly more potent, with the amount of delta-9-tetrahydrocannabinol (Δ^9-THC) found in marijuana seizures rising over threefold, from less than 1.5 to 4.5 percent (El Sholy et al., 2000). Marijuana use alone and/or in combination with alcohol and other drugs is believed to be one of the major contributing factors to violent deaths and accidents among adolescents. It has been reported as being involved in as many as 30 percent of adolescent motor vehicle crashes, 20 percent of adolescent homicides, 13 percent of adolescent suicides, and 10 percent of other unintentional injuries among adolescents (Centers for Disease Control [CDC], 1997; McKeown, Jackson, and Valois, 1997; OAS, 1995a).

Some people think that adolescent substance use is almost a rite of passage and that adolescents will outgrow it: unfortunately the evidence is mixed. From age twelve to twenty the rates of past-month substance use more than double for alcohol (20 to 75 percent), tobacco (18 to 40 percent), and marijuana (8 to 27 percent); by age thirty, alcohol drops off by about 2 percent, tobacco by 5 percent, and marijuana drops off by 15 percent (Anthony and Arria, 1999). (Note that while they follow the same pattern, no other substance peaks over 5 percent.) While some adolescents do stop on their own, most who start using marijuana regularly at an early age have been found repeatedly to continue or increase their use and related problems (e.g., abuse or dependence, dropping out of school, getting in fights, being arrested) (Hofler et al., 1999; Jessor and Jessor, 1975; Perkonigg et al., 1999).

These trends are likely to worsen because the age of onset has been decreasing over the past thirty years (Dennis and McGeary, 1999; Dennis, Babor, Roebuck, and Donaldson, in press). Using data from the National Household Survey on Drug Abuse, the first set of columns of Table 1.1 shows the population estimate and prevalence of adult lifetime users of tobacco, alcohol, marijuana, and other drugs. The next set of columns shows the percent of lifetime users who report one or more symptoms of past-year dependence by age and overall. The last column shows the odds ratio of having problems for those who start using a given substance under the age of fifteen versus those who start over the age of eighteen. For tobacco and alcohol, 32 to 36 percent report one or more problems, with those starting before the age of fifteen being significantly more likely than those starting over the age of eighteen to have current (past-year) problems (odds ratios of 1.49 and 2.74 respectively). For marijuana and other drugs, 49 percent reported one or more problems, with those starting earlier reporting being more likely to have current problems (odds ra-

TABLE 1.1. Percentage of Lifetime Users with 1+ Symptoms of Dependence or Substance-Induced Disorders by Age of First Use

	1998 Lifetime Users[a]		% With 1+ Problems[b]				
			Age of First Use[c]				Odds Ratio[d]
Substance	Population	%	<15	15-17	18+	Total	
Tobacco	151,442,082	69	39	37	30	36	1.49 *
Alcohol	176,188,916	81	45	34	23	32	2.74 *
Marijuana	71,704,012	33	63	51	41	49	2.45 *
Other drugs	38,997,916	18	71	62	48	56	2.65 *

Source: 1998 NHSDA (OAS, 2000) Public Use Tapes.
*p < .05
[a]Based on an estimated total household population size of 218,444,761
[b]Percent with 1+ past-year problems at the time of the interview (mean current age of 41 overall, 43 for alcohol and tobacco users, 36 for marijuana users and 35 for other drug users)
[c]Age at the time of first use of a given substance, which is grouped separately for each row and an average of 20 years earlier
[d]Calculated as [(% under 15)/(1-% under 15)]/[(% 18+)/(1-% 18+)]

tios of 2.45 and 2.65 respectively). While many adolescents who try or use substances do not have problems, a 50 percent or more risk of having continued problems for an average of eleven to twelve years is an unacceptable loss for our nation's public health system. It is also important to note that of all adults reporting one or more symptoms of tobacco, alcohol, or marijuana dependence, 90 percent started using under the age of eighteen (50 percent under the age of fifteen).

The onset and impact of adolescent substance use is also intertwined with a wide range of comorbid (i.e., both cause and consequence) psychological and behavioral conditions including conduct disorder, attention deficient/hyperactivity disorder (ADHD), depression, anxiety, a variety of stress disorders, oppositional defiant disorder (ODD), and reactive attachment disorder (Crowley and Riggs, 1995; Dennis, Scott, et al., 2000; Dennis, Godley, and Titus, 1999; Kaminer, 1994, 1995; Risberg, Stevens, and Graybill, 1995; Robins and McEvoy, 1990). Generally, these studies have found that over 75 percent of the adolescents entering treatment have one or more of these other conditions, with over 50 percent having three or more. In one of the most extensive comparisons across ages and levels of care, the Drug Outcome Monitoring Study (DOMS) (Dennis, Godley, and Titus; 1999; Dennis, Scott, et al., 2000; Godley, Godley, and Dennis, 2001) showed that relative to adults, adolescents were more likely to have externalizing problems such as conduct disorder or ADHD, engage in violent/aggressive behaviors, and are less likely to report internalizing or mood disorders such as depression, anxiety, or stress disorders. Moreover, the rate of these problems was substantially higher among adolescents in inpatient versus outpatient levels of care. While the rate of these problems generally increases with age in the community, in these clinical samples the severity of substance use and comorbid problems were actually higher among females and younger clients: the authors attributed this to a threshold effect in which the problems had to be worse for the system or the families to refer these subgroups to treatment.

THE PUBLIC TREATMENT SYSTEM
FOR ADOLESCENTS IN THE UNITED STATES

Public treatment programs in the United States are required to collect a core set of information for their state, which is then submitted to the federal government as part of the national Treatment Episode Data Set (TEDS). Using reports from the Office of Applied Studies (OAS, 1999; 2000) and public data tapes made available through the University of Michigan (see www.icpsr.umich.edu/SAMHDA), we can assess how the public treatment system for adolescents in the United States has changed from 1992 to 1998 and what it looks like as of 1998 (the most recent data publically available).

TEDS includes nineteen core questions related to demographic characteristics such as gender, race, age, education, and marital status; the primary, secondary, and tertiary substances for which adolescents are being treated, their typical route of administration, frequency of use, and age at first use; the source of referral to treatment; and type of treatment being provided. An additional supplemental data set provided by about 60 percent of the states includes more detailed information on referrals, other client problems, and diagnosis. TEDS is based on treatment admissions, not unique individuals. It is voluntary for clients and has some missing data. It is also voluntary for programs in some states, and some programs either do not report or report too late to be included. TEDS does not include data from exclusively private facilities, those operated by other federal agencies (e.g., the Veterans Administration, Bureau of Prisons, Indian Health Service), treatment provided by individual therapists, or the treatment of codependents. OAS (1999, 2000) estimates that TEDS covers 83 percent of the targeted public treatment system admissions and 67 percent of all admissions (including other federal and private providers). For this chapter we have subset the public use data tapes to the TEDS admissions related to people under the age of eighteen. The public use data are a random sample of the entire data set, so the population estimates here have been weighted to make them equal to the published adolescent treatment population estimates for the whole data set.

Table 1.2 shows the characteristics of adolescent admissions in 1992 and 1998 in terms of population estimate and proportion, as well as the percentage change in each from 1992 to 1998. During this six-year period, the number of admissions grew by 53 percent (from 96,787 to 147,899) and the primary substance for the admission shifted from alcohol to marijuana (though both increased in terms of being primary, secondary, and tertiary problems). Although the system was still dominated by outpatient treatment, substantial growth

TABLE 1.2. Change in Characteristics of Adolescents Entering Substance Abuse Treatment[a]

	Admissions			Relative Proportion[b]		
	1992	1998	Change	1992	1998	Change
Total (Weighted)	96,787	147,899	53%	100%	100%	0%
Gender						
Female	32,277	44,361	37%	33%	30%	−10%
Male	64,297	103,480	61%	66%	70%	5%
Race						
African American (non-Hispanic)	14,570	22,333	53%	15%	15%	0%
Caucasian (non-Hispanic)	61,716	92,782	50%	64%	63%	−2%
Hispanic	10,095	16,587	64%	10%	11%	8%
Other (non-Hispanic)	3,894	7,062	81%	4%	5%	19%
Age						
14 years old or less	24,714	37,316	51%	26%	25%	−1%
15 to 17 years old	72,073	110,583	53%	74%	75%	0%
Education						
0 to 8 years	38,315	58,156	52%	40%	39%	−1%
9 to 11 years	52,386	80,534	54%	54%	54%	1%
12+ years or GED	2,107	3,537	68%	2%	2%	10%
Other						
Employed full-time[c]	1,313	6,301	380%	2%	5%	197%
Employed part-time[c]	5,273	8,320	58%	6%	6%	−2%
Student[c]	41,681	60,011	44%	91%	76%	−16%
Pregnant at admission[d]	389	308	−21%	1%	1%	−42%
Psychological problems[c,e]	7,625	28,025	268%	15%	30%	104%
Homeless or runaway[c]	8,573	2,982	−65%	13%	2%	−82%
Source of Referral						
Criminal justice system	35,321	61,278	73%	36%	41%	14%
School/community agency	26,862	32,060	19%	28%	22%	−22%
Self/family	17,425	25,837	48%	18%	17%	−3%
Other substance abuse provider	7,334	9,221	26%	8%	6%	−18%
Other health care provider	5,322	9,069	70%	5%	6%	12%
Other	4,524	26,232	480%	5%	18%	279%
Prior Treatment						
None	60,485	86,588	43%	71%	71%	0%
1 episode	15,638	22,514	44%	18%	19%	0%
2 episodes	5,088	7,218	42%	6%	6%	−1%
3+ episodes	3,546	5,347	51%	4%	4%	5%

TABLE 1.2 *(continued)*

	Admissions			Relative Proportion[b]		
	1992	1998	Change	1992	1998	Change
Primary Substance Problem						
Marijuana/hashish	21,806	79,572	265%	23%	54%	139%
Alcohol	54,361	35,338	−35%	56%	24%	−57%
Stimulants	1,203	4,125	243%	1%	3%	124%
Hallucinogens	1,661	827	−50%	2%	1%	−67%
Cocaine/crack	3,436	3,237	−6%	4%	2%	−38%
Inhalants	1,460	555	−62%	2%	0%	−75%
Heroin/opiates	736	1,801	145%	1%	1%	60%
Other[f]	474	1,871	294%	0%	1%	158%
None identified by adolescent	11,649	20,573	77%	12%	14%	16%
Pattern of Primary Substance Use						
Weekly use at intake[c]	36,323	63,869	76%	46%	52%	14%
First used under age 15[c]	63,806	100,099	57%	78%	78%	0%
Dependence[c]	7,813	19,343	148%	30%	37%	24%
Primary, Secondary, or Tertiary Substance Problem						
Marijuana/hashish	51,081	109,875	115%	53%	74%	41%
Alcohol	74,809	89,846	20%	77%	61%	−21%
Stimulants	4,876	12,005	146%	5%	8%	61%
Hallucinogens	9,621	9,040	−6%	10%	6%	−39%
Cocaine/crack	9,023	12,191	35%	9%	8%	−12%
Inhalants	4,078	2,406	−41%	4%	2%	−61%
Heroin/opiates	1,501	3,521	135%	2%	2%	53%
Other[f]	3,947	10,019	154%	4%	7%	66%
By Setting						
Outpatient (OP)	70,371	101,604	44%	73%	69%	−6%
Intensive outpatient (IOP)	6,524	16,550	154%	7%	11%	66%
Detoxification or hospital (D/H)[g]	4,164	8,481	104%	4%	6%	33%
Short-term residential(STR)	5,984	8,415	41%	6%	6%	−8%
Long-term residential (LTR)	9,743	12,849	32%	10%	9%	−14%

Source: Office of Applied Studies 1992 and 1998 TEDS public use data set (OAS 1999, 2000).
[a]Based on unweighted sample *n* of 23,662 in 1992 (weight = 4.090) and 35,960 in 1998 (weight=4.113); Change is the change calculated as [(1998-1992)/1992]
[b]May not equal 100% due to rounding and/or missing data
[c]Calculated based on the subset of states and clients reporting
[d]Percent of females
[e]Self-identified psychological problems; note that this appears to grossly underestimate comorbid problems
[f]Including tranquilizers, sedatives, over-the-counter medications, and other identified substances
[g]Included detox hospital inpatient, detox free-standing, detox ambulatory, and hospital-based inpatient

occurred in the number of admissions to intensive outpatient (154 percent) and hospital-based programs (104 percent). As shown in the columns to the right, the treatment system is dominated by white males, aged fifteen to seventeen, who are in (or have dropped out of) high school. They are most likely to use marijuana and alcohol weekly (or more often), have started using before the age of fifteen, and never have been in treatment before. Although only about 8 percent are being treated for stimulant use, this represents a 61 percent increase over the rate in 1992.

While policymakers and researchers have often attempted to compare outpatient and inpatient treatment, these programs have historically served different subgroups of adolescents (CSAT, 1999; Gerstein and Johnson, 1999; Hubbard et al., 1985; Powers et al., 1999; Sells and Simpson, 1979; Simpson, Savage, and Sells, 1978). These differences grew in the 1990s with the increasing use of more explicit patient placement criteria, such as those recommended by the American Society of Addiction Medicine (ASAM, 1996) which have been mandated in several states. Table 1.3 focuses on the characteristics of the treatment system in 1998. Males, African Americans, and adolescents involved in the criminal justice system are more likely to go to intensive outpatient and long-term residential programs. Females, Caucasians, and those referred by other substance abuse treatment or health care providers are more likely to go into detox, hospital, or short-term residential programs. Those in outpatient and intensive outpatient are likely to be younger and entering treatment for the first time. Those entering one of the residential levels of care are more likely to have been in treatment before, use weekly (or more often), and meet criteria for dependence. While the dominant pattern of substance use across levels of care is marijuana and alcohol, adolescents in the residential levels of care are more likely to have problems with marijuana, and (at much lower prevalence rates) cocaine, stimulants, hallucinogens, or other drugs.

THE HISTORY AND EVALUATION
OF ADOLESCENT TREATMENT PRACTICE

From 1915 to 1985, only a handful of evaluations of adolescent substance abuse treatment studies existed and many of these took

TABLE 1.3. Characteristics of Adolescent Admissions in 1998 by Level of Care

	Level of Care[a]					
	OP	IOP	D/H	STR	LTR	Total
Total 1998 Admissions[b]	**101,604**	**16,550**	**8,481**	**8,415**	**12,849**	**147,899**
[Row %]	**(69%)**	**(11%)**	**(6%)**	**(6%)**	**(9%)**	**(100%)**
Gender						
Female	30%	28%	33%	32%	26%	30%
Male	70%	72%	66%	68%	74%	70%
Race						
African American (non-Hispanic)	15%	16%	11%	13%	20%	15%
Caucasian (non-Hispanic)	64%	57%	68%	68%	56%	63%
Hispanic	11%	12%	12%	7%	16%	11%
Other (non-Hispanic)	5%	4%	5%	7%	5%	5%
Age						
14 years old or less	28%	19%	17%	17%	18%	25%
15 to 17 years old	72%	81%	83%	83%	82%	75%
Education						
0 to 8 years	41%	36%	31%	37%	42%	39%
9 to 11 years	53%	58%	59%	57%	53%	54%
12+ years or GED	2%	2%	8%	2%	2%	3%
Other						
Employed full time[c]	4%	6%	4%	1%	12%	5%
Employed part time[c]	7%	5%	7%	2%	1%	6%
Student[c]	72%	89%	83%	81%	89%	76%
Pregnant at admission[d]	1%	1%	0%	0%	1%	1%
Psychological problems[c,e]	32%	17%	30%	30%	23%	30%
Homeless or runaway[c]	3%	1%	2%	4%	3%	2%
Source of Referral						
Criminal justice system	41%	47%	36%	31%	47%	41%
School/community agency	25%	19%	14%	15%	8%	22%
Self/family	18%	15%	20%	15%	15%	17%
Other substance abuse provider	4%	8%	7%	24%	12%	6%
Other health care provider	6%	6%	8%	9%	6%	6%
Other/unknown	6%	6%	15%	5%	12%	7%
Prior Treatment[c]						
None	77%	62%	59%	51%	49%	71%
1 episode	15%	25%	20%	32%	28%	18%

	Level of Care[a]					
	OP	IOP	D/H	STR	LTR	Total
Total 1998 Admissions[b]	**101,604**	**16,550**	**8,481**	**8,415**	**12,849**	**147,899**
[Row %]	**(69%)**	**(11%)**	**(6%)**	**(6%)**	**(9%)**	**(100%)**
2 episodes	4%	8%	9%	10%	12%	6%
3+ episodes	3%	5%	12%	7%	10%	5%
Primary Substance Problem						
Marijuana/hashish	50%	69%	55%	59%	63%	54%
Alcohol	25%	20%	25%	27%	15%	24%
Stimulants	2%	4%	5%	5%	5%	3%
Hallucinogens	0%	1%	1%	1%	1%	1%
Cocaine/crack	1%	2%	4%	4%	6%	2%
Inhalants	0%	0%	0%	0%	1%	0%
Heroin/opiates	1%	1%	5%	3%	2%	1%
Other[f]	2%	0%	1%	0%	1%	1%
None identified by adolescent	6%	1%	1%	1%	5%	5%
Pattern of Primary Substance Use						
Weekly use at intake[c]	39%	57%	66%	76%	63%	48%
First used under age 15[c]	73%	78%	71%	82%	76%	75%
Dependence[c]	26%	61%	80%	67%	82%	37%
Primary, Secondary, or Tertiary Substance Problem						
Marijuana/hashish	69%	88%	77%	91%	85%	74%
Alcohol	59%	68%	63%	73%	58%	61%
Stimulants	6%	11%	11%	15%	11%	8%
Hallucinogens	5%	8%	9%	11%	11%	6%
Cocaine/crack	5%	10%	15%	15%	20%	8%
Inhalants	1%	2%	2%	3%	3%	2%
Heroin/opiates	1%	2%	7%	6%	5%	2%
Other[f]	7%	5%	6%	4%	9%	7%

Source: Office of Applied Studies 1998 TEDS public use data set (OAS, 2000).
[a]Levels of care are outpatient (OP), intensive outpatient (IOP), detoxification or hospital (D/H), short-term residential (STR), and long-term residential (LTR); D/H includes detox hospital inpatient, detox free-standing, detox ambulatory, and hospital-based inpatient.
[b]Weighted based on total reported number of TEDS admissions under age 18 divided by the sample ($n = 35,960$) put in the public domain (constant = 4.113).
[c]Calculated based on the subset of states or clients reporting
[d]Percent of females
[e]Self-identified psychological problems; note that this appears to grossly underestimate comorbid problems
[f]Including tranquilizers, sedatives, over-the-counter medications, and other identified substances

place when adolescents were treated in adult programs or in segregated units with adult models. After the de facto criminalization of narcotics between 1915 and 1920, New York City treated 743 adolescents (under the age of nineteen) addicted to narcotics in segregated units at the Worth Street Clinic. By the 1920s, however, this effort was declared a failure based on internal evaluations (Copeland, 1920; Graham-Mulhall, 1921; Hubbard, 1920).

It took the federal government until the 1930s to establish two federal narcotics "farms" (later called U.S. Public Health Hospitals) that were initially to be dedicated to the treatment of juvenile addiction. But by the time they opened, the average age of a person entering treatment was almost thirty-eight years (Lowry, 1956). From 1947 to 1950, however, adolescent narcotic use increased, and the number of adolescents (under age twenty-one) entering this facility rose from 22 to 440 (1900 percent) (*Conferences,* 1953). New York City also admitted another 250 adolescents per year in a residential treatment program at Riverside Hospital on the Old Welfare Island (Gamso and Mason, 1958). The lack of community resources to help young narcotic addicts in the 1950s triggered new initiatives within cities being hard hit by heroin addiction and these initiatives are the origins of the modern community-based treatment system. These included the creation in the 1950s and early 1960s of addiction wards in local hospitals such as the Detroit Receiving Hospital; Chicago's Bridewell Hospital; and Bellevue, Kings County, Manhattan General, and Metropolitan hospitals in New York City, as well as church-based efforts including such programs as St. Mark's Clinic in Chicago, the Addicts Rehabilitation Center in Manhattan, the Astoria Consultation Service in Queens, Exodus House in East Harlem, and other religiously affiliated programs such as Teen Challenge and the Samaritan Halfway House Society (White, 1998).

Despite the antimarijuana campaigns of the 1920s and 1930s and the de facto criminalization of that drug with the Marihuana Tax Act of 1937, there is little evidence of large numbers of adolescents (or adults) seeking treatment for marijuana until the late 1960s when its use became more common (Anslinger and Cooper, 1937; Anslinger and Tompkins, 1953; Dennis and White, 1999; Rowell, 1929, 1937; Rowell and Rowell,1939). The transition from adolescent admissions for narcotics to admissions for marijuana and alcohol did not start until the late 1960s and early 1970s. This also coincided with a series of national program evaluations of existing practice and attempts to apply adult treatment models to adolescents.

The Drug Abuse Reporting Program (DARP) (Sells and Simpson, 1979; Simpson, Savage, and Sells, 1978) was conducted in the early 1970s using a national stratified and purposive sample of existing community-based programs for narcotics use. The study included data on adolescents (under age twenty) at intake ($n = 5,405$) and a follow-up interview approximately three years later with 587 adolescents who had been treated in methadone maintenance ($n = 119$), therapeutic communities ($n = 238$), outpatient drug free ($n = 158$), and detoxification/other ($n = 72$). Prior to admission, 73 percent of the adolescents used opioids (66 percent weekly or more often), however, the rate of any opioid use ranged from 93 percent of those being treated with methadone to 49 percent of those being treated in outpatient drug free. Even in this early study, marijuana had already emerged as the second most commonly used substance, with 62 percent reporting any use (46 percent weekly use) and ranging from 48 percent among those in methadone programs to 66 percent of the adolescents in outpatient drug free and therapeutic communities. With a median length of stay of about two months, all levels of care substantially reduced opioid use, the rates of alcohol use went up slightly, and the amount of marijuana use remained the same or increased (particularly among those in methadone treatment).

The Treatment Outcome Prospective Study (TOPS) (Craddock, Bray, and Hubbard, 1985; Hubbard et al., 1985) was conducted in the late 1970s and early 1980s using a second national stratified and purposive sample of existing community-based treatment for any kind of drug use. The study included data on adolescents (under age twenty) at intake ($n = 1,042$) and twelve-month post discharge interviews with 256 adolescents who had been admitted to therapeutic communities ($n = 106$) or outpatient treatment ($n = 150$). By this time, 31 percent of the adolescents were being treated primarily for marijuana related problems, followed by admissions primarily related to amphetamines (7 percent), alcohol (5 percent), and only then opioids (4 percent). TOPS found 25 to 50 percent reductions in the rates of daily marijuana use, alcohol use and other drug use, and drug related problems after residential treatment (with a median length of stay of about three months). For adolescent outpatient treatment (with a median length of stay of two months), however, the results were mixed—

with 25 percent or less reductions and several subgroups (e.g., eighteen- to nineteen-year-olds in treatment for less than three months; twelve- to seventeen-year-olds in treatment for more than three months) actually increasing their rates of substance use or other problems.

The Services Research Outcome Study (SROS) (OAS, 1995b) was conducted in the late 1980s to early 1990s using a national probability sample of existing community-based treatment for any kind of substance use. The data include record abstraction and five-year postdischarge follow-ups (that recaptured intake histories) with a total of 156 adolescents (under age eighteen) receiving treatment. Although the data from this study are limited to the percent using five or more times in the five years before and after treatment (with no detailed breakdown for adolescents), it does help to further document the continuing shift toward a pattern of using marijuana (68 percent), alcohol (80 percent), and the smaller roles of cocaine (20 percent) and opioids (2 percent) among adolescent admissions. The median length of stay was two to three months, with 48 percent of the adolescents going back into treatment one or more times in the five years after the index episode (ranging from 65 percent of those who received less than a week of treatment to 40 percent of those who received six or more months). Although the adolescent sample in SROS was very small, it caused considerable concern among policy makers because it found that from the five years before to the five years after treatment, the prevalence of using (5+ times in the past year) substances increased for marijuana (68 to 70 percent), alcohol (80 to 92 percent), cocaine (20 to 29 percent), and heroin (2 to 7 percent).

The National Treatment Improvement Evaluation Study (NTIES) (CSAT, 1999, 2000; Gerstein and Johnson, 1999) was conducted in the early 1990s using a national stratified and purposive sample of community-based treatment programs that had received demonstration grants to enhance treatment. The data include interviews with 236 adolescents (age thirteen to seventeen) at intake and twelve-month postdischarge who received any kind of treatment (no modality breakdowns are available). Again, most adolescents were being treated for marijuana (46 percent) or alcohol (10 percent), with heroin, crack, and cocaine together making up only 14 percent more. With a median length of stay of about two months, NTIES found that residential treatment was associated with reductions in using (5+

times in the past year) marijuana (97 to 72 percent), cocaine (52 to 30 percent), and in alcohol intoxication (52 to 45 percent). Adolescent outpatient treatment, however, was associated with a slight reduction in marijuana use (77 to 69 percent), no change in cocaine use (13 to 13 percent), and a slight increase in alcohol intoxication (32 to 37 percent).

The Drug Abuse Treatment Outcome Studies of Adolescents (DATOS-A) (Grella et al., 1999, 2000; Hser et al., 1999, 2001; Powers et al., 1999; Rounds-Bryant et al., 1998) was conducted in the mid- and late-1990s using a third national stratified and purposive sample of existing community-based treatment for any kind of substance use. The study included data on adolescents (age eleven to nineteen) at intake ($n = 3,382$) and twelve-month postdischarge interviews with 1,785 adolescents that had been admitted to long-term residential ($n = 727$), short-term residential ($n = 613$), and/or outpatient treatment ($n = 445$). By the early 1990s, over 90 percent of the adolescents were using marijuana at intake (58 percent meeting dependence criteria) and 84 percent were using alcohol (27 percent dependent). In contrast, only 15 percent had cocaine dependence and 3 percent opioid dependence. For the year before to the year after treatment, the rates of marijuana (91 to 68 percent) and heavy alcohol use (34 to 20 percent) across modalities went down, while the rates of cocaine use went up slightly (17 to 19 percent).

Substantively, it is important to realize that most of the treatment programs in these evaluations were using adult treatment models with only minimum modifications. Early therapeutic communities such as Odyssey House and Phoenix House started admitted adolescents in the late 1960s and were quickly followed in the 1970s by Crossroads, Gateway Foundation, Inc., Synanon, and Safri House; almost immediately these programs began modifications in order to involve more professionals and families (Kajdan and Senay, 1976). Some of the other early changes made by these and other adolescent programs included:

1. incorporating more psychological and psychiatric assessment, concepts, and services,
2. dealing more flexibly with rule violations,
3. using younger and better educated staff, and
4. using less emphasis on confrontation.

Throughout the 1980s there were increasing calls for more "developmentally appropriate" approaches for working with adolescents (Loree Adams and Nancy Hamilton, personal communication, April 17, 2001). For example, adolescents who had no concept of respecting parents or authority figures were easily confused by the "fuzzy" boundaries between clients and staff. More formal boundaries were needed and the staff's behavior had to be above reproach. Role modeling (for which therapeutic communities (TCs) and twelve-step programs are famous) becomes even more important when it comes to adolescents (Hamilton at Operation PAR, for instance, instituted a "no swearing" policy and other "parenting" types of rules; Adams requires adolescents to "take care" of a teddy bear). Checks on the ability of clients to discipline each other were required, as some could be overly harsh or impulsive. Another key issue was the need for access to formal educational services and the level of intellectual development. Adolescents still think in very concrete (versus abstract) terms; they might say they do not have a drug "problem" but then readily acknowledge having three or more symptoms of dependence. This is not (necessarily) denial, but a gap in their ability to recognize the link between these "concrete" symptoms and the abstract label of a "problem." Obviously this impacts both how assessments are conducted and the kinds of things that can be done in therapy or expected in a living environment. By the end of the 1990s, treatment programs and researchers were only just beginning to address these issues (with most acknowledging a lot of room for more improvement).

These early evaluations of adolescent treatment practice in the community were also methodologically limited by small samples spread over many different programs/undefined approaches, low treatment duration (generally about two months), and marginal follow-up rates (50 to 70 percent). Complicating matters further, none of these studies was based on the kind of manualized approach that is required for easy dissemination to the field and that is increasingly the sine qua non for good substance abuse treatment (Carrol, 1997; Crits-Cristoph and Siqueland, 1996; Institute of Medicine, 1990; Lamb, Greenlick, and McCarty, 1998; Miller et al., 1995; Onken, Blaine, and Battjes, 1997; Ozechowski and Liddle, 2000; Stanton and Shadish, 1997; Weinberg et al., 1998). Several other attempts have been made to develop and evaluate additional models of substance abuse treatment more appropriate for adolescents (e.g., Alford, Koehler, and Leonard, 1991;

Azrin et al., 1994; Borduin, 1999; Brown, Myers, and Vik, 1994; Dakof, Tejeda, and Liddle 2001; Dennis, Babor, et al., 2000; Dennis, Scott, et al., 2000; Godley, Godley, and Dennis, 2001; Godley et al., in press; Henggeler, 1993; Henggeler et al., 1991; Henggeler, Pickrel, and Brondino, 1999; Henggeler et al., 1996; Jainchill, 1997; Joanning et al., 1992; Kaminer and Burleson, 1999; Kaminer et al., 1998; Lewis et al., 1990; Liddle and Dakof, 1995; Szapoznik et al., 1983; Szapocznik et al., 1988; Titus and Godley, 1999; Winters et al., 2000). However, most of these have even smaller sample sizes, were conducted in research or exemplary settings, and suffer from many of the same problems as early evaluations of adolescent treatment practice. Moreover, treatment protocol manuals with sufficient detail to allow another program to replicate their successes are only now becoming available to the field and have yet to be independently replicated in a large number of diverse community-based settings. In short, evaluations of adolescent treatment practice have produced positive but sometimes mixed results, and adolescent treatment research still is many years from demonstrating that its emerging models will be effective and cost-effective in practice.

CSAT'S ADOLESCENT TREATMENT MODEL PROGRAM

One of the ways that CSAT responded to this gap in our knowledge about adolescent treatment was to establish the Adolescent Treatment Model (ATM) program. The goals of the ATM program are to

1. identify currently existing potentially exemplary models of adolescent treatment;
2. collaborate with the treatment providers to formalize their models into disseminable manuals that can be replicated by other programs;
3. determine with whom the model has been tested and the amount of services the adolescents actually received;
4. evaluate the effectiveness, cost, and cost-effectiveness of each model;
5. collaborate on cross-site comparisons of these models with one another and with other studies of adolescent substance abuse treatment; and

6. participate in professional activities to disseminate the resulting models and findings.

CSAT also hopes to make these evidence-based models of treatment available through publication of manuals, through its Addiction Technology Transfer Centers (ATTC), through its Targeted Capacity Expansion (TCE) grants, by working with the states (which received block grant funding), and by making these evidence-based models of treatment available directly to treatment agencies via mailings, clinical conferences, and specialized workshops.

Programs and program evaluators formed partnerships and submitted grant applications that were peer reviewed and the basis for CSAT issuing five awards in 1998 (CSAT GFA No. TI 98-007) and five more awards in 1999 (CSAT GFA No. TI 99-001). Each of these grantees was required to work and be judged on the extent to which they could demonstrate that they: were working with a program that had been in existence for at least two years, had some preliminary data demonstrating program effectiveness, were willing to develop the manual and make it publically available, had a local evaluation plan for assessing the effectiveness of the program, and would be willing to collaborate with the cross-site evaluation of client mix, service mix, client effectiveness, costs, and cost-effectiveness.

The ATM treatment models represent a wide range of levels of care, clinical approaches, provider organizations, geographic locations, and evaluators. The levels of care, programs, and evaluators (described at length in the subsequent chapters of this book) include the following:

- *Outpatient treatment:* EMPACT-SPC in Phoenix, Arizona, evaluated by the University of Arizona Services Research Office
- *Outpatient treatment:* Chestnut Health Systems (CHS) in Bloomington, Illinois, evaluated by CHS' Lighthouse Institute
- *Outpatient treatment:* Epoch Counseling Center in Catonsville, Maryland, evaluated by Friends Research Institute, Inc., Baltimore, Maryland
- *Outpatient family therapy:* The Village, Inc., in Miami, Florida, evaluated by the University of Miami School of Medicine

- *A short-term and intensive inpatient program:* Mountain Manor Treatment Center in Baltimore, Maryland, evaluated by the Johns Hopkins School of Medicine, Baltimore, Maryland
- *A moderate-term residential program on a Native American reservation:* Four Corners Regional Adolescent Center in Shiprock, New Mexico, evaluated by Shiprock Navaho Behavioral Health Board, Inc., and the University of Oklahoma, Oklahoma City, Oklahoma
- *A moderate-term step-down (residential, intensive outpatient, outpatient) treatment program:* CODAC Behavioral Health Services in Tucson, Arizona, evaluated by the University of Arizona.
- *A modified therapeutic community treatment program:* Phoenix Academy in Los Angeles, California, evaluated by Drug Policy Research Center (RAND), Santa Monica, California
- *A modified therapeutic community and step-down (residential, intensive outpatient, outpatient) treatment program:* Dynamic Youth Community, Inc., in Brooklyn, New York, evaluated by the New York Office of Alcoholism and Substance Abuse Services, Albany, New York
- *A modified therapeutic community treatment program:* Thunder Road, in Oakland, California, evaluated by the Public Health Institute

Participants in all programs are predominately marijuana and alcohol using males with criminal justice system involvement. However, significant numbers of adolescents are being treated for cocaine in New York and Tucson, and heroin in New York and Baltimore. Significant numbers of females are being treated in New York, Baltimore, Tucson, Oakland, and Bloomington. Most of the program clients are Caucasians, though there are significant numbers of African Americans in Baltimore, Miami, and Catonsville; Hispanics in Los Angeles, Tucson, Miami, and Phoenix; and Native Americans in Shiprock. These differences are important because prior work has shown that gender identity, ethnic identity, and the degree of acculturation can moderate substance use behaviors (Navarro et al.,1997; Scheier et al., 1997; Vega and Gil, 1998). In addition, the gap between child and parent acculturation may contribute to substance use (Felix-Ortiz, Fernandez, and Newcomb, 1998).

Each of the ATM programs is unique. The goal of manualizing existing programs is to identify the replicable components and allow programs to potentially combine components across manuals into new manual "guided" approaches, which though they vary considerably, generally include: descriptions of the treatment program, facilities, staff, interventions, and services, as well as details about the treatment interventions (e.g., group counseling goals, process, handout materials) and community (e.g., therapeutic milieu, role of clients). Tentative summaries of their current approaches appear in the following chapters, however, it is important to appreciate that these programs continue to evolve their treatment approach.

Each of the program evaluations involves the collection of a core set of measures including treatment transition and follow-up logs, standardized adolescent interviews with the Global Appraisal of Individual Needs (GAIN) (Dennis, 1999) at intake, and follow-up and cost data on the services provided by the ATM program. Intake interviews were conducted no more than two weeks before treatment intake or one week after treatment intake. Follow-up interviews were conducted at six and twelve months postintake for all sites. Individually, sites are also collecting additional measures, additional waves (three- and nine-months postdischarge), abstracting records and/or conducting qualitative studies. The following is a summary of the common data sources and their status.

Developed for the ATM program, the Treatment Transition Log (TTL) is designed to track adolescents as they move through the ATM program (including movement between levels of care). Using multiple rows per unique adolescent, it tracks the site, study ID, treatment program ID, intake date, intake status, referral source (if applicable), prior level of care and site, current program site and level of care, discharge status, discharge date, posttreatment destination, and level of care. As of March 2001, the ten grantees had recruited 1,568 unique adolescents who had a total of 2,205 admissions to one or more levels of care (e.g., step-down, step-up, or readmissions). Approximately 17 percent were in treatment for less than thirty days, 28 percent for thirty-one to ninety days, 28 percent for more than ninety days, and 21 percent were still in treatment. The adolescents were most likely to be transferring in from a juvenile institution (44 percent), the community (32 percent), or from another substance abuse treatment unit. The admissions were spread across outpatient (20 percent), intensive outpatient (12 percent), group homes (19 percent), short-term (thirty days or less) inpatient (8 percent), moderate-term (thirty-one to ninety days) inpatient (19 percent), or long-term (greater than ninety days) residential treatment (13 percent). Of the more than 1,700 adolescents discharged as of March 2001 (counting multiple admissions more than once), 20 percent completed treatment and were discharged to the community, 20 percent transferred to another level of care within the same agency, 3 percent transferred to another substance abuse treatment agency, 13 percent transferred to a criminal justice agency, 3 percent were asked to leave at staff request, and 18 percent left against medical advice.

Developed for the ATM program, the Follow-Up Log (FUL) tracks all people recruited into the study, whether they agreed to participate and, if so what happened to them. For each wave of follow-up being done by a site, it indicates the target date for their follow-up interviews, their current status (not due, completed on time, completed late, unable to gain access, refused, pending), and, if completed, the date of the interview. It generates a summary report by site, and this report is combined and shared across the programs. As of April 30, 2000, the ten grantees had completed 90 percent (1,301 done/1,450 due [excluding those who have died]) of the required six-month interviews and 90 percent of the required twelve-month interviews (1,019/1,137). The New York, Baltimore, Tucson, Arizona, Los Angeles (three-month only), Oakland, Bloomington, and Phoenix sites also completed 92 percent (1,263/1,366) of their optional three-month interviews and 87 percent (699/802) of their optional nine-month interviews. These rates build on follow-up methods developed under earlier CSAT studies (Scott and Dennis, 2000) and represent a major breakthrough for the field by this group of collaborating grantees.

The Global Appraisal of Individual Needs (GAIN) is actually a series of screeners, intake, and follow-up participant interviews that have been normed on both adults and adolescents (Dennis, 1999; Dennis, Godley, and Titus, 1999; Dennis, Scott, et al., 2000), is used as the biopsychosocial clinical assessment at Chestnut Health Systems and is currently one of the most widely used measures in adolescent treatment studies in the United States (Buchan, Tims, and Dennis, 2000; Dennis, Babor, et al., 2000; Dennis et al., in press). There are eight core sections (background, substance use, physical health, risk behaviors, mental health, environment, legal, and vocational) that each contain questions on the recency of problems, breadth of symptoms, and recent prevalence in days or times, as well as lifetime service utilization, recency of utilization and frequency of recent utilization. The items are combined into over 100 scales and subscales that can be used for diagnosis, placement, treatment planning, and outcome monitoring. The GAIN also includes items designed for comparison to the National Household Survey on Drug Abuse (OAS, 1996) and is currently being "valued" for adolescents at the unit (e.g., day, time) level by Dr. Michael French at the University of Miami School of Medicine.

Using data from the first 1,028 adolescents admitted to ATM, we found that the GAIN scales replicated earlier results (Dennis, Scott, et al., 2000; Dennis et al., in press) in terms of high internal consistency on both the summary dimension scales and their more specific subscales, including:

- Internal Mental Distress Index (IMDI-39, .94) and its subscales: Somatic Symptom Index (SSI-4, 0.69), Depressive Symptom Index (DSI-6, .77), Homicidal Suicidal Thought Index (HSTI-4, .83), Anxiety Symptom Index (ASI-10, .77), Traumatic Stress Index (TSI-13, .92), and General Mental Distress Index (GMDI-21, .88)
- Behavior Complexity Index (BCI-33, .91) and its subscales: In-Attention Index (IAI-9, .88), Hyperactivity-Impulsivity Index (HII-9, .81), Conduct Disorder Index (CDI-15, .82), and ADHD-Index (ADHD-18, .90)
- Substance Problem Index (SPI-16 items, alpha = .90) and its subscales: Substance Issues Index (SII-5, .67), Substance Abuse Index (SAI-4; .70), Substance Dependence Index (SDI7, .83), and Substance Use Disorder Index (SUDI-11, .87)
- Violence-Delinquency Index (VDI-22, .90) and its subscales: General Conflict Tactic Index (GCTI-12, .89), Property Crime Index (PCI-6; .75), Interpersonal Crime Index (ICI-7, .67), Drug Crime Index (DCI-4, 0.53), and General Crime Index (GCI-17, .84).

A confirmatory factor analysis using data from the 608 adolescents in the Tucson, Los Angeles, and Oakland sites revealed an outstanding fit between the hypothesized and actual data (Comparative Fit Index or

CFI = .96) (Dennis, Funk, and McDermeit, 2001). Using data from the GAINs for 187 adolescents admitted to residential treatment in the Oakland site, Jasiukaitis and Shane (2001) were able to use discriminant analysis to accurately predict independent and blind psychiatric diagnoses of co-occurring psychiatric diagnoses including ADHD (kappa = 1.00), mood disorders (.85), conduct disorder/obsessive compulsive disorder (.82), adjustment disorder (.69), or the lack of a non-substance use diagnoses (.91), and to discriminate the primary other disorders across these conditions (kappa = .65). In a comparison of fifty-four adolescents entering residential treatment in New York State, Perry and Stark (2001) found that the more detailed GAIN questions were significantly more likely than admission records from New York State's version of the Treatment Episode Data Set (TEDS) to document self-reported needle use, and prior mental health treatment. Also, a tendency (effect size d = .86) for the GAIN existed to identify more prior substance abuse treatment episodes.

A test-retest study of the days of use in the past ninety days and lifetime DSM-IV abuse/dependence symptoms over forty-eight hours or less with a nonATM sample of 210 adolescent entering outpatients reveals consistent but increasing numbers of days of marijuana use (r = .74, 31 versus 34 days), days of alcohol use (r = .74, 6 versus 7 days), abuse/dependence symptoms (r = .73, 4.6 versus 5.3 lifetime), and lifetime diagnosis (Kappa = .55, 40 versus 44 percent lifetime dependence) (Dennis, Babor, et al., 2000; Dennis et al., in press).

The GAIN has also been cross validated with the much more detailed time line followback method using the Form 90 (Miller, 1996; Miller and Del Boca, 1994). A study of 114 adolescents entering residential treatment showed that they produced very similar estimates of the days of alcohol (r = .84) and marijuana use (r = .85), peak blood alcohol content levels (r = .73); after treatment discharge they also produced similar estimates to the days to the first use of alcohol (r = .89) and marijuana (r = .96) (Dennis et al., in press). Self-reports of past-month use by adolescents in residential treatment were also consistent with on-site urine tests for THC (50 ng/ml) at both intake (Kappa = .53) and follow-up (Kappa = .69) (Godley et al., in press). Relative to collaterals, adolescents reported about the same days of alcohol use and about a third more days of marijuana use at intake and follow-up.

The ATM cost study is being conducted by the Capital Consulting Corporation (CCC, 1999), using an accounting methodology based on generally accepted accounting principles (GAAP) and cost accounting standards (CAS) of the American Institute of Certified Public Accountants (AICPA, 2002, <http://www.aicpa.org>). The cost allocation methodology contains a specified allocation basis for each cost center within a substance abuse treatment program, ensuring that costs are uniformly allocated across programs being studied. To date, CCC has completed substance abuse treatment cost profiles for more than 1,000 programs being evaluated under CSAT grants. They provide each grantee with summary and individual level data on the number of service units provided, the average unit cost, and the total (accounting) costs. This includes admission and discharge dates, length of stay, hours of counseling (broken out by individual, family, substance abuse groups, and mental health groups), and units of counseling and other services (e.g., assessment, HIV testing and counseling, medical services, room and board, records management, case management, aftercare, transportation, and education). At the time this chapter was prepared, CCC was about half way through collecting and reporting the cost data.

IMPLICATIONS

The ATM program promises to advance research and actual practice in the area of adolescent substance abuse treatment in several ways. First, ATM will be among the first efforts to manualize and evaluate step-down and/or continuum of care models. Second, it provides large samples of Native American, African American, Hispanic, and female adolescents entering treatment. Third, it provides a wide scope of arrangements between the substance abuse treatment and criminal justice systems that increasingly play a critical role in public policy. Fourth, the ATM grantees have replicated earlier efforts with adolescents (Dennis, Babor, et al., 2000; Dennis, Scott, et al., 2000; Scott and Dennis, 2000) to achieve high follow-up, are doing significant work on measurement, and have been able to address many of the other key barriers that have limited earlier efforts. This book and the ongoing work of CSAT and its ATM grantees promise to lay the foundation for improving actual practice in community-based treatment.

REFERENCES

Alford, G. S., Koehler, R. A., and Leonard, J. (1991). Alcoholics Anonymous-Narcotics Anonymous model inpatient treatment of chemically dependent adolescents: A two-year outcome study. *Journal of Studies on Alcohol, 52,* 118-126.

American Institute of Certified Public Accountants (AICPA) (2002). Generally accepted accounting principles (GAAP) and cost accounting standards (CAS). [Available online at: <http://www.aicpa.org>].

American Society of Addiction Medicine (ASAM) (1996). *Patient placement criteria for the treatment of psychoactive substance disorders* (Second edition). Chevy Chase, MD: Author.

Anslinger, H. and Cooper, C. (1937). Marihuana: Assassin of youth. *American Magazine,* July, 18-19, 150-153.

Anslinger, H. and Tompkins, W. (1953). *The traffic in narcotics.* New York: Funk and Wagnalls.

Anthony, J. C. and Arria, A. M. (1999). Epidemiology of substance abuse in adulthood. In P. J. Ott, R. E. Tarter, and R. T. Ammerman (Eds.), *Sourcebook on substance abuse: Etiology, epidemiology, assessment, and treatment.* Boston: Allyn & Bacon.

Azrin, N. H., Donohue, B., Besalel, V. A., Kogan, E. S., and Acierno, R. (1994). Youth drug abuse treatment: A controlled outcome study. *Journal of Child and Adolescent Substance Abuse,* 3, 1-16.

Borduin, C. M. (1999). Multisystemic treatment of criminality and violence in adolescents. *Journal of the American Academy of Child and Adolescent Psychiatry, 38,* 242-249.

Brown, S. A., Myers, M. G., and Vik, P. W. (1994). Correlates of success following treatment for adolescent substance abuse. *Applied and Preventive Psychology, 3,* 61-73.

Buchan, B. J., Dennis, M. L., Tims, F. M., and Diamond, G. S. (in press). Marijuana use: Consistency and validity of self report, on-site urine testing and laboratory testing. *Addiction.*

Buchan, B. J., Tims, F., and Dennis, M. L. (2000). Consistency and validity of marijuana use measured by self-report, collateral reports, on-site testing and laboratory testing. *Journal of Drug and Alcohol Dependence, 60*(suppl. 1), s26.

Capital Consulting Corporation (1999). Substance Abuse Treatment Cost Allocation and Analysis Template (SATCAAT) (Center for Substance Abuse Treatment contract # 270-97-7001). Rockville, MD: Author.

Carrol, K. M. (1997). New methods of treatment efficacy research. *Alcohol Health and Research World, 21*(4), 352-359.

Center for Substance Abuse Treatment (CSAT) (1998). *Guidance for applicants (GFA) No. TI 98-007, grants for evaluation of treatment models for adolescents.* Rockville, MD: Substance Abuse and Mental Health Services Administration (SAMHSA). Catalog of Federal Domestic Assistance No. 93.230.

Center for Substance Abuse Treatment (CSAT) (1999). *Guidance for applicants (GFA) No. TI 99-001, grants for evaluation of treatment models for adolescents.* Rockville, MD: Substance Abuse and Mental Health Services Administration (SAMHSA). Catalog of Federal Domestic Assistance No. 93.230.

Center for Substance Abuse Treatment (CSAT) (2000). *Adolescents and young adults in treatment.* [Available online at: <www.health.org/nties/young/yungtext.htm>].

Centers for Disease Control (CDC) (1997). *Youth risk behaviors in the United States, 1997.* Rockville, MD: National Center for Chronic Disease Prevention and Health Promotion, CDC 2 Westat Inc. [Available online at <http://www.cdc.gov/epo/mmwr>].

Conferences on drug addiction among adolescents of the New York Academy of Medicine. (1953). New York: Blakiston Company.

Copeland, S. (1920). The narcotic drug evil and the New York City Health Department. *American Medicine, 15,* 17-23.

Craddock, S. G., Bray, R. M., and Hubbard, R. L. (1985). *Drug use before and during drug abuse treatment: 1979-1981 TOPS admission cohorts* [DHHS Publication No. (ADM) 85-1387]. Rockville, MD: National Institute on Drug Abuse.

Crits-Cristoph, P. and Siqueland, L. (1996). Psychosocial treatment for drug abuse: Selected review and recommendations for national health care. *Archives of General Psychiatry, 53,* 749-756.

Crowley, T. J. and Riggs, P. D. (1995). Adolescent substance use disorder with conduct disorder and comorbid conditions. In E. R. Rahdert and D. Czechowicz (Eds.), *Adolescent drug abuse: Clinical assessment and therapeutic interventions* (NIH Publication No. 95-3908, NIDA Research Monograph, 156, pp. 49-111). Rockville, MD: National Institute on Drug Abuse.

Dakof, G. A., Tejeda, M., and Liddle, H. A. (2001). Predictors of engagement in adolescent drug abuse treatment. *Journal of the American Academy of Child and Adolescent Psychiatry, 40*(3), 274-281.

Dennis, M. L. (1999). *Global Appraisal of Individual Needs (GAIN) Administration guide for the GAIN and related measures* (Version 1299). Bloomington, IL: Chestnut Health Systems. Retrieved from <http//www.chestnut.org/li/gain/gadm1299.pdf>.

Dennis, M. L., Babor, T. F., Diamond, G., Donaldson, J., Godley, S. H., Tims, F., Titus, J. C., Webb, C., Herrell, J., and fourteen other people in the CYT Steering Committee. (2000). *The Cannabis Youth Treatment (CYT) experiment: Preliminary findings.* Rockville, MD: Substance Abuse and Mental Health Services Administration, Center for Substance Abuse Treatment. [Available online at <http://www.chestnut.org/li/cyt/findings>].

Dennis, M. L., Babor, T., Roebuck, C., and Donaldson, J. (in press). Changing the focus: The case for recognizing and treating marijuana use disorders. *Addiction.*

Dennis, M. L., Funk, R., and McDermeit, M. (2001). The GAIN's psychopathology measures: A replication and confirmatory factor analysis. Presentation at the CSAT Adolescent Treatment Model Cross-site Meeting, May 15, Bethesda, MD.

Dennis, M. L., Godley, S. and Titus, J. (1999). Co-occurring psychiatric problems among adolescents: Variations by treatment, level of care and gender. *TIE Communiqué* (pp. 5-8 and 16). Rockville, MD: Substance Abuse and Mental Health Services Administration, Center for Substance Abuse Treatment.

Dennis, M. L. and McGeary, K. A. (1999). Adolescent alcohol and marijuana treatment: Kids need it now. *TIE Communiqué* (pp. 10-12). Rockville, MD: Substance Abuse and Mental Health Services Administration, Center for Substance Abuse Treatment.

Dennis, M. L., Scott, C. K., Godley, M. D., and Funk, R. (2000). Predicting outcomes in adult and adolescent treatment with case mix vs. level of care: Findings from the drug outcome monitoring study. *Journal of Drug and Alcohol Dependence, 60*(suppl. 1), s51.

Dennis, M. L., Titus, J. C., Diamond, G., Donaldson, J., Godley, S. H., Tims, F. M., Webb, C., Kaminer, Y., Babor, T., French, M., Roebuck, M. C., Godley, M. D., Hamilton, N., Liddle, H., Scott, C., and the CYT Steering Committee (in press). The Cannabis Youth Treatment (CYT) Experiment: Rationale, study design, and analysis plans. *Addiction.*

Dennis, M. L. and White, W. L. (1999). The legalization debate: Is there a middle ground? In J. Inciardi, (Ed.), *The drug legalization debate, studies in crime, law and justice* (pp. 75-100). Thousand Oaks, CA: Sage.

El Sholy, M. A., Ross, S. A., Mehmedic, Z., Arafat, R., Bao, Y., and Banahan, B. F. (2000). Potency trends of Δ^9-THC and other cannabinoids in confiscated marijuana from 1980-1997. *Journal of Forensic Science, 45*(1), 24-30.

Felix-Ortiz, M., Fernandez, A., and Newcomb, M. D. (1998). The role of intergenerational discrepancy of cultural orientation in drug use among Latina adolescents. *Substance Use and Misuse, 33,* 967-994.

Gamso, R. and Mason, P. (1958). A hospital for adolescent drug addicts. *Psychiatric Quarterly Supplement, 32,* 99-109.

Gerstein, D. R. and Johnson, R. A. (1999). *Adolescent and young adults in the National Treatment Improvement Evaluation Study* (National Evaluation Data Services Report). Rockville, MD: Center for Substance Abuse Treatment.

Godley, S. H., Godley, M. D., and Dennis, M. L. (2001). The assertive aftercare protocol for adolescent substance abusers. In E. Wagner and H.Waldron (Eds.), *Innovations in adolescent substance abuse interventions* (pp. 311-329). New York: Elsevier Science.

Godley, M. D., Godley, S. H., Funk, R. R., Dennis, M. L., and Loveland, D. (in press). Discharge status as a performance indicator: Can it predict adolescent substance abuse treatment outcome? *Journal of Child and Adolescent Substance Abuse.*

Golub, A. and Johnson, B.D. (1994). The shifting importance of alcohol and marijuana as gateway substances among serious drug abusers. *Journal of Studies on Alcohol, 55,* 607-614.

Graham-Mulhall, S. (1921). Experiences in narcotic drug control in the state of New York. *New York Medical Journal, 113,* 106-111.

Grella, C., Hser, Y., Anglin, M., Joshi, V., and Rounds-Bryant, J. (1999). *Comorbidity among adolescents in drug treatment: Treatment processes and outcomes from the Drug Abuse Treatment Outcome Studies.* Paper presented at the College of Problems of Drug Dependence conference, Acapulco, Mexico, June. [Available online at <http://www.datos.org>].

Grella, C. E., Hser, Y. I., Joshi, V., and Rounds-Bryant, J. (2000). Drug treatment outcomes for adolescents with comorbid mental and substance use disorders. *Journal of Nervous and Mental Disease, 189,* 384-392.

Henggeler, S. W. (1993). Multisystemic treatment of serious juvenile offenders: Implications for the treatment of substance-abusing youths. In L. S. Onken, J. D. Blaine, and J. J. Boren, (Eds.), *Behavioral treatments for drug abuse and de-*

pendence (pp. 181-200, Research Monograph 137). Rockville, MD: National Institute on Drug Abuse.

Henggeler, S. W., Borduin, C. M., Melton, G. B., Mann, B. J., Smith, L. A., Hall, J. A., Cone, L., and Fucci, B. R. (1991). Effects of multisystemic therapy on drug use and abuse in serious juvenile offenders: A progress report from two outcome studies. *Family Dynamics of Addiction Quarterly, 1,* 40-51.

Henggeler, S. W., Pickrel, S. G., and Brondino, M. J. (1999). Multisystemic treatment of substance-abusing and dependent delinquents: Outcomes, treatment, fidelity, and transportability. *Mental Health Services Research, 1,* 171-184.

Henggeler, S. W., Pickrel, S. G., Brondino, M. J., and Crouch, J. L. (1996). Eliminating (almost) treatment dropout of substance abusing or dependent delinquents through home-based multisystemic therapy. *American Journal of Psychiatry, 153,* 427-428.

Hofler, M., Lieb, R., Perkonigg, A., and Schuster, P. (1999). Covariates of cannabis use progress in a representative sample of adolescents: A prospective examination of vulnerability and risk factors. *Addiction, 94*(11), 1679-1694.

Hser, Y., Grella, C., Hsieh, S., and Anglin, M. (1999). *National evaluation of drug treatment for adolescents.* Paper presented at the College on Problems of Drug Dependence conference, Acapulco, Mexico, June.

Hser, Y. I., Grella, C. E., Hubbard, R. L., Hsieh, S. C., Fletcher, B. W., Brown, B. S., and Anglin, M. D. (2001). An evaluation of drug treatments for adolescents in four U.S. cities. *Archives of General Psychiatry, 58,* 689-695.

Hubbard, R. L., Cavanaugh, E. R., Craddock, S. G., and Rachal, J. V. (1985). Characteristics, behaviors, and outcomes for youth in the TOPS. In A. S. Friedman and G. M. Beschner (Eds.), *Treatment services for adolescent substance abusers* (pp. 49-65). Rockville, MD: National Institute on Drug Abuse.

Hubbard, S. (1920). The New York City Narcotic Clinic. *Monthly Bulletin of the Department of Health of New York, 10*(2), 33-47.

Institute of Medicine (1990). *Broadening the base of treatment for alcohol problems.* Washington, DC: National Academy Press.

Jainchill, N. (1997). Therapeutic communities for adolescents: The same and not the same. In G. DeLeon (Ed.), *Community as method: Therapeutic communities for special population and special settings* (pp. 161-177). Westport, CT: Praeger Publishers/Greenwood Publishing Group.

Jasiukaitis, P. and Shane, P. (2001). Discriminant analysis with the GAIN predicts staff psychiatrist baseline diagnoses for an adolescent residential treatment sample (CSAT grant no. TI-11432). Presentation at the CSAT Adolescent Treatment Model Cross-site Meeting, May 15, Bethesda, MD.

Jessor, R. and Jessor, S.L. (1975). Adolescent development and the onset of drinking. *Journal of Studies on Alcohol, 36,* 27-51.

Joanning, H., Quinn, W., Thomas, F., and Mullen, R. (1992). Treating adolescent drug abuse: A comparison of family systems therapy, group therapy, and family drug education. *Journal of Marital and Family Therapy, 18,* 345-356.

Johnson R. A. and Gerstein, D. R. (1998). Initiation of use of alcohol, cigarettes, marijuana, cocaine, and other substances in US birth cohorts since 1919. *American Journal of Public Health 88*(1), 27-33.

Kajdan, R. A. and Senay, E. C. (1976). Modified therapeutic communities for youth. *Journal of Psychoactive Drugs, 8*(3), 209-214.

Kaminer, Y. (1994). *Adolescent substance abuse: A comprehensive guide to theory and practice.* New York: Plenum Press.

Kaminer, Y. (1995). Pharmacotherapy for adolescents with psychoactive substance use disorders. In E. Rahdert and D. Czechowicz (Eds.), *Adolescent drug abuse: Clinical assessment and therapeutic interventions* (NIDA Research Monograph, 156, pp. 291-324). Rockville, MD: National Institute on Drug Abuse.

Kaminer, Y. and Burleson, J. A. (1999). Psychotherapies for adolescent substance abusers: 15-month follow-up of a pilot study. *American Journal on Addictions, 8,* 114-119.

Kaminer, Y., Burleson, J. A., Blitz, C., Sussman, J., and Rounsaville, B. J. (1998). Psychotherapies for adolescent substance abusers: A pilot study. *Journal of Nervous and Mental Disorders, 186,* 684-690.

Kandel, D. B. and Yamaguchi, K. (1985). Developmental patterns of the use of legal, illegal and medically prescribed psychotropic drugs from adolescence to young adulthood. In C.L. Jones and R.J. Battjes (Eds.), *Etiology of drug abuse: Implications for revention, NIDA Research Monograph 56* (pp. 193-235). Rockville, MD: National Institute on Drug Abuse.

Kandel, D. B. and Yamaguchi, K. (1993). From beer to crack: Developmental patterns of involvement in drugs. *American Journal of Public Health, 83,* 851-855.

Kandel, D. B., Yamaguchi, K., and Chen, K. (1992). Stages of progression in drug involvement from adolescence to adulthood: Further evidence for the gateway theory. *Journal on Studies on Alcohol, 53,* 447-457.

Lamb, S., Greenlick, M. R., and McCarty, D. (Eds.) (1998). *Bridging the gap between practice and research: Forging partnerships with community-based drug and alcohol treatment.* Washington, DC: National Academy Press.

Lewis, R. A., Piercy, F. P., Sprenkle, D. H., and Trepper, T.S. (1990). Family-based interventions for helping drug-abusing adolescents. *Journal of Adolescent Research, 50,* 82-95.

Liddle, H. and Dakof, G. (1995) Family-based treatment for adolescent drug abuse: State of the science. In E. Rahdert and E. Czechowics (Eds.), *Adolescent drug abuse: Clinical assessment and therapeutic interventions.* NIDA Monograph No. 156 (DHHS Publication No. 95-3908) Rockville, MD: National Institute on Drug Abuse.

Lowry, J. (1956). The hospital treatment of the narcotic addict. *Federal Probation, 15*(20 December), 42-51.

McKeown, R. E., Jackson, K. L., and Valois, R. F. (1997). The frequency and correlates of violent behaviors in a statewide sample of high school students. *Family and Community Health, 20*(4), 38-53.

Miller, W. R. (1996). *Form 90A structured assessment interview for drinking and related behaviors.* (NIH Publication No. 96-4004, NIAAA Research Monograph Series). Bethesda, MD: National Institute on Alcohol Abuse and Alcoholism.

Miller, W. R., Brown, J. M., Simpson, T. L., Handmaker, N. S., Bien, T. H., Luckie, L. F., Montgomery, H. A., Hester, R. K., and Tonigan, J. S. (1995). What works? A methodological analysis of the alcohol treatment outcome literature. In R. K. Hester and W. R. Miller (Eds.), *Handbook of alcoholism treatment approaches: Effective alternatives* (pp. 12-44). Boston: Allyn and Bacon.

Miller, W. R. and Del Boca, F. K. (1994). Measurement of drinking behavior using the Form 90 family of instruments. *Journal of Studies on Alcohol,* (Supplement No. 12), 112-118.

Monitoring the Future [MTF] (1999). *Percent past-year drug and alcohol use among twelfth graders: 1975-1999 Monitoring the future.* [Available online at <http://monitoringthefuture.org>.]

Navarro, J., Wilson, S., Berger, L. R., and Taylor, T. (1997). Substance abuse and spirituality: A program for Native American students. *American Journal of Health Behavior, 21*(1), 3-11.

Newcomb, M. D. and Bentler, P. M. (1986). Frequency and sequence of drug use: A longitudinal study from early adolescence to young adulthood. *Journal of Drug Education, 16,* 101-120.

Newcomb, M. D. and Bentler, P. M. (1990). Antecedents and consequences of cocaine use: An eight-year study from early adolescence to young adulthood. In L. Robins (Ed.) *Straight and devious pathways from childhood to adulthood* (pp. 158-181). Cambridge: Cambridge Press.

Office of Applied Studies (OAS) (1995a). *Drug Abuse Warning Network. Annual medical examiner data 1995* (Series D-1, prepared by CSR, Inc). Rockville, MD: Author.

Office of Applied Studies (OAS) (1995b). *Services Research Outcomes Study.* Rockville, MD: Substance Abuse and Mental Health Services Administration. [Available online at <http://www.drugabusestatistics.samhsa.gov>.]

Office of Applied Studies (OAS) (1996). *Preliminary estimates from the 1995 National Household Survey on Drug Abuse.* (Advance Report, 18). Rockville, MD: Office of Applied Studies, Substance Abuse and Mental Health Services Administraiton.

Office of Applied Studies (OAS) (1999). *Treatment Episode Data Set (TEDS) 1992-1997: National admissions to substance abuse treatment services.* Rockville, MD: Author. [Available online at <http://www.icpsr.umich.edu/ SAMHDA>.]

Office of Applied Studies (OAS) (2000). *Treatment Episode Data Set (TEDS) 1993-1998: National admissions to substance abuse treatment services.* Rockville, MD: Author. [Available on line at <http://www.icpsr.umich.edu/SAMHDA. html>.]

Onken, L. S., Blaine, J. D. and Battjes, R. J. (1997). Behavioral therapy research: A conceptualization of a process. In S.W. Henggeler and A.B. Santos (Eds.), *Innovative approaches for difficult-to-treat populations* (pp. 477-485). Washington, DC: American Psychiatric Press.

Ozechowski, T. and Liddle, H. A. (2000). Family-based therapy for adolescent drug abuse: Knowns and unknowns. *Clinical Child and Family Psychology Review, 3*(4), 269-298.

Perkonigg, A., Lieb, R., Hofler, M., Schuster, P., Sonntag, H., and Wittchen, H.U. (1999). Patterns of cannabis use, abuse and dependence over time: Incidence, progression and stability in a sample of 1228 adolescents. *Addiction, 94*(11), 1663-1678.

Perry, P. D. and Stark, D. M. (2001). Dynamic Youth, Inc. program evaluation: Examination of GAIN and state administrative data (CSAT grant no. TI 11423).

Presentation at the CSAT Adolescent Treatment Model Cross-site Meeting, May 15, Bethesda, MD.

Powers, K., Hser, Y., Grella, C., and Anglin, M. (1999). *Differential assessment of treatment effectiveness on property crime and drug dealing among adolescents.* Paper presented at the College on Problems of Drug Dependence, Acapulco, Mexico, June. [Available online at <http://www.datos.org>.]

Risberg, R. A., Stevens, M. J., and Graybill, D. F. (1995). Validating the adolescent form of the substance abuse subtle screening inventory. *Journal of Child and Adolescent Substance Abuse, 44,* 25-41.

Robins, L. N. and McEvoy, L. (1990). Conduct problems as predictors of substance abuse. In L. N. Robins and M. Rutter (Eds.), *Straight and devious pathways from childhood to adulthood* (pp. 182-204). Cambridge: Cambridge University Press.

Rounds-Bryant, J.L., Kristiansen, P.L. Fairbank, J.A., and Hubbard, R.L. (1998). Substance use, mental disorders, abuse, and crime: Gender comparisons among a national sample of adolescent drug treatment clients. *Journal of Child and Adolescent Substance Abuse, 7*(4), 19-34.

Rowell, E. (1929). *Battling the wolves of society: The narcotic evil.* Mountain View, CA: Pacific Press.

Rowell, E. (1937). *Dope: Adventures of David Dare.* Nashville, TN: Southern Publishing.

Rowell, E.A. and Rowell, R. (1939). *On the trail of marijuana, the weed of madness.* Mountain View, CA: Pacific Press.

Scheier, L.M., Botvin, G.J., Diaz, T., and Ifill-Williams, M. (1997). Ethnic identity as a moderator of psychosocial risk and adolescent alcohol and marijuana use: Concurrent and longitudinal analyses. *Journal of Child and Adolescent Substance Abuse, 6,* 21-48.

Scott, C.K. and Dennis, M.L. (2000). A cost-effective approach to achieving over 90 percent follow-up in outcome monitoring with substance abuse treatment clients. *Journal of Drug and Alcohol Dependence. 60* (suppl.1), s200.

Sells, S. B. and Simpson, D. D. (1979). Evaluation of treatment for youth in the Drug Abuse Reporting Program. In G. Beschner and A. S. Friedman (Eds.), *Youth drug abuse: Problems, issues, and treatments* (pp. 571-628). Lexington, MA: Lexington Books.

Simpson, D. D., Savage, L. J., and Sells, S. B. (1978). *Data book on drug treatment outcomes.* Follow-up study of the 1969-1977 admissions to the Drug Abuse Reporting Program. (IBR Report 78-10). Fort Worth, TX: Texas Christian University.

Stanton, M. D. and Shadish, W. R. (1997). Outcome, attrition, and family/marital treatment for drug abuse: A meta-analysis and review of the controlled, comparative studies. *Psychological Bulletin, 122,* 170-191.

Szapoznik, J., Kurtines, W., Foote, F., Perez-Vidal, A., and Hervis, O. (1983). Conjoint versus one person family therapy: Some evidence for the effectiveness of conducting family therapy through one person. *Journal of Consulting and Clinical Psychology, 51,* 889-899.

Szapocznik, J., Perez-Vidal, A., Brickman, A. L., Foote, F. H., Santisteban, D., Hervis, O., and Kurtines, W. M. (1988). Engaging adolescent drug abusers and their families in treatment: A strategic structural systems approach. *Journal of Consulting and Clinical Psychology, 56,* 552-557.

Titus, J. C. and Godley, M. D. (1999). *What research tells us about the treatment of adolescent substance use disorders.* Paper presented at the Governor's Conference, Chicago, IL, August. [Available online at <http://www.chestnut.org/li/cyt/findings>.]

Vega, W. A. and Gil, A. G. (Eds.) (1998). *Drug use and ethnicity in early adolescence.* New York: Plenum Press.

Weinberg, N., Rahdert, E., Colliver, J.D., and Glantz, M.D. (1998). Adolescent substance abuse: A review of the past 10 years. *Journal of the American Academy of Child and Adolescent Psychiatry, 37,* 252-261.

White, W. (1998). *Slaying the dragon: The history of addiction treatment and recovery in America.* Bloomington, IL: Chestnut Health Systems.

Winters, K. C., Stinchfield, R. D., Opland, E. O., Weller, C. and Latimer, W.W. (2000). The effectiveness of the Minnesota Model approach in the treatment of adolescent drug abusers. *Addiction, 94*(4), 601-612.

SECTION II:
OUTPATIENT TREATMENT MODELS

Chapter 2

The Teen Substance Abuse Treatment Program: Program Design, Treatment Issues, and Client Characteristics

Sally J. Stevens
Barbara D. Estrada
Theodora Carter
Lynn Reinardy
Valerie Seitz
Tara Swartz

INTRODUCTION

The Teen Substance Abuse Treatment (TSAT) program is a three-month intensive outpatient treatment program administered by EMPACT-SPC for adolescent substance users living in Maricopa County, Arizona. Most of what is now Maricopa County was included as part of the Territory of New Mexico until 1863 when the Arizona Territory was established. The growth of Phoenix and other settlements along the Salt River resulted in the creation of Maricopa County which was officially established on February 14, 1871. It was the first new county of the original four counties of Territorial Arizona. The county was named in honor of the Maricopa Indians, who

Financial assistance for this study was provided by the Substance Abuse and Mental Health Service Administration—Center for Substance Abuse Treatment (SAMHSA-CSAT) grant # KD1 TI11892. The opinions expressed in this chapter are those of the authors and do not reflect official positions of SAMHSA-CSAT.

Please address correspondence to: Sally J. Stevens, Services Research Office, University of Arizona, 3912 S. 6th Ave, Tucson, AZ 85714; E-mail : sstevens@dakotacom. net; Phone: (520) 434-0334; Fax: (520) 434-0336.

were known to have inhabited the area as early as 1775. Maricopa County's outer geographical boundaries were set in 1881 with a land area of 9,226 square miles. Currently 14,441 square miles are incorporated. It is the fourteenth largest county in the United States, spanning 132 miles from east to west and 103 miles from north to south. Maricopa County has a population of more than 2,800,000 people, making it the fourth most populous county in the nation. The ethnic breakdown is approximately 71.9 percent Anglo, 20.5 percent Hispanic, 3.5 percent African American, 1.9 percent Native American, 1.5 percent Asian American, and 0.7 percent of unknown origin (Maricopa County at a Glance, 2000).

EMPACT-SPC began in 1987 as the Suicide Prevention Center, under the umbrella of Interfaith Counseling Services which was located southeast of Phoenix in Tempe, Arizona. By early 1989, as a result of the children's mental health bill, the agency became one of the first local agencies to offer in-home family counseling services. Eschewing a more typical medical model, EMPACT counseling staff evaluate the functioning level of an individual and their family and provide treatment within the context of the family. Services expanded with the addition of mobile crisis staff who intervene by phone or in person, twenty-four hours a day, in behavioral crises involving youth and families. In 1990 these services became independent of Interfaith and the name was changed to EMPACT-SPC. Because of large urban sprawl in Maricopa County, EMPACT-SPC added a second West Side office located in Glendale, Arizona. The two EMPACT-SPC sites provide prevention programs for eleven of the twenty-nine cities in the county.

As the agency established itself as a major nonprofit center for treatment, several programs were added through a variety of funding sources. Contracts from the Arizona Department of Health Services (ADHS), Division of Economic Security (DES), funded after school clubs, and Child Protective Services (CPS) funded such programs as Intensive Family Preservation and Parent Aide Services. Most in-office and in-home family therapy has been funded through the Regional Behavioral Health Authority (RBHA) allocating funds from ADHS, Division of Behavioral Health. RBHA evolved from three local entities serving Maricopa County, which were consolidated to one entity called ComCare (a nonprofit), then assumed by the current, for profit, ValueOptions. Meanwhile EMPACT-SPC crisis services grew to include eighteen teams of therapists working in conjunction with local Urgent Care Centers and a transportation provider to handle Maricopa County's adult and children's crisis needs.

Early in EMPACT's history, substance abuse treatment was identified as a key area of need and funding was sought and obtained. For adult services, Maricopa County Adult Probation funds treatment groups as a result of Proposition 200, a bill that allowed for treatment of first-time drug offenders. Adult Parole funds COOL, a treatment program for adults leaving the prison system. DES funds an intensive outpatient program for adults with children in the custody of CPS due to child abuse or neglect. Most recently EMPACT-SPC became the pilot site for a family recovery program. Funded through state agency cost sharing, this project provides intensive wraparound services to families involved with CPS where the adult(s) are involved with substance abuse.

To address the needs of the substance abuse among juveniles, EMPACT-SPC developed a treatment program in 1994 through a grant from the Center of Substance Abuse Treatment (CSAT). This program, Positive Alternatives to Drugs Requires Encouragement and Support (PADRES), was a three-year collaborative effort between EMPACT-SPC, the Department of Youth Treatment and Rehabilitation (DYTR), and TASC, Inc., which provides a specialized treatment intervention to juveniles ages thirteen to seventeen on supervised release from the Arizona Department of Juvenile Corrections. When funding for PADRES ended, the TSAT program was implemented.

TEEN SUBSTANCE ABUSE TREATMENT PROGRAM DESCRIPTION (TSAT)

Overview of the TSAT Program

The TSAT program opened in 1997 to meet the need for an intensive outpatient program for juveniles ages twelve to seventeen with substance abuse problems and their families. In Maricopa County, intensive outpatient treatment is defined as any counseling service in which participants receive nine or more hours of service per week. Juvenile probation has been the primary referral source for the TSAT program, with most probationers' involvement in TSAT being court ordered. In recent years the number of clients referred from the Regional Behavioral Health Authority, ValueOptions, has increased bringing greater diversity in the type of youth being served.

TSAT is a ninety-day program from intake to graduation. Evaluated on an individual basis, an extension is sometimes granted for the juvenile to continue with services after ninety days of treatment. Additional reasons for this extension include: level of sobriety (significant reduction in drug use was not achieved); irregular attendance; or indication for the need to step the client down from intensive outpatient to an aftercare level of services, such as one or two groups per week.

The treatment goals for individuals enrolled in TSAT include

1. reduced or eliminated substance use,
2. improved decision making,
3. improved family functioning,
4. reduced or eliminated criminal involvement, and
5. reduced out-of-home placements.

To achieve these goals TSAT staff, clients, and family members of the client work together to strengthen the family's ability to manage crises, support sobriety, and to reinforce good decision making and appropriate behavior of all family members. Juveniles and family members are assisted in utilizing age-appropriate coping and decision making skills. Family patterns that are identified as dysfunctional are addressed and effort is made to replace unhealthy interactions with healthier interactions. Multiple treatment components are utilized along with random drug use monitoring. To ensure treatment compliance, strategies to reduce barriers that keep juveniles and their family members from receiving treatment, such as lack of transportation, are implemented.

TSAT Program Approach

The TSAT program approach is based upon cognitive behavioral therapy (CBT) and family systems therapy (FST). CBT is best thought of as a family or collection of methods rather than any single technique (McGuire, 1996). It can be and has been used in both individual and group therapy. CBT programs use behavioral learning techniques to change the adaptive behaviors of clients so that they have a new repertoire of skills enabling them to function without the use of drugs. CBT teaches clients functional behaviors (i.e., social skills, problem solving, lifestyle activities) that may have deteriorated due to drug use—or may never have initially been developed. CBT also teaches clients to self-manage affects through programs and/or activities which address issues such as impulse control, anger management, and cognitive restructuring. In addition, CBT provides training in relapse prevention, which given the nature of substance abuse and addiction, is critically needed (Najavitis, Weiss, and Liese, 1996). Outcome studies have indicated the effectiveness of CBT approaches with numerous adult populations such as male probationers (Kownacki, 1995; Ross, Fabiano, and Diemer-Ewles, 1988, 1995), incarcerated males enrolled in substance abuse treatment (Peters et al., 1993), cocaine using methadone patients (Rosenblum et al., 1999), and women with histories of rape and childhood trauma (Foa, Steketee, and Rothbaum, 1989; Richards and Rose, 1991; Steketee and Foa, 1987). While less is known about the effectiveness of the CBT for working with adolescent substance abusers, it is thought to be a promising approach.

Family systems theory looks to the family and larger social systems for clues to the development and reoccurrence of substance use. Working within this framework, counselors treat the family as the patient, addressing family structure and family interactions. Family characteristics such as roles and boundaries are identified and counselors work to assist families in restructuring malfunctions in the family system (Stevens-Smith and Smith, 1998). Families can express symptoms just as an individual family member's substance use can be the symptom of the larger malfunction within the family. While the adolescent may be the "client in treatment," the entire family may receive treatment within this approach.

TSAT Entrance Criteria

All juveniles accepted into the program are evaluated as having significant substance abuse problems or diagnosed as being alcohol or drug dependent. Clients are not accepted in the program if the level of their substance involvement has been experimental or relatively minor. Such intense contact with longer-term addicted or heavily using clients is seen as being a threat to inducting early users into, not out of, the drug culture. In addition to a substance-related diagnosis, clients are also accepted for treatment who have co-occurring disorders such as unipolar or bipolar depression, ADD/ADHD, conduct disorder and oppositional defiant disorder, eating disorders, anxiety and panic disorders, and PTSD. However, clients experiencing significant psychotic symptoms that would hinder their ability to participate and benefit the TSAT program are screened as inappropriate for enrollment. In addition, adolescents who are evaluated as needing inpatient services (i.e., hospitalization, long-term residential) are not admitted into the TSAT program. Adolescents needing inpatient services who are referred by Juvenile Probation work with their probation officer to find an appropriate placement, while those referred from Value Options work with TSAT staff to secure an appropriate inpatient placement.

Because Maricopa County is geographically spread over a large area, access to treatment is typically a problem if one does not have transportation. However, given EMPACT-SPC's commitment to making services available to all clients, access to treatment is not a barrier for TSAT clients. To enable TSAT clients to participate in the program and arrive at one of the two treatment sites in a timely manner, transportation is provided for clients within the geographic boundaries of approximately 400 square miles surrounding each of the EMPACT treatment sites. For clients living in remote areas of the county, staff assist the family in arranging for a pick-up and drop-off location. Clients can also receive bus tokens from Maricopa County Juvenile Probation to assist with commuting to and from their treatment site. In addition, TSAT's inclusion of home-based therapy also helps to reduce transportation problems, although this is not the primary reason for provision of home-based services.

TSAT Program Components

The design of the TSAT program includes three components: (1) in-home family and individual counseling, (2) teen group, and (3) multifamily group. All TSAT participants receive all of the treatment components.

In-Home Family and Individual Counseling

In-home family and individual counseling both use a brief, solution-focused approach, blending the cognitive-behavioral and family systems approach with techniques which entail getting clients to become aware of their feelings and the motivating forces for their behaviors. Family sessions are influenced by tenets from family therapy, including the notion that the family can express symptoms. Family strengths are identified and interventions are designed to build on the strengths of the client and family. Successful treatment is seen to begin with a clear understanding and agreement among the therapist, the client, and the family members regarding the goals of the therapy. In-home therapy sessions are scheduled most frequently in the early evenings and on Saturdays. The first in-home family session includes an in-depth assessment of the youth and the biopsychosocial and familial issues that encompass the case. The assessment includes obtaining information about basic demographics, health status (including medication history), alcohol and drug history, mental health, criminal involvement, family background and interaction patterns, education and vocation, and social functioning. Although assessment is ongoing throughout treatment, this initial assessment provides the basis for the individualized treatment plan in which the adolescent's treatment goals and objectives are outlined. It is particularly important that this assessment is conducted in the home so that the therapist can gain a sense of the family structure, setting, and dynamics.

Although TSAT therapists encourage attendance of all family members involved in the case, they must be able to adapt the session to whomever attends each session as this may change during the course of treatment. Family members are often substance involved themselves and this must be addressed by the therapist. Drug-involved family members vary in the degree to which they are open about their substance use thereby presenting a challenge to therapists to remain flexible in their approach. At a minimum, substance abuse treatment referrals are offered. Family therapists who work with families who are open to counseling with regard to family drug involvement address intergenerational drug use, patterns of use, effect of use on family dynamics, and family recovery plans, including accountability and support. Typically, the therapist begins the session by "checking in" with the client and family members to get a general feel for what has occurred since the previous visit. The treatment goals and objectives are reviewed during each visit and modified if needed. Crisis plans for dealing with issues such as health emergencies, gang involvement incidents, experiences of relapse, and family confrontations are developed with families as well as with the family's support systems such as case managers, probation officers, primary care physicians, and educational professionals. Significant issues from the family's past are addressed through discussion with the purpose of allowing the client and family to decrease psychological and psychiatric symptoms, conflict or disengagement levels, and to build positive hierarchy and communication skills. When appropriate, parenting skills are taught to help parents set and maintain household rules and regain a position of authority within the family.

Discharge planning begins at the initial in-home family session with the identification of solutions to the identified problem. Teens and parents are encouraged to move toward self-sufficiency. The treatment design reflects this movement toward self-sufficiency. The first month of the program indicates six hours per week of home-based services that is decreased to four hours per week for the second month. Home-based services are then reduced to two hours per week for the final month. These levels serve as general guidelines, however; the specific level of therapy for each family is determined by the staff and family per the family's needs. When appropriate, family members are referred to drug treatment and to community resources such as church involvement; Department of Economic Security for food stamps, child support, medical coverage; self-help/twelve-step groups; and parenting and support groups. Therapists also help the adolescent clients connect to other social service agencies that provide health care, assistance with enrollment into school, enrollment into job skills programs, or agencies that assist with obtaining employment. Related needs of the clients and their immediate family members such as health care, transportation, housing, and recreational resources are also addressed by the therapy staff.

Teen Group

The teen group is held three times a week for three hours. The East Side TSAT site holds teen groups on Mondays, Wednesdays, and Fridays from 3:00 to 6:00 p.m. while the West Side site holds the groups on Mondays, Tuesdays, and Thursdays from 3:00 to 6:00 p.m. These time periods were chosen because they resulted in the highest rate of attendance. Participating adolescents are finished with their school day and are not yet engaged in other activities. TSAT staff are often able to pick the adolescents up at their school, decreasing problems with communication and transportation.

As with the in-home individual and family therapy component, the primary therapeutic approach in addressing client education, awareness, and behavior change is cognitive behavioral. The teen group also begins by "checking in" with each client for an update on what has occurred since the previous group. This is followed by engagement in curriculum unless an imminent crisis within the group or group dynamic exist that need immediate attention. Significant flexibility in the order and method (i.e., group discussion, worksheets, readings, movies) of curriculum delivery is maintained. This flexibility allows TSAT staff to be able to work with the diverse and emergent needs of each group as well as the specific needs of the individuals who comprise the group. Curriculum units include (1) substance abuse, (2) recovery, (3) skill building, (4) health, and (5) relapse prevention, each of which has several developed sessions from which to choose. (See Table 2.1 for a list of TSAT curriculum units.) Within the substance abuse curriculum unit there are seven developed curriculum sessions. For example, in one of the sessions clients are given information on signs of alcoholism while another session focuses on stages of addiction, and a third details drug categories and their physical effects. The recovery curriculum unit includes eight sessions on topics such as motivation and willingness to change, addiction versus rational thinking, and a speaker series which includes recovering individuals—many of whom were former TSAT clients. Within the skill-building curriculum unit, nine sessions have been developed such as anger management, goal setting, and alcohol and drug refusal skills. The eight developed sessions in the unit on health include sessions on such topics as HIV and other sexually transmitted diseases (STDs), healthy boundaries, and sober fun/natural highs. Because relapse occurs often with adolescents, addressing their addiction problem is important. The relapse prevention curriculum unit includes sessions on topics such as relapse triggers, relapse warning signs, and developing "clean" or drug-free plans.

In general, the TSAT teen group curriculum is an interactive curriculum in which some sessions are somewhat interactive (e.g., signs of substance abuse and addiction) while others are highly interactive (e.g., drug refusal skills). In addition, clients are encouraged to be open during teen group regarding issues they are experiencing. Com-

TABLE 2.1. TSAT Curriculum Units and Sessions

Unit	Session
Substance Abuse	Signs of Substance Abuse and Addiction
	Addiction: Tolerance, Withdrawal, Cross Addiction
	Self-Medication
	Drug Categories/Physical Effects of Drugs
	Tobacco/Nicotine
	Postacute Withdrawal
	Drug of Choice—Interactive Exercise
	Chemical Addiction and Substance Abuse Workshop
Recovery	Cognitive Disorders
	Motivation and Willingness to Change
	Responsibility
	Identity and Diversity
	Addicted versus Rational Thinking
	Consequences of Substance Abuse
	Healthy versus Unhealthy Recovery
	Recovery Stories Speakers Series
	12-Step Programs
Skill Building	Anger Management
	Avoiding Pitfalls "Hole in the Sidewalk"
	Coping Strategies
	Taking Responsibility
	Decision Making
	Goal Setting
	Communication Skills
	Refusal Skills—Role-Play
	Values Clarification
Health	HIV and Other STDs
	Depression
	Physical Exercise and Fitness
	Future-Day Fantasy
	Healthy Boundaries
	Healthy Living
	Positive Feedback "Right On"
	Sober Fun/Natural Highs
Relapse Prevention	Relapse Cycle
	Relapse Triggers
	Relapse Warning Signs
	Support Networks
	Developing Clean Plans

mon issues concern fighting/disagreements within the family, past and present trauma, difficulty with significant other, and work and school problems. The adolescents learn to identify their feelings and begin to connect with others since many adolescents within the group often share common feelings. The development of coping skills is strongly emphasized. Monthly sober-fun activities are organized. Indoor rock-climbing, laser tag, hiking, basketball, bowling, and other activities provide clients with alternatives to drug use and criminal behavior.

Multifamily Group

A three-hour multifamily group meeting occurs monthly, taking the place of the teen group. Because family members cannot typically attend a 3:00 to 6:00 p.m. session, the multifamily group is scheduled from 6:00 to 9:00 p.m. As with the in-home individual and family therapy and teen group components, the multifamily group begins with "checking in" with the families. Family members share with one another their current progress, solutions, support, and resources. Families in TSAT are seen to have unique strengths while sharing certain commonalties of their shared struggles. They are encouraged to gain a sense of potential solutions and to decrease any experience of isolation or stigma as a result of substance abuse and family problems. Information is shared on topics such as adolescent development, post-acute withdrawal, and roles in addicted families. The parents, teens, and significant others discuss issues such as how parents can work with their teens to learn coping skills, effective discipline techniques, and ways in which family members can engage with one another more positively. Activities are facilitated and processed that relate to communication, values, cooperation, and trust. Occasionally, events such as an art or talent show are organized. A potluck dinner is served during the multifamily group, and transportation is arranged for those in need.

Monitoring of Drug Use

To monitor clients' level of drug use, TSAT staff collaborate with Maricopa County's Treatment Alternative to Street Crime (TASC) program. TASC, a local drug-testing facility, is an offender case management program designed to link drug-using offenders within the criminal justice system to community-based drug treatment as an alternative or supplement to criminal penalties.

TSAT clients are brought to TASC one time per week, with the day of testing chosen randomly. The results of the urinalysis are sent to probation (and/or a case manager) and are also shared with the client's family as well as the therapeutic teen group as a means of monitoring sobriety. Incidences of relapse are used as an opportunity for the clients to learn more about their own relapse triggers and the limitations of their current personal recovery program. Clients are not typically discharged for multiple drug use infractions. Any client suspected of being under the influence of drugs or alcohol during group is brought to the testing facility during group. Clients who refuse to provide a urine sample are taken home. All major behavioral infractions are reported to the client's probation officer and/or case manager.

TSAT Staffing Pattern

The staffing pattern for the TSAT program includes a master's level program coordinator who oversees both the East Side and West Side sites. The program coordinator also oversees and facilitates the teen group and multifamily group at the East Side location. A second master's level certified therapist oversees and facilitates the activities at the West Side site. The two master's level therapists also provide most of the in-home individual and family sessions, although several "contract" therapists also carry a caseload for this component. Although utilizing contract therapists is more cumbersome in terms of coordination and communication, it does allow for more variability in counseling style as well as gender and ethnic diversity. The benefits of being able to provide some client matching is viewed by TSAT staff to outweigh the increased complexity of coordination and communication. All therapists are required to keep their paperwork up to date on each adolescent on their caseload. EMPACT-SPC management staff conduct regular internal audits of all case files while external audits are conducted by Commission of Accreditation of Rehabilitative Facilities (CARF), EMPACT-SPC's contracting organization and by the Arizona State Behavioral Health Licensing Board.

Each site has two program assistants who not only assist with the teen and multifamily group but also provide transportation, oversee vehicle maintenance, coordinate the urine screen testing, update and communicate with probation officers and caseworkers, organize the potluck for the multifamily group, make reminder telephone calls, and organize the monthly sober-fun activities. Program assistants are required to have a bachelor's degree and two years' experience or an associate's degrees and four years of field experience.

EVALUATION DESIGN

Three types of evaluation activities have been implemented by the University of Arizona-Services Research Office (UofA-SRO) research team who have been contracted to evaluate the TSAT program. These include: (1) a treatment outcome study, (2) a qualitative study, and (3) a cost study. Aggregated findings from each of the evaluation activities are shared with program staff on a regular and as-needed basis. During the intake process the UofA-SRO evaluation activities are explained to the adolescents and their parents or guardians. If interested in participating in the evaluation component, two sets of consent forms are signed; one by the adolescent and the other by a parent or guardian. Of the adolescents enrolled in TSAT, 90 percent agreed to participate in the evaluation component.

Treatment Outcome Study

The treatment outcome evaluation activities include (1) a baseline assessment conducted within seven days of intake and (2) follow-up assessments at three, six, nine, and twelve months from the date of intake. The baseline interview takes approximately 1.5 to 3 hours, while the follow-up assessments take 1 to 2.5 hours. Variation in the time of the assessment interview is typically due to:

1. the client's experiences during the reference period (i.e., substance use, criminal activity, education, employment),
2. the client's ability to recall his or her activities during the reference period,

3. the client's command of the English language (some report Spanish as the first language), and
4. the client's ability to stay focused on the interview.

Clients are not paid for the baseline interviews but they are paid $25.00 for each of the follow-up assessment interviews. The baseline and follow-up assessments include:

1. Global Appraisal of Individual Needs (GAIN)—Initial (GAIN-I) and follow-up (GAIN-M-90) (see Dennis et al., 2003)
2. Hispanic acculturation scale (see Stevens et al., 2003)
3. HIV/AIDS knowledge and risk assessment (see Stevens et al., 2003)
4. Environmental stress inventory (see Stevens et al., 2003)
5. Adolescent relapse coping questionnaire (see Stevens et al., 2003)
6. Cognitive functioning questionnaire, which assesses adolescents' cognitive abilities including problem solving, inferencing, and abstract reasoning along with their knowledge and concepts of disease

Qualitative Study

The qualitative study component includes (1) in-depth case studies of selected TSAT participants, (2) examination of the treatment process, and (3) the study of identity and diversity.

In-Depth Case Studies

The case study component includes qualitative sessions with eight adolescents during treatment and up to six months after treatment discharge. The UofA-SRO ethnographer meets with the adolescents approximately once a week during treatment and approximately two times per month once the youth has completed or left treatment. All of the case study data are transcribed, verbatim, from the audiotaped sessions. From the transcribed case study notes the data are coded into ten categories. These categories include

1. self,
2. family,
3. friends,
4. neighborhood,
5. legal involvement,
6. drug use,
7. drug treatment,
8. mainstream connections,
9. future expectations, and
10. ethnographic notes.

In addition, the ten broad categories include many subcategories. These qualitative data are used to illuminate the treatment process as well as to help interpret findings from the quantitative component.

Treatment Process

The UofA-SRO research staff examines the treatment process by having the TSAT counselors assess each client's progress through treatment and the client's perception of what treatment components have assisted his or her process of change. The following scales and assessments are used to obtain this information:

- Counselor rated—progress scale (see Stevens et al., 2003)
- Client rated—satisfaction scale (see Stevens et al., 2003)

Identity and Diversity

These topics are explored through the observation of special activities. The treatment staff address the issue of adolescent identity through the adolescent's participation in an art show which is held during a multifamily group session. In preparation, the adolescents are given a camera to take pictures of themselves or of other images that reflect upon who they are. These pictures are developed and then placed on poster board. In addition, clients are encouraged to make collages from newspaper pictures or from pictures of themselves in earlier years; to write poetry; and draw and/or paint pictures. The

UofA-SRO ethnographer attends the art show and, with permission, audiotape records each client's artwork explanation—as the client articulates how the art reflects self-identity.

TSAT staff also address diversity. Diversity is explored through an outing to the Heard Museum, an American Indian historical and contemporary museum located in central Phoenix. Once at the Heard Museum, clients are asked to reflect upon the large hand-painted murals depicting the history—including the colonization—of the American Indian. The UofA-SRO ethnographer questions each youth about his/her thoughts, perceptions, feelings, and interpretation of the murals. Clients permission to audiotape record their responses is obtained in advance. As with other qualitative evaluation activities, audiotape transcription, coding, and analysis is conducted.

Cost Study

A cost study examining the cost of treatment will be conducted by Capital Consulting Corporation during the third and final year of the CSAT evaluation grant. Cost of treatment matched with treatment outcomes will be examined across the ten ATM funded programs (see Dennis et al., 2003).

CLIENT POPULATION DESCRIPTION

Between January 2000 and October 2000, thirty-two adolescents were enrolled in the TSAT program. As described in Table 2.2, the majority of TSAT clients are male (81.3 percent). Most are between the ages of fifteen and sixteen (59.4 percent), although 25 percent are younger (thirteen to fourteen). The youth are predominately white (43.8 percent) although a sizable portion are Hispanic (31.3 percent). Almost all (93.8 percent) live at home with their parents. Close to half (43.7 percent) are in school, while 37.5 percent are unemployed, and 12.5 percent are working full time. The last school grade completed by TSAT clients was ninth to tenth grade (53.1 percent), followed by sixth to eighth grade (40.7 percent). The majority of clients felt that the drug they most needed treatment for was marijuana (65.6 percent), with smaller percentages reporting needing treatment for methamphetamine (12.5 percent), and hallucinogens (6.3 percent), or not needing treatment at all (9.4 percent). Seventy-one percent of the youth met the cri-

TABLE 2.2. Cross-Site Variables (N = 32)

Item	N	%
Gender		
Male	26	81.3
Female	6	18.7
Age		
11-12	0	0.0
13-14	8	25.1
15-16	19	59.4
17-18	5	15.6
19 and over	0	0.0
Ethnicity		
American Indian/Alaskan Native	0	0.0
Asian or Pacific Islander	2	6.3
Black	2	6.3
White	14	43.8
Hispanic (Puerto Rican, Mexican, Cuban, other)	10	31.3
Mixed/some other group	4	12.6
Current living situation		
A house or apartment (yours or parents)	30	93.8
A foster home or public housing	0	0.0
A friend's or relative's house or apartment	2	6.3
A nursing home, hospital, inpatient or residential	0	0.0
Jail, detention center, or other correctional institution	0	0.0
Temporary or emergency shelter	0	0.0
Vacant buildings	0	0.0
Any other housing situation	0	0.0
Present work or school situation		
Working full time	4	12.5
Working part time	2	6.3
Unemployed or laid off	12	37.5
Have a job, but not working because of treatment, illness, seasonal	0	0.0
In school or training only (even if not in session now)	14	43.7

TABLE 2.2 *(continued)*

Item	N	%
In jail or prison	0	0.0
Some other work situation (no school/no work)	0	0.0
Substance dependence (meeting criteria)	22	71.0
Substance treatment needed for		
Any kind of alcohol	0	0.0
Marijuana, hashish, etc.	21	65.6
Crack, freebase cocaine, other cocaine	2	6.3
Amphetamine/methamphetamine	4	12.5
Inhalants	0	0.0
Heroin	0	0.0
"Acid" or other hallucinogens	2	6.3
Some other drug	0	0.0
None	3	9.4
Age when first got drunk or used any drugs		
Below 15	31	100.0
15-18	0	0.0
Over 18	0	0.0
Last grade or year completed in school		
< 6	0	0.0
6-8	13	40.7
9-10	17	53.1
11-12	2	6.3
> 12	0	0.0

	Mean	SD
Times in life arrested, charged with a crime and booked	4.09	4.03
Substance use—last 90 days		
Days used alcohol, marijuana, or other drugs	30.81	22.97
Days drunk or high for most of the day	19.31	21.92
Days in a jail (or other place) where you could not use drugs	21.13	24.33
Times in life admitted to drug treatment or counseling	1.06	1.24

teria for drug dependence based on the year prior to treatment entry. All of the youth reported getting drunk or using drugs before age fifteen, while recent alcohol and drug use was reported on average to be 30 of the past 90 days (Standard Deviation 22.97). The adolescents, including those who reported no use, reported being drunk or high for most of the day on average of 19 of the last 90 days (SD 21.92), although they also reported living in a place where they could not use drugs on average of 21.13 days of the past 90 days (SD 24.33). Finally, TSAT clients reported being arrested, charged, and convicted of a crime an average of 4 times (SD 4.03). Not including their enrollment into TSAT, on average they had been admitted to a drug treatment or counseling facility 1.0 times (SD 1.24).

DISCUSSION

The TSAT program utilizes a cognitive behavioral and family systems approach for working with adolescent substance abusers, most of whom are probationers. While cognitive behavioral approaches have been shown to be successful for working with various adult populations, less is known about the effectiveness of this approach for working with substance abusing adolescents. Preliminary findings, prior to the implementation of the CSAT adolescent treatment models (ATM) study, indicated that adolescents who participated in the TSAT program were able to reduce their drug use and related negative behaviors. To substantiate these findings and ascertain more clearly which clients are assisted by their involvement in the TSAT program and the type and level of changes made, the current study was implemented. Examination of outcome data along with the treatment process data should illuminate the impact of the TSAT program on enrolled clients, while the cost study will assist policymakers, clinicians, and researchers to understand the cost effectiveness of the program when compared to the nine other CSAT-funded exemplary programs involved in this initiative.

REFERENCES

Dennis, M.L., Dawud-Noursi, S.D., Muck, R.D., and McDermeit, M. (2003). The need for developing and evaluating adolescent treatment models. In S.J. Stevens and A.

Morral (Eds.), *Adolescent substance abuse treatment in the United States: Exemplary models from a national evaluation study* pp. 3-56, Binghamton, NY: The Haworth Press, Inc.

Foa, E.B., Steketee, G., and Rothbaum, B.O. (1989). Behavioral/cognitive conceptualizations of posttraumatic stress disorder. *Behavior Therapy, 20,* 155-176.

Kownacki, R.J. (1995). The effectiveness of a brief cognitive-behavioral program on the reduction of antisocial behaviour in high-risk adult probationers in a Texas community. In R.R. Ross and R.D. Ross (Eds.), *Thinking Straight: The Reasoning and Rehabilitation Program for Delinquency Prevention and Offender Rehabilitation* (pp. 249-257). Ottawa, Canada: Air Training and Publications.

Maricopa County at a Glance (Retrieved September 4, 2000). The World Wide Web: <http://www.maricopa.gov/default/default.asp?bhcp=1>.

McGuire, J. (1996*). Cognitive Behavioral Approaches: An Introductory Course on Theory and Research.* Liverpool, UK: Department of Clinical Psychology, University of Liverpool.

Najavitis, L.M., Weiss, R.D., and Liese, B.S. (1996). Group cognitive behavioral therapy for women with PTSD and substance use disorder. *Journal of Substance Abuse Treatment, 13*(1) 13-22.

Peters, R.H., Kearns, W.D., Murrin, M.R., Dolente, A.S., and May II, R.L. (1993). Examining the effectiveness of in-jail substance abuse treatment. *Alcohol and Drug Rehabilitation, 19,* 1-39.

Richards, D.A. and Rose, J.S. (1991). Exposure therapy for posttraumatic stress disorder: Four case studies. *British Journal of Psychiatry, 158,* 836-840.

Rosenblum, A., Magura, S., Palij, M., Foote, J., Handelsman, L., and Stimmel, B. (1999). Enhanced treatment outcomes for cocaine-using methadone patients. *Drug and Alcohol Dependence, 54,* 207-218.

Ross, R.R., Fabiano, E.A., and Diemer-Ewles, C. (1988). Reasoning and rehabilitation. *International Journal of Offender Therapy and Comparative Criminology, 32,* 29-35.

Ross, R.R., Fabiano, E., A., and Diemer-Ewles, C. (1995). The Pickering Project for high risk probationers. In R.R. Ross, and R.D. Ross (Eds.), *Thinking Straight: The Reasoning and Rehabilitation Program for Delinquincy Prevention and Offender Rehabilitation* (pp. 145-153). Ottawa, Canada: Air Training and Publications.

Steketee, G. and Foa, E.B. (1987). Rape victims: Posttraumatic stress responses and their treatment: A review of the literature. *Journal of Anxiety Disorders, 1,* 69-86.

Stevens, S.J., Hasler, J., Murphy, B.S., Taylor, R., Senior, M., Barron, M., Garcia, P., Polois, Z. (2003). La Cañada adolescent treatment program: Addressing issues of drug use, gender, and trauma. In S.J. Stevens and A.R. Morral (Eds.), *Adolescent Substance Abuse Treatment in the United States: Exemplary Models from a National Evaluation Study* (pp. 333-376). Binghamton, NY: The Haworth Press, Inc.

Stevens-Smith, P. and Smith, R.L. (1998). *Substance Abuse Counseling: Theory and Practice.* Upper Saddle River, NJ: Prentice-Hall, Inc.

Chapter 3

Chestnut Health Systems' Bloomington Outpatient and Intensive Outpatient Program for Adolescent Substance Abusers

Susan Harrington Godley
Richard Risberg
Loree Adams
Alan Sodetz

Chestnut Health Systems' (CHS) Bloomington outpatient and intensive outpatient programs for adolescent substance abusers are part of a larger system of adolescent services (for ages twelve through eighteen years old) that includes early intervention services, day treatment, and residential treatment. CHS is a private not-for-profit behavioral health care corporation with a volunteer board of directors that offers both substance abuse and mental health services to consumers of all ages. It was one of the first organizations in Illinois to receive funding from the state for adolescent treatment after having begun as a substance abuse treatment agency in 1975. The corpora-

Financial assistance for this study was provided by SAMHSA's Center for Substance Abuse Treatment (CSAT) Grant No. TI11894. The opinions expressed herein are those of the authors and do not reflect official positions of the government. The authors appreciate the valuable work of Michael Dennis, Bryan Garner, Sam Lyons, Lora Passetti, Melissa McDermeit, Judy Miller, and Laura Slown in the preparation of this manuscript.

Please address correspondence to: Susan H. Godley, Chestnut Health Systems, 720 W. Chestnut, Bloomington, IL, 61701; Phone: 309-827-6025; Fax: 309-829-4661; e-mail: <sgodley@ chestnut.org>.

tion has a second location for adolescent treatment in southwestern Illinois that was one of the four Cannabis Youth Treatment study sites (Dennis et al., in press). The Adolescent Treatment Model funding was awarded to CHS in the fall of 1999 and at the time of this writing about 33 percent of the sample had been recruited for the evaluation study.

The adolescent substance abuse treatment program has been in existence since 1985 and is now the largest adolescent provider in the state, with 4 percent of all public admissions (Dennis, Hristova, and Foss, 1999). Although annual program changes have occurred, the outpatient program underwent major revisions in 1993. These revisions were in response to a low census (averaging twelve to sixteen clients) and the recognition that many youth in need of services were not being served. Prior to 1993, the outpatient (OP) and intensive outpatient (IOP) programs primarily served clients who were receiving aftercare services postresidential treatment. In that year, two case managers were hired to conduct outreach activities to increase referrals, a new curriculum was designed for outpatient skills groups, and transportation for clients was provided to and from treatment. In 1998 and 1999 the average daily census for the program was forty-five clients.

The treatment program is located in and serves McLean County in central Illinois, which is the largest geographical county in Illinois covering close to 1,200 square miles. With an estimated 1997 population of 138,569, it includes a mix of more that twenty rural communities and the metro area of Bloomington (57,707) and Normal (42,219). The county's major employment sectors are service (25 percent), finance—particularly insurance—(18 percent), and government (17 percent). The twin cities are home to two major universities, Illinois State University and Illinois Wesleyan University. According to the estimated 1995 census, the county population is approximately 5 percent African American, 2 percent Hispanic, and 94 percent white. Of the residents age twenty-five and over, 33 percent have a high school degree (or its equivalent) and 52 percent have some post-high school education. The county is the third fastest growing in the state and has a healthy economic base as evidenced by an unemployment rate of 2.1 percent in 1999.

OVERVIEW

Theoretical Rationale

As is typical of community-based treatment programs that have developed over a number of years with the input of various professionals, the program is based on a blended therapeutic approach. It draws upon four theories of behavioral and emotional change (Rogerian, behavioral, cognitive, and reality therapy) and includes twelve-step concepts and approaches. Rogerian concepts include unconditional positive regard, acceptance, building rapport, and empowering the client (Rogers, 1951, 1959). Behavioral approaches include focusing on skills building/learning, behavior modification techniques, and habit control (Chiauzzi, 1991; Hester and Miller, 1989; Kazdin, 2000). Cognitive theory emphasizes evaluating perceptions and thoughts, and changing thinking patterns by reframing and cognitive restructuring (Ellis et al., 1988; Walen, DiGiuseppe, and Dryden, 1992; Yankura and Dryden, 1990). Reality therapy focuses on choices and their consequences, emphasizing that experiencing the consequences of their actions will help teach clients about responsibilities, and that their life problems are directly related to the choices they make (Glasser, 1976, 1992). There is also a strong emphasis on the early detection of substance use, the identification of attention deficit and hyperactivity disorder (ADHD) and conduct disorder (Adams and Wallace, 1994; Risberg, Stevens, and Graybill, 1995), and family involvement (Risberg and Funk, 2000). These principles and consideration of development issues associated with adolescence shape and guide all treatment interventions for clients and their families.

Facility, Accreditation, and State Requirements

All levels of care, as well as medical and psychiatric services, are located in one facility. Of youths (under age twenty-one) admitted to Chestnut, 63 percent are seen in outpatient settings; statewide 84 percent of adolescent admissions are in outpatient settings (Dennis, Hristova, and Foss, 1999). All programs are accredited by the Joint Commission on the Accreditation of Healthcare Organizations (JCAHO) and are required under state regulations to conduct a needs assessment, use diagnostic practices, use patient placement criteria to determine the level of care, and develop an individualized treatment plan. A diagnosis is assigned according to the *Diagnostic and Statistical Manual of Mental Disorders,* Fourth Edition (DSM-IV; American Psychiatric Association [APA], 1994) and level of care determined according to the Patient Placement Criteria for the Treatment of Psychoactive Substance Use Disoders-2 (PPC-2; American Society of Addiction Medicine [ASAM], 1996).

Program Components

Components of the program include the following:

1. A standardized biopsychosocial assessment using the Global Appraisal of Individual Needs (GAIN-I) and interviews with collaterals (e.g., parents, probation officers, counselors, and school officials)
2. Placement into (outpatient) level of care based on the patient placement criteria of ASAM (1996)
3. An individualized treatment plan based on component number one
4. Cognitive-behavioral, skill, knowledge-based, and counseling group sessions
5. Individual therapy sessions
6. Family Night program and a limited number of family counseling sessions
7. Transportation
8. Psychiatric services
9. Hepatitis B and C, HIV and TB prevention, HIV/TB testing, and counseling
10. Random urine screens, and
11. On-site GED classes, which are offered in the evenings

Weekly Time in Treatment

The OP and IOP programs provide a continuum of care ranging from one to twelve hours per week. OP provides from one to eight hours of treatment per week, while IOP provides from nine to twelve hours of treatment per week. The differences between the OP and IOP programs are in the intensity of treatment. The content of certain groups varies based on client abuse severity and treatment history. Most therapy is group based, but individual sessions are provided to address individual needs (i.e., younger adolescents or females who have special issues) and for treatment planning and/or crisis intervention.

RECRUITMENT, ASSESSMENT, AND PLACEMENT OF CLIENTS

Recruitment

Recruitment for outpatient services is primarily based on strong linkages with other social service agencies, criminal justice authorities, and schools. The CHS adolescent program has early intervention/student assistant program specialists in twenty-two schools in the county and has linkage agreements with over 100 juvenile justice, mental health, child welfare, and other service providers. In addition, attempts are made to inform the community at large about the program through advertising and special events. Most of the referrals to the program are by telephone. During referral calls, enough information is gathered to determine whether substance abuse may be a problem and if further exploration is warranted. If a client is in crisis, he or she is provided immediate assistance, otherwise the adolescent and a parent or guardian are scheduled for an assessment within ten business days.

Assessment and Client Placement

The next step in the admission process is a comprehensive assessment that is provided at no cost to the adolescent or the family that includes a biopsychosocial assessment based on the GAIN-I (Dennis et al., 1996), interviews with collaterals, and a urine test if indicated. (Typically, the costs of assessments are reimbursed by the state substance abuse authority.) The GAIN-I is completed via an interview by a case manager or a substance abuse therapist. This instrument includes over 1,500 questions and 100 scales (see Dennis et al., 2003, for a description of the GAIN-I). Urine tests are conducted in the event that an adolescent denies any substance abuse.

All assessments are staffed with a clinical supervisor or other senior clinical staff member to determine the appropriate treatment recommendation. Potential recommendations include

1. no treatment at this time,
2. referral to an early intervention specialist in the adolescent's school,
3. referral outside of CHS for other types of services such as family counseling or mental health counseling,
4. placement in OP or IOP,
5. placement in day treatment, or
6. placement in residential treatment.

Treatment recommendations are determined based on ASAM's PPC-2 (1996) per Illinois state guidelines. While ASAM criteria provide general guidelines, each client's particular situation is taken into account. Many factors enter into the recommendation for level of care and a client's projected length of stay. Some of these factors include previous treatment involvement, time spent incarcerated, the age of the client, psychiatric issues, level of social skills, level of denial/defensiveness, and the nature of their recovery environment (e.g., gang involvement, substance use in the home, and the availability of Alcoholics Anonymous/Narcotics Anonymous [AA/NA] meetings). If the staffing recommendation is outpatient treatment, the goal is for the client to leave the assessment appointment with a scheduled time for an admission session with his or her primary counselor.

A review of screening and admission statistics for an eleven-month period revealed that approximately 25 percent of the adolescents screened by telephone for OP or IOP services were admitted within four weeks of their assessment. Out of the 265 adolescents who were screened by telephone, 86 percent completed the assessment process. Of these, 66 percent were recommended for outpatient treatment. Fifty-one percent of the adolescents recommended for one of the outpatient modalities were admitted within twenty-eight days of their assessment. The remainder either did not set up an admission appointment at CHS or failed to attend repeated appointments. During this period, most referrals were made by a juvenile detention center (23 percent) or family members (22 percent). Other referral sources included probation and parole (17 percent), schools (12 percent), self (3 percent), other substance abuse treatment providers (3 percent), judges (3 percent), the state's child welfare agency (2 percent), and other sources (6 percent). In addition, 6 percent of the admissions were adolescents who "stepped down" into outpatient from residential treatment.

CHARACTERISTICS OF CLIENTS

Table 3.1 provides data regarding the demographic and clinical characteristics of the program based on the first seventy-six cases that agreed to participate in the ATM study. The majority of the clients were male (75 percent), white (78 percent), attended school in the past ninety days (93 percent), and lived with a single parent (51 percent). Half were either fifteen or sixteen years old, and most (71 percent) be-

TABLE 3.1. Characteristics of CHS Outpatient and Intensive Outpatient Clients at Intake (N = 76)

Item	N	%
Gender		
Male	57	75
Female	19	25
Age		
11-12	0	0
13-14	12	16
15-16	38	50
17-18	25	33
19 and over	1	1
Ethnicity		
American Indian/Alaskan Native	1	1
Asian or Pacific Islander	1	1
Black	8	11
White	59	78
Hispanic (Puerto Rican, Mexican, Cuban, other)	2	3
Mixed/some other group	5	7
Current living situation		

TABLE 3.1 *(continued)*

Item	N	%
A house or apartment (yours or parents)	66	87
A foster home or public housing	4	5
A friend's or relative's house or apartment	3	4
A nursing home, hospital, inpatient, or residential	0	0
Jail, detention center, or other correctional institution	3	4
Temporary or emergency shelter	0	0
Vacant buildings	0	0
Any other housing situation	0	0
Present work or school situation		
Working full-time	4	5
Working part-time	8	11
Unemployed or laid off	9	12
Have a job, but not working because of treatment, illness, seasonal	1	1
In school or training only (even if not in session now)	48	63
In school or training at all in past 90 days	71	93
In jail or prison	1	1
Some other work situation	5	7
Substance dependence (meeting criteria)	37	49
Substance treatment needed for*		
Any kind of alcohol	28	37
Marijuana, hashish, etc.	62	81
Crack, freebase cocaine, other cocaine	1	1
Amphetamine/methamphetamine	0	0
Inhalants	1	1
Heroin	0	0
"Acid" or other hallucinogens	4	5
Some other drug	1	1
Age when first got drunk or used any drugs		
Below 15	54	71
15-18	22	29
Over 18	0	0

Item	N	%
Last grade or year completed in school		
< 6	0	0
6-8	19	25
9-10	44	58
11-12	13	17
> 12	0	0
Legal custody		
Parents together	21	28
Parents separated	2	3
Single parent	39	51
Other family	2	3
County/state	2	3
Juvenile or correctional facility	0	0
18 or older	6	8
Other	4	5
Times in life arrested and charged with a crime and booked		
0 times	20	26
1-2 times	34	45
3+ times	22	29
Times in life admitted to drug treatment or counseling		
0 times	51	67
1-2 times	21	28
3+ times	4	5

	Mean	SD
Times in life arrested, charged with a crime, and booked	2.2	2.7
Substance use—last 90 days		
Days used alcohol, marijuana, or other drugs	24.5	12.1
Days drunk or high for most of the day	8.4	6.2
Days in a jail (or other place) where you could not use drugs	9.1	21.0
Times in life admitted to drug treatment or counseling	.5	1.0

*Calculated from client self-report of need for treatment unless client reports no need for treatment, then calculated from therapist determination. Total will be greater than 100 percent.

gan experimenting with alcohol or drugs before age fifteen. Eighty-one percent reported using or needing treatment for marijuana, 37 percent for alcohol, 5 percent for hallucinogens, and 3 percent for other drugs. In the ninety days prior to their assessments, they reported an average of twenty-five days using alcohol, marijuana, or other drugs; eight days when they were drunk or high for most of the day; and nine days in jail or another place where they could not use drugs. Sixty-seven percent reported that this was their first substance abuse treatment episode, while 28 percent reported having one or two prior treatment episodes. They reported being arrested, charged with a crime, and booked an average of two times. Sixty-five percent reported current involvement with the criminal justice system.

As described previously, placement in level of treatment is based on presenting clinical characteristics. An earlier study of admission data from this program revealed that those admitted to an outpatient modality were similar to those admitted to residential treatment with regard to demographic variables, but were significantly different on several clinical variables (Godley, Godley, and Dennis, 2001). For example, the outpatient clients were more likely to report fewer prior substance abuse treatment episodes and lower weekly alcohol and drug use. Those admitted to outpatient treatment were less likely to report symptoms of physiological dependence and more likely to only report symptoms of abuse. These findings suggest that the program is successful in meeting its expressed goal of treating adolescents with less severe symptoms in less restrictive levels of care.

DESCRIPTION OF TREATMENT COMPONENTS

Master Treatment Plan

Once the client is admitted to treatment, the therapist works with the adolescent to develop a master treatment plan (MTP) based on findings from the assessment process. The MTP includes

1. an approval sheet which is signed by the client, therapist, and supervisor;
2. a listing of the client's strengths and weaknesses as perceived by the client, family, and staff;

3. a listing of different skill groups and individual sessions the client is required to attend, the expected frequency of attendance, a listing of other family members that are expected to be involved in the adolescent's treatment, and a description of how issues (e.g., medical) that might impact participation in treatment will be addressed, and

4. specific treatment objectives and interventions by each ASAM dimension that needs to be addressed, the responsible staff, and time frame.

For OP and IOP treatment, the three ASAM conditions that are typically addressed in the MTP are emotional/behavioral conditions and complications, relapse potential, and recovery environment. In order to address any one dimension, numerous objectives and interventions can occur. For example, in order to address relapse prevention the MTP could include

1. weekly urine screens and blood alcohol content (BAC) tests;
2. completed relapse prevention skills groups;
3. writing and sharing a drug history with parents and talking with parents on a weekly basis about how the individual will maintain sobriety and how his or her parents can be supportive, and
4. a smoking cessation intervention.

Progress notes are made in relation to each particular treatment objective that is addressed.

Individual Sessions

Most OP and IOP services are group based. However, individual sessions are always conducted to develop the MTP and to review progress toward accomplishing MTP goals. Individual sessions may be used to lessen a client's resistance to treatment and to address special needs, since the development of a strong therapeutic alliance may occur best in an individual counseling situation. Often adolescents are resistant to treatment because they have been coerced into treatment by the criminal justice system or parents. The therapist approaches this situation by acknowledging that the youth is in treatment because of others and acts as a resource to help the client complete the program. Examples of special needs that would be addressed in individual sessions are developmental and gender-specific issues. For example, if an adolescent was young chronologically and/or developmentally and expected to have difficulty with group dynamics in a treatment group of older teenagers, the treatment team could decide that individual treatment would be most appropriate. And even though the program offers gender-specific counseling groups, a therapist can always choose to address sensitive issues, such as sexual preference or sexual abuse, in individual sessions.

Cognitive-Behavioral, Skill, Knowledge-Based, and Counseling Group Sessions

As has been noted, group treatment is the primary mode of treatment delivery. Assignment to the number and type of groups is based on the assessment and the client's personalized MTP goals and objectives. To accommodate different client schedules for school and work, OP treatment groups are offered from 4 to 7 p.m., Monday through Thursday, and from 10 a.m. to 12 p.m. on Tuesdays and Thursdays. Most clients attend the evening groups. Each type of group described in the following is composed of eight to twelve modules that are repeated cyclically. All the different types of group are offered during the course of each week. Group sessions last forty-five minutes and twenty-three different group sessions occur every Monday through Thursday. Frequently, more than one type of group is conducted simultaneously.

The treatment group schedule is designed to accommodate three different types of clients with differing needs. The first schedule is designed for clients appropriate for OP services and these clients are scheduled for one to eight hours of groups per week. A typical OP client is entering treatment for the first time, has a supportive recovery environment, has demonstrated some success at maintaining sobriety, has a relatively mild DSM-IV diagnosis (i.e., usually an abuse diagnosis or one mild dependency diagnosis and no significant psychiatric issues), and/or is motivated to stop abusing substances. The length of stay in OP is based on individual needs and is highly variable, although generally it would be for two months or more. The second schedule is designed for clients appropriate for IOP services and these clients are scheduled for nine to twelve hours of groups per week. IOP clients, as compared to OP clients, have more severe DSM-IV diagnoses, are in need of more structure and support, may have been unable to maintain sobriety at the OP level of care, and have a higher level of resistance/denial. Participation in IOP services tends to average around four weeks because it is used as a transitional level of care. During this period, the counselor assesses if the adolescent can maintain sobriety and if so, the client is transferred to OP. If the adolescent cannot maintain sobriety during four weeks of IOP, the counselor will work toward a transfer to a more intensive level of treatment (i.e., day or residential treatment). The third type of clients are those in aftercare or continuing care following a successful residential treatment episode. These individuals are scheduled for two to four hours of groups each week for at least two months following their discharge from residential treatment.

The three different tracks of groups allow for an individualized approach to treatment. Clients are in groups with others who are struggling with similar issues including denial, resistance, maintaining or not maintaining sobriety, building a supportive recovery environment, and developing goals related to making significant life changes versus only stopping using in order to avoid legal consequences. A client's group schedule changes in response to his or her progress or lack of progress, although other interventions are also used to address a client's recovery status. The following section provides an overview of the types of groups that are offered.

Types of Treatment Groups

Orientation groups. Two types of groups are used to orient clients who have had little or no prior experience in substance abuse treatment. One group provides an overview of treatment expectations including how to behave in group counseling situations, how to bring up issues, and how to assertively confront and support peers. It also provides information about recovery groups outside of CHS and introduces the twelve-step philosophy including the concepts of acceptance, powerlessness, denial, unmanageability, and spirituality.

A second orientation group is specifically designed for those who are resistant to treatment. Clients are aided in recognizing and acknowledging the life difficulties caused by their substance use. They develop a list of problems related to use and the consequences resulting from them and identify substance use patterns and drug history. A recovering substance user is a guest speaker. Group members are encouraged to confront other members' honesty when discussing these issues.

Drug education. This is a didactic group providing information about drugs and alcohol, specific behavioral and emotional effects of chemical use, and driving under the influence. It is targeted toward clients who have had minimal prior substance abuse education. Activities include viewing and discussing educational videos, completing written treatment work, and participating in games designed to increase clients' knowledge of substance use and its consequences.

Relapse prevention. The purpose of this didactic group is to help clients identify problem situations and substance abuse triggers that occur in their daily life. The concepts of relapse, substance use triggers, high risk situations, and relapse prevention are introduced. Based on analysis of their individual situations, clients are helped to develop survival plans that are customized to their own needs.

Life skills. This is a didactic group that includes instruction for a number of life skill areas. Topics addressed include hepatitis/AIDS/HIV/TB education, basic health care, job hunting, budgeting, and educational/vocational issues. The group is interactive and often involves outside speakers, discussion, and role-playing.

Self-esteem. This group is designed to increase each member's self-awareness, self-esteem, and increase healthy coping strategies. Activities include reviewing videos, role-playing, art therapy, and guided visualization.

Leisure education. This group uses therapeutic recreational activities to build the following skills: ability to identify positive social activities, self-esteem and self-awareness enhancement, positive risk taking, appropriate self-disclosure, cooperation and teamwork, assertiveness, communication, feelings, and stress management.

Emotions/communication. The goal of this didactic group is to help clients develop assertive, expressive, and open-minded communication skills and communicate a recovery image.

Working recovery/decision making. The purpose of this group is to help clients maintain recovery. Clients in this group have already learned many of the skills and concepts of recovery. Support networks and AA/NA, habit control, developing a new "clean" image, and dealing with "using" friends and family and "using" situations are also discussed. Clients develop and implement a recovery plan.

Clients also review decision-making skills and practice making recovery-oriented decisions.

Art therapy. This group is for clients at all stages in their recovery efforts. It introduces a pleasant and creative way to learn new skills and provide additional support for self-expression.

Counseling. Counseling groups provide opportunities for clients to bring up personal issues. Clients are encouraged to focus on how they can effectively deal with problems or issues in their lives. Peers are asked to give feedback and relate the issues to their own personal experiences. Counseling groups are also offered in all male and all female formats.

Family Nights and Family Sessions

The program recognizes the critical role that family plays in recovery. Each week, family members are asked to participate in a two-hour Family Night with other families who have adolescents in treatment. In addition, family sessions with individual families may be provided on a limited basis. The first hour of Family Night includes family members of the adolescent client only, not the client. Issues that may be addressed include a discussion of family roles, drug education, relapse signs, denial, coping styles, enabling, detachment, parenting skills, goals and objectives, adolescent development, and AIDS education. In the second half of Family Night the adolescents join their families for group counseling during which an opportunity for sharing, processing, and problem-solving occurs. Topics that are addressed depend on the needs of the families present. For example, one of the parents could describe a communication problem in her family and under the close supervision of all therapists present, the family member would be encouraged to share feelings, switch roles, and then share and give feedback. Other members of the group would also be encouraged to share and offer feedback.

CRITICAL ISSUES CENTRAL TO TREATMENT

Contact with Other Professionals Involved with the Adolescent

The program acknowledges the importance of the system of care and recognizes that many of the youth who participate in treatment are served by multiple agencies and institutions (e.g., child welfare, schools, probation, mental health). During the admission process, adolescents are asked if they are willing to sign release of information forms regarding staff contact with other agencies. Therapists maintain communication with other professionals involved in the adolescent's life to help ensure continuity of care.

Urine Screens

Clients are typically asked to provide weekly or bimonthly urine screens. If a staff member suspects use, the client may be asked to provide a urine screen or Breathalyzer test at any time. Family and other professionals (i.e., parents, school officials, probation officers) may also request that clients be tested. Positive urine screens are considered a treatment issue. Clients are generally required to notify the significant people (e.g., parents, probation officers) in their lives about any positive urine screens since the program teaches that taking responsibility for behavior is an important part of recovery.

Tobacco Policy

CHS addresses tobacco use as it would any other drug of abuse/addiction. Skill groups provide information about the short- and long-term effects of nicotine. Clients are taught that managing tobacco use is similar to managing the use of other drugs and alcohol. Medical interventions such as nicotine gum, transdermal patches, and Zyban are explained. If an adolescent is addicted to nicotine, his or her treatment plan would include goals of addressing nicotine education and skills training in coping strategies supportive of nicotine cessation. In addition, all clients are required to follow treatment rules that include no tobacco use while at CHS.

Hepatitis, HIV/TB Prevention, Testing, and Treatment

Hepatitis, HIV, and TB prevention and education programs are incorporated into treatment. The program uses educational videos as well as selective activities from a curriculum that has been approved by the Centers for Disease Control: *Be Proud! Be Responsible!* (Jemmott, Jemmott, and McCaffree, 1999). This curriculum is based on social cognitive theory, the theory of reasoned action, and the theory of planned behavior. Both test decision counseling and on-site HIV testing are available, optional, and free of charge. The test decision process includes a problem solving approach that helps adolescents identify their risks and future prevention options. In all the adolescent programs at CHS, approximately 150 youths annually ask to participate in test decision counseling and about half of those choose to be tested for HIV. CDC and Illinois Department of Public Health guidelines for test decision counseling are followed and both blood and oral HIV tests are offered. As required by state law, all test results are confidential and this information is not placed in the client's clinical record. If an adolescent tests positive for HIV, the HIV coordinator would continue to meet regularly with him or her for education and counseling with the goal of linking the individual to appropriate crisis services, medical care, and HIV case management services.

Dual Diagnosis Issues

Clients with dual diagnoses, or who are suspected of having psychiatric issues, are referred to the CHS consulting child and adolescent psychiatrist. These referrals are common. Therapists consult with the psychiatrist regarding particular clients and have the opportunity to review written psychiatric assessment reports prepared on assessed clients. If a client is prescribed psychotropic medication, then compliance is viewed as a critical issue with this adolescent. Therapists work with the psychiatrist in encouraging medication compliance. Family members are involved and educated regarding the important role they can play in encouraging medication compliance.

Age Issues

Program staff are also sensitive to a client's age when determining the appropriate treatment regimen. Since chronological age is not always as important as developmental age, a client's level of functioning is determined through both observation and collaborative reports. In the event that younger clients are mocked by older clients, therapists are trained to intervene early and try to engage older clients to be positive role models and supportive of the younger clients. Staff members have also learned that younger clients tend to profit from increased individual attention.

Gender Issues

The outpatient staff is sensitive to gender issues in several ways. Clinical assessment information related to gender is used when assigning a therapist. Both male and female therapists are available. Skills groups address issues such as relationships, sexuality, role models, and normalizing confusion about societal stereotypes of masculinity and femininity. Gender counseling groups are offered when appropriate. Team staff meetings may discuss gender issues with specific clients and develop a plan for addressing related problems. Referrals are made to agencies such as Planned Parenthood and the Rape Crisis Center when appropriate. If identity issues are suspected, the therapist may have the client complete the Minnesota Multiphasic Personality Inventory for Adolescents (MMPI-A). Results from the MMPI-A can provide insight into the client's coping strategies and issues with which she or he is struggling. These issues can then be addressed in the individual's treatment plan. Both the psychiatrist and the nurse are other resources that can be used by the treatment team in addressing these issues.

Cultural Issues

Although the outpatient population is primarily white (as is the population in the county), the program serves a higher proportion of African Americans and Hispanics then in the general population base. The outpatient staff includes members of these ethnic groups and staff receive training to improve their cultural competency. A Latino interventionist is primarily responsible for recruitment and retention of Latino/Latina youth and ensuring that the program is culturally sensitive to this community.

Cultural issues are relevant to nearly all outpatient clients in the following way: use of alcohol and other drugs will eventually immerse clients in the culture of addiction (White, 1990) and the culture of addiction involves many aspects of clients' lives. The clothes and jewelry that drug-using adolescents wear, how they talk and what they talk about, who they associate with and how they interact, what activities they participate in, and their values and goals can all be strongly influenced by the culture of addiction. Through discussion, clients' awareness of these drug culture issues is heightened. When gang involvement has been a part of a client's lifestyle, a referral to another local agency who has a gang intervention program is usually indicated; CHS staff work with the other agency's staff to provide a united treatment team across agencies.

Ancillary Services: Transportation, Medical, and GED

Other ancillary services are provided as needed including transportation to and from individual and group sessions, medical examinations, and on-site GED classes.

DETERMINING READINESS
FOR DISCHARGE OR TRANSFER

Ultimately, OP and IOP clients are either transferred to another level of care (e.g., to residential treatment or from IOP to OP) or discharged from all CHS services. A client's movement between treatment components or discharge from services is directly tied to the progress made on the MTP goals and objectives. As described previously, when the MTP is developed, behavioral expectations and time frames for accomplishing objectives are outlined along ASAM dimensions. Each client is discussed at least weekly in a staff meeting to evaluate his or her progress on specific objectives related to different ASAM dimensions. Therapists provide explicit feedback to clients explaining how they have progressed and/or how they have not demonstrated progress. Indicators of change related to MTP objectives can be physiological, behavioral, and emotional/attitudinal. Transfer or discharge recommendations are made by the treatment team rather than an individual therapist to insure objectivity surrounding these decisions.

Clients are discharged or transferred with one of the following three dispositions: as planned (AP), against staff advice (ASA), or at staff request (ASR). An AP discharge indicates that the client has accomplished most, if not all, of the MTP objectives. At the time of discharge, recommendations are made regarding future expectations for the client. These expectations often include continued AA/NA involvement, following through with legal obligations and leaving urine screens at probation, maintaining contact with a school counselor, and/or seeking psychiatric follow-up for medication management. An ASA discharge most commonly results when a client refuses to attend his or her scheduled groups (e.g., lack of contact). An ASR discharge is reserved for those clients who cannot maintain behavioral stability in the treatment setting such that their disruptive behavior is detrimental to the treatment of other clients. Transfers, whether to increase or decrease the intensity of treatment or to change the focus of treatment (referral to a psychiatric facility, hospital, or long-term behavioral facility), are considered AP, assuming the client is willing to follow through with the recommendation.

Discussion of cases at frequent staffings, weekly supervision, and weekly contact with the client, family, and collaterals provide therapists with the information and strategies to justify a client's level of care and discharge status.

DESCRIPTION OF STAFF AND CLINICAL
SUPERVISION PROCESS

The current staffing pattern for the adolescent outpatient program includes a program coordinator who reports to the director for adolescent treatment, three outpatient therapists, two case managers, one Latino interventionist, and a part-time counselor. The state of Illinois mandates that all staff who provide direct services to clients must be certified or licensed at the time of hire or within two years of employment in the field. Different levels of certification are available through the Illinois Alcohol and Other Drug Abuse Professional Certification Association. Licensure is through the Illinois Department of Professional Registration and is based on an individual's area of study and experience.

The program coordinator has ten years' experience with CHS, is licensed and certified, and has a master's degree in counseling psychology. He is responsible for hiring, training, weekly clinical supervision, conducting staff meetings, and facilitating treatment groups. In addition, he oversees the daily operations of the program (e.g., census, program reports, etc.), as well as program development. The outpatient therapists are licensed or license-eligible and have master's degrees in counseling or social work with one to six years of experience. They are responsible for developing the MTP with clients, ongoing assessment, reviewing treatment progress, report writing, discharge planning, and facilitating individual, family, and group sessions. Case managers are bachelors level certified substance abuse counselors. One provides on-site screenings/evaluations of youth from the target counties. The other provides off-site screenings/evaluations at the local county's juvenile detention center, facilitates drug education groups, admissions, and a minimal amount of outpatient treatment. The Latino interventionist is bilingual and has five years' experience working with youth. He works to engage and retain Latino youth in need of substance abuse treatment. The part-time counselor helps provide transportation to groups for youth, completes paperwork, and assists in the facilitation of skill groups.

Certain personality characteristics, skills, and knowledge are assessed during the hiring process to increase the likelihood that treatment staff will relate effectively to adolescents. Potential employees are evaluated for their patience, an understanding of developmental stages and general age-specific issues, a desire to work specifically with adolescents, and their knowledge of the substance dependence and recovery process. The program philosophy holds that while being in recovery is an asset in many situations, it is certainly not a prerequisite to providing treatment to adolescents. Presently, three of the eight staff members are in recovery. The combination of recovering and nonrecovering staff has worked well in the program. Relating to clients therapeutically and effectively appears more dependent on a counselor's basic therapeutic skills including his or her empathy, consistency, skill at maintaining boundaries and confronting unacceptable behavior, and ability to avoid enabling behaviors and being manipulated.

The clinical supervision process is considered essential to staff and program development. All staff members receive one hour of individual supervision per week. It is an organizational belief that providing substance abuse treatment is stressful and complex and that it is necessary for the clinical supervision process to provide staff with ongoing training, guidance, and support. Supervision accomplishes these tasks by (1) focusing on the mechanics of the job, for example, specific functions including treatment planning and documentation; (2) professional issues including job expectations, career goals, program planning, and training; and (3) personal issues as they relate to the staff person's ability to perform his or her job. The weekly supervision hour and availability at other times is seen as the most important ingredient to maintaining the "health" of the treatment team.

CONCLUSION

Participation in the Adolescent Treatment Model (ATM) research study funded by SAMSHA's Center for Substance Abuse Treatment provides the opportunity to carefully study a program that has evolved over fifteen years. The program's strengths appear to be its comprehensive assessment process, ability to individualize the treatment process, therapeutic approach which is based on established theories of behavioral and emotional change with attention to developmental appropriateness, master's level therapists trained in social work or psychology who are provided with regular clinical supervision, emphasis on involving families in the treatment process, and regular contact with collaterals.

The program has regularly used discharge status as an indicator of treatment success. A review of forty-one clients discharged since the advent of the ATM study suggests that approximately 56 percent of the adolescents had "as planned" discharges. At best, however, this indicator is only a gross measure of treatment success. A recent analysis of the relationship between adolescents' discharge status and therapeutic outcomes after discharge from a substance abuse residential treatment program revealed that the planned discharge group did not report superior outcomes ninety days after discharge (Godley et al., in press). CSAT funding allows for a more discriminating test of program effectiveness and mediating variables. Program outcomes will be analyzed by comparing outcome data at three, six, nine, and twelve months post intake to existing CHS GAIN data from other adolescent studies including one that evaluated five other outpatient protocols under CSAT's Cannabis Youth Treatment study (Dennis et al., in press), concurrent data on adolescents assigned to residential treatment under a NIAAA study (Godley, Godley, and Dennis, 1997), and benchmark data from the same program collected on adolescents admitted between August, 1996, and September, 1997, as part of an earlier study (Dennis et al., 1999). These analyses will provide evidence about the merit of replicating the CHS model elsewhere and, if promising, the treatment manual that is currently being developed will enhance the ability of other practitioners to adopt this approach.

REFERENCES

Adams, L. and Wallace, J.L. (1994). Residential treatment for the ADHD adolescent substance abuser. *Journal of Child and Adolescent Substance Abuse, 4,* 35-44.

American Psychiatric Association (1994). *Diagnostic and Statistical Manual of Mental Disorders* (DSM-IV) (Fourth Edition). Washington, DC: Author.

American Society of Addiction Medicine (1996). *Patient Placement Criteria for the Treatment of Psychoactive Substance Use Disorders* (Second Edition). Chevy Chase, MD: Author.

Chiauzzi, E. (1991). *Preventing Relapse in the Addictions: A Biopsychosocial Approach.* New York: Pergamon.

Dennis, M.L., Dawud-Noursi, S., Muck, R.D., and McDermeit, M. (2003). The need for developing and evaluating adolescent treatment models. In S.J. Stevens and A. Morral (Eds.), *Adolescent Substance Abuse Treatment in the United States: Exemplary Models from a National Evaluation Study* (pp. 3-26). Binghamton, NY: The Haworth Press, Inc.

Dennis, M.L., Hristova, L., and Foss, M. (1999). *Special Runs on Illinois' Electronic DASA Automated Reporting and Tracking System (DARTS) Data Base on All Publicly Funded Treatment for 154,255 Patients Served (68264 Unique Individuals) for Fiscal Year 1997 (7/96 to 6/97).* Bloomington, IL: Chestnut Health Systems. (Done under NIDA Grant R01 DA11977.)

Dennis, M.L., Titus, J.C., Diamond, G., Donaldson, J., Godley, S.H., Tims, F.M., Webb, C., Kaminer, Y., Babor, T., Roebuck, M.C., et al. (in press). The Cannabis Youth Treatment (CYT) experiment: Rationale, study design, and analysis plans. *Addiction.*

Dennis, M.L., Webber, R., White, W., Senay, E., Adams, L., Bokos, P., Eisenberg, S., Fraser, J., Moran, M., Ravine, E., Rosenfeld, J., and Sodetz, A. (1996). *Global Appraisal of Individual Needs (GAIN), Volume 1: Administration, Scoring and Interpretation,* Bloomington, IL: Lighthouse Institute, Chestnut Health Systems.

Dennis, M., Scott, C.K., Godley, M.D., and Funk, R. (1999). *Comparisons of Adolescents and Adults by ASAM Profile Using GAIN Data from the Drug Outcome Monitoring Study (DOMS).* Bloomington, IL: Chestnut Health Systems (http://www.chestnut.org/LI/downloads/asam98.pdf).

Ellis, A., McInerney, J.F., DiGiuseppe, R., and Yeager, R.J. (1988). *Rational-Emotive Therapy with Alcoholics and Substance Abusers.* Elmsford, NY: Pergamon Press.

Glasser, W. (1976). *Positive Addiction.* New York: Harper and Row.

Glasser, W. (1992). Reality therapy. In J.F. Zeig (Ed.), *The Evolution of Psychotherapy: The Second Conference.* New York: Brunner/Mazel, Inc.

Godley, S.H., Godley, M.D., and Dennis, M.L. (2001). The assertive aftercare protocol for adolescent substance abusers. In E. Wagner and H. Caldron (Eds.), *Innovations in Adolescent Substance Abuse Interventions* (pp. 311-329). New York: Elsevier Science Ltd.

Godley, M., Godley, S.H., and Dennis, M.L. (1997). *Assertive Aftercare Project.* Funded by the National Institute on Alcohol Abuse and Alcoholism, Grant Number: AA10368. Project Period: June 1997 to May 2002.

Godley, M.D., Godley, S.H., Funk, R.R., Dennis, M.L., and Loveland, D. (in press). Discharge status as a performance indicator: Can it predict adolescent substance abuse treatment outcome? *Journal of Child and Adolescent Substance Abuse.*

Hester, R.K. and Miller, W.R. (Eds.) (1989). *Handbook of Alcoholism Treatment Approaches: Effective Alternatives.* New York: Pergamon.

Jemmott, L.S., Jemmott, J.B., and McCaffree, K.A. (1999). *Be Proud! Be Responsible! Strategies to Empower Youth to Reduce Their Risk of AIDS.* New York: Select Media, Inc.

Kazdin, A.E. (2000). *Behavior Modification in Applied Settings* (Sixth Edition). Chicago: Dorsey Press.

Risberg, R.A. and Funk, R.R. (2000). Evaluating the perceived helpfulness of a family night program for adolescent substance abusers. *Journal of Child and Adolescent Substance Abuse, 10*(1), 51-67.

Risberg, R.A., Stevens, M.J., and Graybill, D.F. (1995). Validating the adolescent form of the substance abuse subtle screening inventory. *Journal of Child and Adolescent Substance Abuse, 44*(4), 25-41.

Rogers, C.R. (1951). *Client-Centered Therapy.* Boston: Houghton Mifflin.

Rogers, C.R. (1959). A theory of therapy, personality, and interpersonal relationships as developed in the client-centered framework. In S. Koch (Ed.), *Psychology: A Study of a Science.* New York: McGraw-Hill.

Walen, S.R., DiGiuseppe, R., and Dryden W. (1992). *A Practical Guide to Rational-Emotive Therapy.* New York: Oxford University Press.

White, W.L. (1990). *The Culture of Addiction and the Culture of Recovery.* Bloomington, IL: Lighthouse Training Institute.

Yankura, J. and Dryden W. (1990). *Doing RET—Albert Ellis in Action.* New York: Springer Publishing.

Chapter 4

Evaluation of a Group-Based Outpatient Adolescent Substance Abuse Treatment Program

Robert J. Battjes
Emily A. Sears
Elizabeth C. Katz
Timothy W. Kinlock
Michael Gordon
The Epoch Project Team

STATEMENT OF THE PROBLEM

Adolescent substance use and misuse is a major public health problem. For example, a recent Monitoring the Future report indicated that, in fiscal year (FY) 1999, 12 percent of eighth graders and 22 percent of tenth graders reported use of any illicit substance during the past 30 days; these rates have been stable for the past few years (Johnston, O'Malley, and Bachman, 2000). According to the Baltimore County Bureau of Substance Abuse, during the 1999-2000

In addition to the above listed authors, the Epoch Project Team includes Cyndy Adams, Richard Bateman, Teal Beatty, Gary Brown, Trevor Bush, Stacy Frank, Diana Givens, Charles Hall, Barbara Lingenfelter, Donna Lucker, Jan Marshall, Katherine Nunn, Heather Reisinger, Anna Soisson, Robert Storey, Gail Swanbeck, Marsha Swilley, and Judy Walsh.

This work was produced under Grant No. KD1 TI 11874 funded by the Center for Substance Abuse Treatment, Substance Abuse and Mental Health Services Administration, U.S. Department of Health and Human Services. The contents are solely the responsibility of the authors and do not necessarily represent the official views of the funding agency.

Please address correspondence to Robert J. Battjes, D.S.W., Social Research Center, Friends Research Institute, 1229 W. Mount Royal Avenue, Baltimore, MD 21217.

school year, approximately 300 adolescents received assessments re-sulting from substance-related school expulsions, and an additional 844 adolescents received drug education through a school-based county program (Jackie Foreman, personal communication, Febru-ary 2001). According to the Maryland Alcohol and Drug Abuse Ad-ministration (ADAA), 802 adolescents were admitted to treatment in Baltimore County during 2000 (Vickie Kaneko, personal communi-cation, February 2001).

Given the magnitude of the adolescent drug problem in the United States in general, and in Maryland specifically, it is somewhat sur-prising that there are relatively few outcome studies evaluating pro-grams for adolescents who are chemically dependent (Ralph and McMenamy, 1996). The majority of studies on adolescent substance use focus on factors that contribute to initial drug use and overall drug trends throughout the country. Although a number of studies have shown that adolescent substance abusers who receive treatment fare better than those who do not (Catalano et al., 1990-1991), research suggests that no single treatment approach is superior (Henggeler, 1997). Moreover, aspects of treatment that contribute to effectiveness have not been identified. The Center for Substance Abuse Treat-ment's (CSAT) Adolescent Treatment Model (ATM) program pro-vides an opportunity to address gaps in past research and to develop and evaluate effective adolescent treatment programs.

OVERVIEW OF EPOCH COUNSELING CENTER AND THE EVALUATION TEAM

The ATM project in Baltimore County, Maryland, is designed to (1) develop and evaluate a group-based, adolescent treatment program, and (2) evaluate the impact on treatment engagement, retention, and outcome of adding a single motivational interview at the beginning of treatment. The project involves collaboration between two components of Friends Research Institute, Inc.: Epoch Counseling Center (Epoch) and the Social Research Center. Epoch Counseling Center is respon-sible for delivering the treatment interventions. Epoch has five treat-ment facilities and has been offering outpatient substance abuse treat-ment services to adults, adolescents, youth-at-risk, and families for the last thirty years. Two of the facilities, located in Catonsville and

Lansdowne, have served residents of western and southwestern Baltimore County since 1971 and 1993, respectively. The other three facilities are located in eastern and southeastern Baltimore County, including one facility in Essex, open since 1976, and two facilities located in Dundalk, open since 1990 and 1998. The populations served by these facilities are largely low to middle income, with the Lansdowne and Essex facilities serving economically depressed areas marked by high rates of unemployment. The service area populations are predominantly white, with the Catonsville facility also serving a sizeable African-American population.

Epoch Counseling Center is a private nonprofit agency that receives funding from various grants. The primary source of support comes from the Maryland ADAA of the Department of Health and Mental Hygiene. ADAA funding supports the infrastructure of the five facilities and allows the use of a sliding fee scale. In addition to funds from ADAA, Epoch also receives funding from the Baltimore County Office of Safe and Drug-Free Schools, part of the Baltimore County Department of Education. This funding supports placement of prevention specialists and addictions counselors in Baltimore County public schools as part of the Maryland Student Assistance Program (MSAP). Epoch's MSAP counselors offer drug abuse assessments and educational, consultative, and other supportive services to students, teachers, principals, and guidance counselors in sixteen local schools.

Epoch's clinical program is contracted to serve 510 individuals at any given time. In FY 1998, for example, Epoch admitted a total of 324 adolescents, which represented 30 percent of all admissions for that year. Approximately 70 to 80 percent of the adolescents were referred from the Maryland Department of Juvenile Justice, 10 percent through Epoch's MSAP program, and the remainder from other sources.

The Social Research Center (SRC) is a private nonprofit research organization that has been conducting substance abuse research for over thirty years, including etiologic, prevention, and treatment research. The SRC investigators, in collaboration with Epoch counselors, are responsible for developing and evaluating the adolescent treatment program.

THEORETICAL BACKGROUND

Epoch's Standard Adolescent Treatment Program

The Epoch Counseling Center adolescent treatment program is based on both social learning theory, which explains substance use initiation, and conditioning theory, which explains continuation. First, the program is based on the assumption that substance use is a learned behavior (Bigelow, Brooner, and Silverman, 1998) that is affected by an interaction between adolescents' perceptions of their social environment and the pharmacological properties of the substances used. Consistent with social learning theory (Abrams and Niaura, 1987; Bandura, 1977), modeling plays an important role in the initiation of substance use. Research has shown, for example, that children with little or no prior drinking experience hold beliefs about the effects of alcohol (Miller, Smith, and Goldman, 1990; Query, Rosenberg, and Tisak, 1998). These early beliefs develop through exposure to substance use by salient role models and affect subsequent use by the adolescent (Aas et al., 1998). Longitudinal studies have shown that children initiated drinking earlier when they believed that alcohol produced positive effects than when they believed that it produced negative effects (Killen et al., 1996; Smith et al., 1995).

Whereas modeling influences initiation of substance use, conditioning, or associative learning, influences escalation of substance use. The theory of operant conditioning specifies that behaviors that are followed by reinforcement will be repeated (Skinner, 1953). Thus, substance use continues or increases because adolescents learn that using substances leads to positive outcomes. According to classical conditioning (Pavlov, 1927), with continued use adolescents associate substances with cues that are present in the environment most or every time they use. Exposure to these cues produces thoughts about using, strong cravings for the substance, and, with some substances, withdrawal-like symptoms (e.g., heroin, 1973). Presumably, adolescents use in the presence of these cues to reduce the aversive feelings they elicit.

Lack of parental supervision, poor parent-child relationships, and permissive parenting styles are also considered to be important factors in both the initiation and progression of substance use. For example, less after-school supervision (Richardson et al., 1993) and high levels of conflict between adolescents and their parents (Duncan et al., 1998) were associated with greater involvement in substance use. This may be because adolescents who are unsupervised, and those who avoid going home due to high levels of conflict, have more opportunities to associate with deviant peers, learn the effects of substances, and associate substance use with a wider array of cues. In addition, parents who were perceived to be less authoritative and more permissive had children who reported more involvement with alcohol and tobacco, whereas parents who were perceived to be more authoritative, less permissive, and less authoritarian had less deviant children (Cohen and Rice, 1997). Permissive parenting may contribute to adolescent substance use to the extent that such parents do not provide punishment for their adolescents' deviant behavior. Thus, adolescents are insulated from some of the negative consequences of their use.

Treatment at Epoch is designed to teach adolescents the skills necessary to disassociate substance use from the myriad of cues with which it has become associated. Adolescents learn, for example, relaxation exercises that can be used to manage strong urges to use. Lessons on assertiveness provide adolescents with the skills necessary to resist social pressure, whereas anger management and self-esteem lessons focus on addressing the psychological and emotional factors that are often associated with relapse. In addition to assisting clients in modifying strategies so that they are effective in the adolescents' environment, counselors also address the personal and environmental consequences (e.g., fear of rejection, environment that supports drug use over abstinence) that prevent the adolescent from utilizing these skills. Treatment at Epoch also focuses on the family and is designed to reduce family conflict, teach parenting skills, and teach strategies parents can use to help their adolescents achieve and maintain abstinence.

Motivational Interviewing

Because client motivation is an important determinant of treatment engagement and outcomes (e.g., Joe, Simpson, and Broome, 1998), this project is also examining the effects of a treatment induction technique designed to increase client readiness to change. Motivational interviewing (Miller, 1989, 1996), the most widely implemented induction technique, is a procedure designed to facilitate behavioral change by helping clients explore and resolve ambivalence about the need for change (Rollnick and Miller, 1995). Substantial evidence of its effectiveness exists with alcoholic adults (Miller, 1996; Miller and Rollnick, 1991), drug-dependent women in a hospital emergency department (Andersen, 1985), marijuana users (Stephens et al., 1994), heroin addicts in methadone maintenance (Saunders, Wilkinson, and Phillips, 1995), and drug-abusing probationers undergoing treatment in a therapeutic community (Blankenship, Dansereau, and Simpson, 1999). Yet, relatively little attention has been paid to developing and evaluating such approaches with adolescents. A recent study demonstrated positive long-term effects of a brief motivational intervention on drinking of entering college freshman (Marlatt et al., 1998). Similarly, short-term reductions in drinking frequency were observed when teenage patients admitted to a hospital emergency department with positive blood alcohol levels received a 45-minute motivational intervention (Wagner et al., 1999).

EPOCH'S ADOLESCENT PROGRAM

Intake Assessment

Adolescents seeking treatment at Epoch are first screened, using the American Society for Addiction Medicine: Patient Placement Criteria (ASAM, 1996) to determine their eligibility for outpatient treatment. Youth who are considered ineligible for Epoch's services (e.g., in need of detoxification) are referred to higher levels of care (e.g., detoxification, inpatient). Those who are considered suitable for outpatient treatment complete an extensive assessment battery that includes the Global Appraisal of Individual Needs (GAIN) (see Dennis et al., 2003) and the Problem Oriented Screening Instrument for Teenagers (POSIT) (Hall et al., 1998; Knight et al., 2000; McLaney et al., 1994). The GAIN is a structured interview that takes approximately two hours to administer. It is designed to assess both lifetime and recent problem areas that affect and are affected by substance use, including drug history, family history of substance use and psychiatric problems, family environment, adolescents' legal involvement, school performance, current mental health status, etc. The POSIT is a nationally recognized self-administered questionnaire assessing substance-related problems and is required for use by all adolescent substance abuse treatment programs that receive funding from the Maryland ADAA.

Treatment Induction Session

Upon completion of the intake assessment, clients are scheduled for one of two types of treatment induction within one week following admission.

Motivational Interviewing

Approximately one-half of adolescent clients receive a motivational interview based on the work of Miller and his colleagues (Miller, 1983; Miller and Rollnick, 1991; Miller and Sanchez, 1994). In this project the motivational interview consists of two carefully planned and individualized treatment phases delivered within one 75-minute counseling session. The first treatment phase focuses on obtaining information about problems associated with substance use, decisional considerations (i.e., costs and benefits of continuing versus discontinuing substance use), future plans, and building client commitment to initiate or continue change. This phase of the session involves using reflective listening, rolling with resistance, and structured feedback to elicit self-motivational statements. The second phase continues the motivation enhancement process by working with clients to develop an action plan; that is, a specific plan for how change will be achieved. A change plan worksheet is used to guide development of the client's action plan. This instrument is then used as a basis for recapitulation, a strategy in which the counselor offers a broad summary of what has transpired during the session. Specifically, the recapitulation emphasizes the client's self-motivational statements, plans for change, and the perceived consequences of changing versus not changing. The ultimate goal of this session is to have the client make a formal commitment to discontinue substance use.

Counseling Overview

Other clients receive a sixty to seventy-five-minute individual counseling session that focuses on increasing a client's understanding of the treatment process. This session is intended as an attention control used for research purposes. Rather than focusing on motivational issues and the problems that brought adolescents into treatment, counselors describe the treatment experience and explore adolescents' expectations of the program during this counseling overview session. A number of aspects of counseling may be examined, including: defining counseling and the counseling relationship; discussing how different treatment modalities work together to effect change; and discussing adolescents' thoughts or concerns about starting treatment.

Treatment Planning

Following the treatment induction session, clients are scheduled to meet with their assigned counselor to develop the treatment plan, which serves as the framework, albeit a "work-in-progress," for the client's treatment. It is used to delineate the primary concerns for treatment as short- and long-term objectives. Areas addressed in the treatment plan include issues related to achieving abstinence, education, employment, legal problems, family problems, communication skills, and anger management.

Epoch's Standard Adolescent Treatment Program

Once the treatment plan has been formulated, clients found suitable for group treatment enter Epoch's standard course of treatment. While the adolescent programs have historically varied among the five Epoch facilities, Epoch and Social Research Center staff are currently collaborating to develop a common adolescent treatment protocol for use at all five facilities. The Epoch adolescent program is designed as a flexible, semi-structured, twenty-week program in which group therapy is the primary treatment approach. Clients are required to attend one, seventy-five-minute group counseling session each week. New adolescent clients are admitted continuously.

Group counseling sessions are divided into two phases. Phase 1 is a drug education group consisting of four sessions and focuses on educating clients about the effects of substances, the progression of substance use, the process of relapse, and the impact of genetics and family environment on substance use and abuse. Clients who do not successfully complete phase 1 either repeat that phase or are referred for a higher level of care at the counselor's discretion. Phase 2 is a fifteen-week skills building group. The focus of phase 2 is on development of skills needed to initiate abstinence or to avoid relapse. Groups are primarily psychoeducational, however, each session allows for processing of emerging issues, didactic presentation of the session topic and subsequent discussion/processing of that topic. Group topics for the two treatment phases are presented in Box 4.1.

In addition to group counseling, Epoch offers individual and family counseling sessions and parent educational support groups. Clients are required to attend a minimum of three individual sessions. The initial session at the beginning of treatment focuses on formulating the treatment plan, the second session occurs at around week thirteen and focuses on updating the treatment plan, and the final session focuses on developing a recovery plan (i.e., plan for how the client will remain sober following treatment). In addition, a minimum of four family counseling sessions is required during treatment, addressing family environmental factors that affect a client's substance use. Depending on need and on family composition, family sessions

---

BOX 4.1. Group-Based Adolescent Drug Abuse Treatment

Phase 1: Drug Education, Sessions 1-4
   1.   Physical, Psychological, and Behavioral Effects of Substance Use
   2.   Progression of Substance Use; Self-Diagnosis
   3.   Relapse
   4.   Family Influence
Phase 2: Skills Building/Relapse Prevention, Sessions 5-19
   5.   Goals Group I
   6.   Coping with Stress
   7.   Coping with Hurdles in Recovery
   8.   Managing Thoughts About Using
   9.   Process Group I
  10.   Self-Esteem
  11.   Outside Speaker: STDs/HIV
  12.   Assertiveness: Relationships
  13.   Process Group II
  14.   Goals Group II
  15.   Assertiveness: Drink/Drug Refusal
  16.   Anger
  17.   Process Group III
  18.   Physical Health
  19.   Increasing Pleasurable Activities

can involve parent/caretaker(s) alone or with the client and/or other family members. Additional individual and/or family counseling sessions are offered per client request and/or may be offered or mandated at the discretion of the counselor. In general, clients are seen once during a typical week, however, they can receive up to three sessions in one week if additional individual and/or family sessions are also scheduled.

Parent educational support groups offer both information and support to adolescents' parents/caretakers. Parents/caretakers are expected to attend a minimum of four parenting groups throughout the course of treatment (see Box 4.2 for topics). With the exception of the Catonsville site, however, the sites have had little success in implementing these groups due to lack of interest on the part of parents. Therefore, the facilities have increased their focus on family counseling, using these sessions as a means to encourage parent educational support group attendance.

In addition to these program components, Epoch strongly recommends that adolescents attend at least one twelve-step meeting during the course of their treatment. This introduction to twelve-step recognizes that adolescents often need additional support both during and following treatment and that they may also provide support to others.

BOX 4.2. Parent Educational Support Group

Regular Topic Selections
1. Enabling
2. Family Communication Patterns
3. Stages of Addiction
4. Parenting Styles
5. Understanding Adolescence
6. Limit Setting
7. Anger Management
8. Maintaining Recovery After Treatment

Optional Topics
1. Single Parenting
2. Codependency and Boundary Issues
3. Discussion of Video: "Seven Worst Things Parents Do"
4. Pattern Popping: Breaking Destructive Patterns

Staffing

Epoch's adolescent treatment staff includes counselors, responsible for both group and individual contacts, and family therapists, responsible for both family and parent group contacts. However, counselors at some of the smaller clinics also provide family/parent services, while one of the larger clinics has one staff member providing family therapy and another providing parent educational support group services. Adolescent staff are either bachelor's or master's level clinicians with an average of five years clinical experience.

Procedure for Department of Juvenile Justice Clients

As mentioned earlier, approximately 70 to 80 percent of adolescent referrals to Epoch are made through the Department of Juvenile Justice (DJJ). Although adolescents with criminal histories and/or patterns of delinquent behavior seem to have poorer outcomes than nondelinquent youths (Henggeler, 1993), Epoch and DJJ staffs are attempting to improve outcomes through close collaboration that integrates treatment and juvenile justice efforts. The amount of contact between Epoch counselors and DJJ officers varies from weekly to monthly, depending on the case involved. Most notably, counselors contact DJJ officers immediately in the event of a drug-positive urine test or missed appointment that was not previously canceled. Similarly, DJJ officers keep the counselors abreast of any change in status of an adolescent following legal proceedings. Adolescents involved with the juvenile justice system understand that noncompliance with outpatient treatment will lead directly to a referral for inpatient treatment, or, if left to their DJJ officer, the possibility of house arrest or "lock-up" at a state juvenile facility.

Additional Program Requirements

All clients are expected to comply with random urine screenings. Although tests are typically conducted on a monthly basis, more frequent testing may result if adolescents provide drug-positive urine samples. Any decision to increase testing frequency is at the counselor's discretion. Positive tests are typically discussed and processed in group counseling sessions. Failure to provide requested urine samples is initially treated as a clinical issue in either an individual or group counseling session and will result in termination should a client continue to refuse testing.

Clients are required to comply with program rules and policies. For example, the state of Maryland mandates that failure to have face-to-face contact with a client within a thirty-day period will automatically result in termination. Clients who demonstrate behavioral signs of intoxication, make threats, and/or engage in any form of violence, or who fail to pay incurred fees may be terminated from the program. Clients who are unable to achieve abstinence during treatment will be referred to a higher level of care prior to being discharged.

Criteria for Successful Completion

Clients are considered to have successfully completed the treatment program if they

1. have been abstinent for the 30 days prior to discharge;
2. have attended all group and individual counseling sessions;
3. have completed all treatment plan goals; and
4. have paid their fees in full.

Parent/caretaker attendance at four family counseling sessions and four parent educational support group sessions is also required for successful completion; however, where parents refuse to participate in treatment despite efforts on the part of the counselor and the adolescent, the adolescent is allowed to complete treatment successfully as long as all other requirements are fulfilled.

PROGRAM EVALUATION PROCEDURES

Inclusion/Exclusion Criteria

Adolescent substance abusers aged fourteen to eighteen years of age who apply for treatment at any of the five Epoch locations are recruited to participate in this evaluation study. Adolescents younger than fourteen and adolescents aged eighteen who are out of high school are excluded from the study, as they are inappropriate for the group-based program. Adolescents who are unsuitable for outpatient treatment or group counseling, according to ASAM criteria, are also excluded. A parent or legal guardian and the adolescent must sign the research consent form. The target sample size is 300 subjects.

Assignment to Treatment Induction Approaches

In order to avoid the potential for contamination if *experimental* subjects (i.e., those receiving motivational interviewing) and *comparison* subjects (i.e., those receiving the counseling overview) were treated together (Cook and Campbell, 1979), a crossover design is being used whereby facilities are initially designated as experimental or comparison. Halfway through the enrollment period, experimental sites will become comparison sites and vice versa. Facilities are grouped based on geography to facilitate implementation of the induction techniques, with one group comprising western and southwestern Baltimore County (Catonsville and Lansdowne) and the other group comprising eastern and southeastern Baltimore County (Essex and the two Dundalk offices). Initial assignment of facility groups to treatment induction conditions was determined randomly by a coin toss.

Timing of Assessments

Intake

In addition to the GAIN and POSIT discussed previously, participants complete instruments designed to evaluate coping skills, self-esteem, and self-efficacy. The instruments administered at intake include the Rosenberg Self-Esteem Scale (Rosenberg, 1965, 1979); the Social Skills Rating System (Gresham and Elliot, 1990); the Drinking-Related Locus of Control Scale (Donovan and O'Leary, 1978; Hirsch, McCrady, and Epstein, 1997); and the Adolescent Relapse Coping Questionnaire (Myers and Brown, 1996). Because motivation is an important predictor of outcome, the Circumstances, Motivation, and Readiness Scales (DeLeon and Jainchill, 1986) and the Desire for Help Scale (Simpson, 1992; Simpson and Joe, 1993; Knight, Holcum, and Simpson, 1994) are also administered.

Two-Week Assessment

To assess the short-term effectiveness of the motivational intervention, study participants complete the Circumstances, Motivation, and Readiness Scales and the Desire for Help Scale one week after the treatment induction session and immediately prior to their treatment planning session.

Six-Week Assessment

Approximately six weeks after beginning treatment, study participants are administered the Working Alliance Inventory (Youth) (Horvath and Greenberg, 1989) and the Client Evaluation Scales (Simpson and Chatham, 1995), to determine the quality of their relationships with their counselors and their attitudes toward treatment. At this time, counselors also complete the Counselor Rating of Client (Simpson and Chatham, 1995), which assesses treatment engagement and participation. Clients who terminate or are discharged from treatment before completion will be interviewed regarding their attitudes toward treatment, reasons for termination, any treatment concurrently received, and plans for subsequent treatment.

Six- and Twelve-Month Assessments

Longer-term outcome evaluation is based on participant interviews conducted six and twelve months following intake using the GAIN (monitoring version) and supplemental instruments.

Process Measures

Treatment process data, including attendance, urine screening results, counselor assessments, reasons for termination, and school and juvenile justice system data supplements client self-reported and inventory data. Urine drug screening is conducted at all post-treatment assessments for verification of self-reported substance use. Subjects are not reimbursed for their initial assessment since this is a standard interview for clinical as well as research purposes, but are reimbursed $10 for the two- and six-week assessments, and $20 for the six-month and $25 for the twelve-month assessments.

Ethnographic Component

Twenty-five youths are being selected from the sample to be studied more intensively using an ethnographic strategy that maximizes subject differences. This component of the study involves several in-depth ethnographic interviews conducted outside the program both during and following treatment. Primary emphasis of these interviews will be on the youths' self-perceptions in relation to their substance use, linked with perceptions of their program experiences in particular and their social worlds in general. Key for the analysis is the question of whether and how these perceptions change, and how youths explain these changes. This ethnographic component is focused on several orienting questions:

1. Does a widely shared program experience exist or does it vary substantially among youths?
2. Assuming some variation, does the variation cluster among youth in some systematic way?
3. Are variations in program experience related to outcomes?

SUBJECT CHARACTERISTICS

Characteristics of the first sixty-two clients enrolled in the study as of January 15, 2001, are summarized in Table 4.1. Participants were predominantly male (89 percent) and largely white (68 percent) or African American (23 percent). Nearly all lived in a house or apartment, either of their own or their parents (85 percent) or that of a friend or relative (11 percent). Over half (53 percent) were under the legal custody of a single parent, whereas most of the remainder were under the custody of their parents together (27 percent) or separated (11 percent). Thirty-two percent met criteria for substance dependence. Forty-eight percent identified needing treatment for marijuana/hashish, 8 percent for alcohol, and 8 percent other drugs, while the remainder denied needing treatment. Participants reported using alcohol or other drugs a mean of 25.0 days in the last 90 days, being drunk or high most of the day on 8.4 days of those days, and being in jail or other place where they could not use drugs 9.5 of those days. Just 11 percent of participants had never been arrested, charged, and

TABLE 4.1. Characteristics of the Study Sample as of January 15, 2001 (N = 62)

Item	N	%
Gender		
Male	55	89
Female	7	11
Age		
13-14	9	15
15-16	31	50
17-18	22	35
Ethnicity		
American Indian/Alaskan Native	1	2
Asian or Pacific Islander	1	2
Black	14	23
White	42	68
Hispanic (Puerto Rican, Mexican, Cuban, other)	0	0
Mixed/some other group	3	5
Current living situation		
A house or apartment (yours or parents)	53	85
A friend's or relative's house or apartment	7	11
Any other housing situation	1	2
Present work or school situation		
Working full time	10	16
Working part time	7	11
Unemployed or laid off	11	18
In school or training only (even if not in session now)	34	55
In school or training at all in the past 90 days	47	76
Substance dependence (meeting criteria)	20	32
Substance treatment needed for		
Any kind of alcohol	5	8
Marijuana, hashish, etc.	30	48
Crack, freebase cocaine, other cocaine	2	3
Heroin	1	2

Item	N	%
"Acid" or other hallucinogens	2	3
Age when first got drunk or used any drugs		
Below 15	50	81
15-18	9	15
Last grade or year completed in school		
<6	1	2
6-8	12	19
9-10	33	53
11-12	16	26
Legal Custody		
Parents together	17	27
Parents separated	7	11
Single parent	33	53
Other Family	3	5
Other	1	2
Times in life arrested, charged with a crime, and booked		
0	7	11
1-2	37	60
3+	18	29
Times in life admitted to drug treatment or counseling		
0	32	52
1-2	23	37
3+	7	11

	Mean	SD
Times in life arrested, charged with a crime and booked	2.2	2.3
Substance use—last 90 days		
Days used alcohol, marijuana, or other drugs	25.0	29.6
Days drunk or high for most of the day	8.4	17.5
Days in a jail (or other place) where you could not use	9.5	21.3
Times in life admitted to drug treatment or counseling	0.9	1.5

booked, while the mean number of times arrested, charged, and booked was 2.2. This was the first treatment admission for 52 percent of participants, while most of the remainder (37 percent) had one or two prior treatment admissions.

CONCLUSION

Adolescent substance use and misuse is a significant problem in the United States. Yet relatively little attention has been paid to evaluating treatment programs for adolescents who are chemically dependent (Ralph and McMenamy, 1996). CSAT's Adolescent Treatment Model program evaluates existing and new adolescent treatment programs throughout the country. The Epoch Counseling Center and Social Research Center are collaborating to develop an adolescent group-based outpatient treatment program that is both comprehensive and feasible for implementation in community-based facilities and are evaluating this treatment model and also the addition of a one-session motivational interview at the beginning of treatment. If found effective, these interventions may help to improve adolescent treatment services delivered in Maryland as well as nationally.

REFERENCES

Aas, H.N., Leigh, B.C., Anderssen, N. and Jakobsen, R. (1998). Two year longitudinal study of alcohol expectancies and drinking among Norwegian adolescents. *Journal of Addictions, 93,* 373-384.

Abrams, D.B. and Niaura, R.S. (1987). Social learning theory. In H.T. Blane and K.E. Leonard (Eds.), *Psychological Theories of Drinking and Alcoholism* (pp. 131-178). New York: Guilford.

American Society of Addiction Medicine (ASAM) (1996). *American Society of Addiction Medicine: Patient Placement Criteria for the Treatment of Substance-Related Disorders,* Second Edition. Bethesda, MD: ASAM.

Andersen, M.D. (1985). Personalized nursing: An effective intervention model for use in drug-dependent women in an emergency room. In R.S. Ashery (Ed.), *Progress in the Development of Cost-Effective Treatment for Drug Abusers* (pp. 67-82). Rockville, MD: NIDA.

Bandura, A. (1977). *Social Learning Theory.* Englewood Cliffs, NJ: Prentice-Hall.

Bigelow, G.E., Brooner, R.K., and Silverman, K. (1998). Competing motivations: Drug reinforcement vs. non-drug reinforcement. *Journal of Psychopharmacology, 12,* 8-14.

Blankenship, J., Dansereau, D.F., and Simpson, D.D. (1999). Cognitive enhancements of readiness for corrections-based treatment for drug abuse. *The Prison Journal, 79,* 431-445.

Catalano, R.F., Hawkins, J.D., Wells, E.A., and Miller, J. (1990-1991). Evaluation of the effectiveness of adolescent drug abuse treatment, assessment of risks for relapse, and promising approaches for relapse prevention. *International Journal of the Addictions, 25,* 1085-1140.

Cohen, D.A. and Rice, J. (1997). Parenting styles, adolescent substance use, and academic achievement. *Journal of Drug Education, 27,* 199-211.

Cook, T.D. and Campbell, D.T. (1979). *Quasi-Experimentation.* Chicago: Rand McNally.

DeLeon, G. and Jainchill, N. (1986). *Circumstance, Motivation, Readiness, and Suitability for Substance Abuse Treatment (CMRS).* New York: Phoenix House Foundation, Inc.

Dennis, M., Dowud-Noursi, S., Muck, R., and McDermeit, M. (2003). The need for developing and evaluating adolescent treatment models. In S.J. Stevens and A.R. Morral (Eds.), *Adolescent Substance Abuse Treatment in the United States: Exemplary Models from a National Evaluation Study* (pp. 3-26). Binghamton, NY: The Haworth Press, Inc.

Donovan, D.M. and O'Leary, M.R. (1978). The drinking-related locus of control scale: Reliability, factor structure, validity. *Journal of Studies on Alcohol, 39*(5).

Duncan, S.C., Duncan, T.E., Biglan, A., and Ary, D. (1998). Contributions of the social context to the development of adolescent substance use: A multivariate latent growth modeling approach. *Journal of Drug and Alcohol Dependence, 50,* 57-71.

Gresham, F.M. and Elliot, S.N. (1990). *Social Skills Rating System.* Circle Pines, MN: American Guidance Service.

Hall, J.A., Richardson, G., Spears, J., and Rembert, J.K. (1998). Validation of the POSIT: Comparing drug using and abstaining youth. *Journal of Child and Adolescent Substance Abuse, 8*(2), 363-376.

Henggeler, S.W. (1993). Behavioral treatments for drug abuse and dependence. In L.S. Onken, J.D. Blaine, and J.J. Boren (Eds.), *Multisystemic Treatment of Serious Juvenile Offenders: Implications for the Treatment of Substance Abusing Youths* (pp. 181-199). National Institute on Drug Abuse Research Monograph 137. Rockville, MD: National Institute on Drug Abuse.

Henggeler, S.W. (1997). Treating drug abusers effectively. In J.A. Egerston, D.M. Fox, and A.I. Leshner (Eds.), *The Development of Effective Drug-Abuse Services for Youth* (pp. 253-279). New York: Blackwell Publishers.

Hirsch, L.S., McCrady, B.S., and Epstein, E.E. (1997). The Drinking-Related Locus of Control Scale: The factor structure with treatment-seeking outpatients. *Journal of Studies on Alcohol,* March, 162-166.

Horvath, A.O. and Greenberg, L.S. (1989). Development and validation of the Working Alliance Inventory. *Journal of Counseling Psychology, 36,* 223-233.

Joe, G.W., Simpson, D.D., and Broome, K.M. (1998). Effects of readiness for drug abuse treatment on client retention and assessment of process. *Addiction, 93,* 1177-1190.

Johnston, L.D., O'Malley, P.M., and Bachman, J.G. (2000). *Monitoring the Future: National Survey Results on Drug Abuse, 1975-1999,* Volume 1: *Secondary School Students.* Bethesda, MD: National Institute on Drug Abuse.

Killen, J.D., Hayward, C., Wilson, D.M., Haydel, K.F., Robinson, T.N., Taylor, C.B., Hammer, L. D., and Varady, A. (1996). Predicting onset of drinking in a community sample of adolescents: The role of expectancy and temperament. *Addictive Behaviors, 21,* 473-480.

Knight, J.R., Goodman, E., Pulerwitz, T., and Durant, R.H. (2000). Reliabilities of short substance abuse screening tests among adolescent medical patients. *Pediatrics, 105,* 948-953.

Knight, K., Holcum, M., and Simpson, D.D. (1994). *TCU Psychosocial Functioning and Motivation Scales: Manual on Psychometric Properties.* Fort Worth, Texas: Institute of Behavioral Research, Texas Christian University.

Marlatt, G.A., Baer, J.S., Kivlahan, D.R., Dimeff, L.A., Larimer, M.E., Quigley, L.A., Somers, J.M., and Williams, E. (1998). Screening and brief intervention for high-risk college student drinkers: Results from a two-year follow-up assessment. *Journal of Consulting and Clinical Psychology, 66,* 604-615.

McLaney, M.A., Richardson, G., Spears, J., and Rembert, J.K. (1994). A validation study of the Problem Oriented Screening Instrument for Teenagers (POSIT). *Journal of Mental Health, 3,* 363-376.

Miller, P.M., Smith, G.T., and Goldman, M.S. (1990). Emergence of alcohol expectancies in childhood: A possible critical period. *Journal of Studies on Alcohol, 51,* 343-349.

Miller, W.R. (1983). Motivational interviewing with problem drinkers. *Behavioural Psychotherapy, 11,* 147-172.

Miller, W.R. (1989). Increasing motivation for change. In R.K. Hester and W.R. Miller (Eds.), *Handbook of Alcoholism Treatment Approaches* (pp. 67-80). New York: Pergamon.

Miller, W.R. (1996). Motivational interviewing: Research, practice, and puzzles. *Addictive Behaviors, 21,* 835-842.

Miller, W.R. and Rollnick, S. (1991). *Motivational Interviewing: Preparing People to Change Addictive Behaviors.* New York: Guilford Press.

Miller, W.R. and Sanchez, V.C. (1994). Motivating young adults for treatment and lifestyle change. In G. Howard (Ed.), *Issues in Alcohol Use and Misuse by Young Adults* (pp. 55-82). Notre Dame, IN: University of Notre Dame Press.

Myers, M.G. and Brown, S.A. (1996). The Adolescent Relapse Coping Questionnaire: Psychometric validation. *Journal of Studies on Alcohol, 57,* 40-46.

Pavlov, I.P. (1927). *Lectures on Conditioned Reflexes.* New York: International Publishers.

Query, L.R., Rosenberg, H., and Tisak, M.S. (1998). The assessment of young children's expectancies of alcohol versus a control substance. *Journal of the Addictions, 93,* 1521-1529.

Ralph, N. and McMenamy, C. (1996). Treatment outcomes in an adolescent chemical dependency program. *Adolescence, 31,* 91-107.

Richardson, J.L., Radziszewska, B., Dent, C.W., and Flay, B.R. (1993). Relationship between after-school care of adolescents and substance use, risk taking, depressed mood, and academic achievement. *Pediatrics, 92,* 32-38.

Rollnick, S. and Miller, W.R. (1995). What is motivational interviewing? *Behavioral and Cognitive Psychotherapy, 23,* 325-334.

Rosenberg, M. (1965). *Society and the Adolescent Self-Image.* Princeton, NJ: Princeton University Press.

Rosenberg, M. (1979). *Conceiving the Self.* New York: Basic Books.

Saunders, B, Wilkinson, C., and Phillips, M. (1995). The impact of a brief motivational intervention with opiate users attending a methadone program. *Addiction, 90,* 415-424.

Simpson, D.D. (1992). *TCU Forms Manual: Drug Abuse Treatment for AIDS-Risk Reduction (DATAR).* Fort Worth, TX: Institute of Behavioral Research, Texas Christian University.

Simpson, D.D. and Chatham, L.R. (1995). *TCU/DATAR Forms Manual.* Fort Worth, TX: Institute of Behavioral Research, Texas Christian University.

Simpson, D.D. and Joe, G.W. (1993). Motivation as a predictor of early dropout from drug abuse treatment. *Psychotherapy, 30,* 357-367.

Skinner, B.F. (1953). *Science and Human Behavior.* New York: Macmillan.

Smith, G.T., Goldman, M.S., Greenbaum, P.E., and Christiansen, B.A. (1995). Expectancy for social facilitation from drinking: The divergent paths of high-expectancy and low-expectancy adolescents. *Journal of Abnormal Psychology, 104,* 32-40.

Stephens, R.S., Roffman, R.A., Cleaveland, B.L., Curtin, L., and Wertz, J. (1994). *Extended versus Minimal Intervention with Maryland Dependent Adults.* Paper presented at the Annual Meeting and the Association for the Advancement of Behavior Therapy, November. San Diego, CA.

Wagner, E.F., Brown, S.A., Monti, P.M., Myers, M.G., and Waldron, H.B. (1999). Innovations in adolescent substance abuse intervention. *Alcoholism: Clinical and Experimental Research, 23*(2), 236-249.

Wikler, A. (1973). Dynamics of drug dependence: Implications of a conditioning theory for research and treatment. *Archives of General Psychiatry, 28,* 611-616.

SECTION III:
FAMILY-ORIENTED OUTPATIENT
TREATMENT MODELS

Chapter 5

Family Therapy for Early Adolescent Substance Abuse

Cynthia Rowe
Elizabeth Parker-Sloat
Seth Schwartz
Howard Liddle

INTRODUCTION

Early adolescence is one of the most sensitive periods in the life cycle. It is a transitional period during which young adolescents experience physical changes (Paikoff and Brooks-Gunn, 1990), new feelings and perspectives about their sense of self and relationships (Archer, 1982), and significant shifts in socially ascribed roles (Dunham, Kidwell, and Wilson, 1986). The "developmental reorganization" (Cicchetti and Toth, 1992) that occurs between late childhood and adolescence makes early adolescence a time of heightened vulnerability to emotional and behavior problems and substance use disorders. Moreover, problems during this critical period increase vul-

Completion of this work was supported by grants from the Center for Substance Abuse Treatment (CSAT, Grant No. 1 KD1 TI11871, H. Liddle, Principal Investigator) and the National Institute on Drug Abuse (Grant No. P50 DA11328, H. Liddle, Principal Investigator; Grant No. T32 DAO7297, H. Liddle, Principal Investigator). The opinions expressed in this chapter are those of the authors and do not reflect official positions of CSAT or NIDA.

Correspondence concerning this chapter should be addressed to Cynthia Rowe or Howard Liddle, Center for Treatment Research on Adolescent Drug Abuse (M711), Department of Epidemiology and Public Health, University of Miami School of Medicine, P.O. Box 019132, Miami, FL 33101. Phone: (305) 243-6434; Fax: (305) 243-3651. Electronic mail may be sent to <crowe@med.miami.edu> or <hliddle@med.miami. edu>.

nerability to a range of negative outcomes throughout adolescence and into adulthood. Generally, the earlier youths begin to use drugs and experience related problems, the more serious the consequences (Tarter et al., 1999), and the more difficult it is to steer them on to a positive developmental course.

Given the increased susceptibility to problem behaviors during the early adolescent transition, this is a critical period for intervention efforts (compare Cicchetti and Richters, 1993). Furthermore, the difficulty of treating severe drug abuse in late adolescence and adulthood has motivated researchers and clinicians in the drug abuse field to identify effective "early interventions" that may halt the progression of deviance before negative behavioral patterns become highly resistant to change (Hogue and Liddle, 1999). Unfortunately, as is true for adolescent drug abusers generally, few empirically supported treatments for young adolescent drug abusers exist (Liddle and Dakof, 1995), and those that have demonstrated efficacy remain inaccessible to community providers (Institute of Medicine, 1998).

The purpose of this chapter is to describe interventions designed for early adolescents within a family-based treatment model, multidimensional family therapy (MDFT) (Liddle, Dakof, and Diamond, 1991; Liddle, 1992; Liddle, in press). MDFT is an empirically supported outpatient approach for treating adolescent drug abusers (CSAT, 1999; CSAP, 2000; Liddle and Hogue, 2001; NIDA, 1999; Mendel, 2000). Different versions of MDFT have been developed and tested in various clinical studies. These studies have explored the effectiveness of the approach according to different patient characteristics (e.g., comorbidity, adolescents referred for residential care) and treatment delivery conditions (e.g., adding in-home sessions, case management, and varying weekly dose and intensity of service delivery). We are currently investigating the effectiveness of the model as a stand-alone intervention in community settings, as well as the feasibility of transporting MDFT into other settings and modalities with therapists who have a range of educational backgrounds and therapeutic experience. Among other ongoing studies, MDFT is currently being implemented and evaluated with young adolescent drug abusers at The Village, Inc., Miami, Florida, a nonprofit community drug abuse treatment center, which provides a wide range of drug treatment services to adolescents and adults.

The current project is a randomized clinical trial comparing the effectiveness of MDFT in comparison to a standard group therapy model for adolescent drug abuse. Youth meeting criteria for the "Village Heat Program" are randomly assigned to either MDFT or group treatment upon admission to The Village. Bachelor's and master's level therapists provide the therapy. In both treatment conditions, adolescents receive therapy sessions (either family or group) twice a week as well as case management services. Youths in both conditions receive between twelve and sixteen weeks of treatment. Therapists receive training in their respective manuals and ongoing weekly supervision by an expert in the therapy model.

Table 5.1 describes the characteristics of adolescents seen in this controlled trial. Adolescents in this project are twelve to fifteen years old and meet ASAM criteria for outpatient drug abuse treatment. Because MDFT is being tested as an early intervention model in this study, youth with drug use or delinquency problems warranting intensive outpatient services are not appropriate for this level of treatment. Thus, adolescents with an extensive psychiatric and juvenile justice history are excluded from the program. Youths must also have a family member willing to participate in therapy and assessments. Most youths have had between one and two arrests but very few have had previous drug treatment. The sample is approximately 50 percent Hispanic and 50 percent African American. Males make up slightly over 80 percent of the sample. The majority of youths in the program are living at home with their parents and are enrolled in school. Adolescents report using an average of fourteen days out of the past ninety, and marijuana is the substance of choice for almost all youths in the study. Referrals to the program come primarily from school counselors and the Juvenile Assessment Center of Miami-Dade County's juvenile justice system.

Comprehensive articulations of the theory and interventions of the MDFT model have been provided in previous publications (Liddle, Dakof, and Diamond, 1991; Liddle, 1995, 1999). This chapter highlights MDFT interventions that have direct clinical relevance for early adolescents, given the known developmental risk factors during this period.

TABLE 5.1. Characteristics of Youth in the Village Heat Program

Item	N	%
Gender		
Male	25	83
Female	5	17
Age		
11-12	2	7
13-14	15	50
15-16	13	43
17-18	0	0
19 and over	0	0
Ethnicity		
American Indian/Alaskan Native	0	0
Asian or Pacific Islander	0	0
Black	15	50
White	1	3
Hispanic (Puerto Rican, Mexican, Cuban, other)	14	47
Mixed/some other group	0	0
Current living situation		
A house or apartment (yours or parents)	23	77
A foster home or public housing	4	13
A friend's or relative's house or apartment	1	3
A nursing home, hospital, inpatient or residential	0	0
Jail, detention center, or other correctional institution	0	0
Temporary or emergency shelter	0	0
Vacant buildings	0	0
Any other housing situation	2	7
Present work or school situation		
Working full time	0	0
Working part time	0	0
Unemployed or laid off	0	0
Have a job but not working	0	0

Item	N	
In school or training only (even if not in session now)	30	100
In jail or prison	0	0
Some other work situation	0	0
Substance dependence (meeting criteria)	0	0
Substance treatment needed for		
Any kind of alcohol	6	20
Marijuana, hashish, etc.	30	100
Crack, freebase cocaine, other cocaine	0	0
Amphetamine/methamphetamine	0	0
Inhalants	0	0
Heroin	0	0
"Acid" or other hallucinogens	0	0
Some other drug	0	0
Age when first got drunk or used any drugs		
Below 15	30	100
15-18	0	0
Over 18	0	0
Last grade or year completed in school		
< 6	0	0
6-8	25	83
9-10	5	7
11-12	0	0
> 12	0	0

	Mean	SD
Times in life arrested, charged with a crime, and booked	2.00	1.46
Substance use—last 90 days		
Days used alcohol, marijuana, or other drugs	14.27	14.61
Days drunk or high for most of the day	6.47	11.76
Days in jail (or other place) where you could not use drugs	3.70	6.70
Times in life admitted to drug treatment or counseling	.13	.35

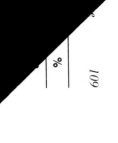

IMENSIONAL FAMILY THERAPY:
'ENTAL AND ECOLOGICAL APPROACH

·oach has evolved over the past seventeen years
·ogram designed to develop and evaluate family-
:atment for adolescents (this work is summarized
ɪe, 2001). MDFT identifies several pathways to
ɪultiple systems involved in maintaining dysfunc-
....dolescent drug users. Grounded in developmental
and ecological theory, MDFT interventions are based in knowledge
about the challenges and critical tasks of individual maturation, as
well as the impact of contextual factors on the individual's development (Liddle et al., 2000).

Therapists in MDFT work simultaneously in four domains corresponding to the most important areas of the youth's life. Each domain
is operationalized in a therapeutic module, which prescribes core
content and generic relationship and intrapersonal themes which become targets of intervention. In each module, change occurs in sequentially applied steps, with therapists helping family members build
on their successes in sessions and outside of therapy. Therapists are
active and directive in inspiring change in each domain. The four domains and corresponding therapeutic modules are

1. The individual adolescent
2. The parents and other individual family members
3. The family's transactional patterns
4. Family members' interactions with extrafamilial systems.

The model specifies particular interventions to initiate change within
each module. The *adolescent* module focuses on the individual adolescent within the family and in social systems, principally peer
groups. The *parent* module enhances parenting skills in the areas of
monitoring and limit-setting, rebuilding emotional attachments with
the adolescent, and increasing participation in the adolescent's life
(Schmidt, Liddle, and Dakof, 1996). The parent module's work also
includes assessment of and attention to the personal and psychological functioning of the parent as an individual, in addition to their parental role. The *family interaction* module facilitates change in family
relationship patterns by providing an interactional context wherein
family members are helped to validate the perspectives of other mem-

bers, decrease conflict, increase communication, and improve problem solving (Diamond and Liddle, 1996). The *extrafamilial* module establishes collaborative relationships among all systems to which the adolescent is connected (e.g., school, juvenile justice, recreational).

MDFT is based on a developmental psychopathology framework and targets the multiple ecological factors maintaining drug use and other problem behaviors (Liddle, 1999), with the ultimate aim to place the adolescent on an adaptive developmental trajectory. Factors that contribute to adolescent drug abuse can be traced to earlier difficulties (Conger and Ge, 1999), including poor parent-adolescent relationships (Steinberg, 1991), early behavior problems (Patterson, Bank, and Stoolmiller, 1990), and peer rejection and negative peer affiliation (Loeber, 1989). Risk and protective factors provide targets and guidelines for early intervention. Within MDFT, interventions are designed to bolster protective mechanisms and alter the cumulative effects of multiple risk factors (Liddle, 2000; Liddle et al., 2000).

MDFT interventions highlighted here encompass the important domains of (1) the adolescent's developing sense of self, (2) peer relationships, and (3) relationships with parents. These domains represent the most important spheres of influence and change during early adolescence. MDFT interventions in each of these areas are based on developmental research and the risk and protective factors framework. Relevant research findings that inform our clinical work in each domain are presented in the following, including examples of interventions utilized in actual MDFT clinical cases. (Names and identifying circumstances have been altered to protect confidentiality.)

THE SELF OF THE EARLY ADOLESCENT AND CLINICAL IMPLICATIONS

Identity development is one of the major tasks of adolescence. It occurs through a combination of role modeling, identification processes, and validation from others (Adams, 1985). Accordingly, relationships with both parents and peers are critical in the process of identity formation. Close, responsive family relationships engender youth with a healthy sense of identity and self-efficacy (Jackson,

Dunham, and Kidwell, 1990), whereas families characterized by a lack of warmth, involvement, and structure tend to promote apathy, lack of direction, and low self-efficacy (Adams, Dyk, and Bennion, 1987). In addition, peer group membership and interactions with peers strongly impact the young adolescent's development of self-worth and identity. Young adolescents tend to select peers who are at their own level of identity development (Akers, Jones, and Coyl, 1998). For instance, a young adolescent who is confused about his or her sense of self and in a state of "identity diffusion" is likely to gravitate to others who are exploring similar identity issues. Furthermore, young adolescents tend to internalize the sense of identity that they construct together with peers (Pugh and Hart, 1999).

Researchers have linked problems in identity development to drug use and delinquency in adolescence. Drug use is most common and pervasive in young adolescents who are characterized as identity diffuse and have problems with identity development (Jones, 1992, 1994). In addition, Oyserman and Markus (1990) uncovered a relationship between "possible selves"—"the elements of the self-concept that represent the individual's goals, motives, fears, and anxieties" (p. 113)—and delinquency status. These authors showed that delinquents were much more negative and pessimistic in describing the person they expected and hoped to become than were nondelinquents. While public school youth focused on achievements to define their possible selves, delinquents rarely predicted school or job success in their futures, and most often saw themselves becoming criminals or drug addicts. The clinical relevance of these findings is that possible selves provide direction for the adolescent's actions, thus skilled clinicians can use these representations to explore alternatives to the way the adolescent is living his life. Jackson-Gilfort and Liddle (in press) illustrate how we use these ideas in the context of crafting and testing culturally specific MDFT interventions with African-American adolescents.

Research findings discussed previously are directly applicable to our clinical work with adolescents and families in MDFT. MDFT therapists spend much of the early stage of therapy getting a picture of what the teenager's life is like, how the teen feels about himself or herself and about the path his or her life is taking. These discussions are important in building the therapeutic alliance (Diamond et al., 1999), but also in helping the adolescent explore his or her evolving identity and hopes and dreams for the future, or "possible selves." It is the therapist's job to help the adolescent link these "possible selves" to concrete, manageable steps that they can monitor and fine-tune together. With younger adolescents, the process of uncovering the adolescent's sense of who he or she is and who he or she would like to be is particularly important, since during this time feelings and thoughts about oneself are most in flux and vulnerable to negative influences. Therapists also utilize this time to reinforce their role as advocate for, supporter of, and collaborator with the teen.

In the following vignette with a fourteen-year-old teenager, the therapist summarizes for the adolescent his impressions after a lengthy discussion of the teen's family relationships, past and current friendships, and school experiences. The therapist makes the connection between the person the adolescent wants to be and the specific steps he will have to take to get there, and then provides encouragement that these new realities are possible.

THERAPIST: You've got a strong sense of yourself, huh? It sounds like you've done some thinking and you have some ideas about how you want your life to look.

CHRIS: Yeah. When I was young, when I was little, I looked up to my older brother. But now, since I was like twelve, I just want to be my own self. I don't want to be like him.

TH: When you look at the people in your life, are there certain things that you know you'd like to have turn out the same way? Or you're going to find your own direction?

C: [*Adolescent nods in agreement.*]

TH: It sounds like there are some clear things that you've said today that I just want to keep in mind because we're going to come back to them—and one of them is that you really want this year to be different than last year, you want to do your work, you want to pass, and it also sounds like you want to go on to high school. It sounds like when you get there you want to make sure that you meet new people who aren't going to have a bad influence on you, so that you can do your work there too. You're serious about graduating high school, and I believe that you can do it. And I want to help you stay on track and make sure that happens.

MDFT therapists attend to the ways in which the young adolescent's drug use, delinquency, and other problems factor into the sense of who he or she is and who he or she would like to be. For many teens, the drug or street subculture becomes a way of life and they begin to take on the associated negative identity as they gravitate toward these kinds of peers. Oyserman and Markus (1990, p. 114) hypothesize that "adolescents who are not successful in constructing and maintaining positive selves in the conventional domains of the family, friends, or school are likely to seek alternative ways to define the self." Often, therapists can help adolescents uncover more positive feelings they had when they were younger, and offer ways to reclaim a more positive identity by changing their behaviors, as in the following exchange between a fourteen-year-old and her therapist.

GLORIA: I'm not as good of a person as I used to be. 'Cause before, I acted better and I would go to school, and I would get As and Bs. But that was when I was young, like before I was in seventh grade.

THERAPIST: Is that something you would like to get back? That feeling of knowing you were doing what your parents asked you to do, getting good grades, feeling good about yourself? Because I think it's tough being your age—I know I wouldn't want to be your age again. I think it's a tough time, but I also believe you can really turn things around and feel good about the way your life is going again. That is one of the things I think you can get out of therapy. I really believe you can do it, and I want to help you get there.

MDFT therapists understand the complex interrelationships of self, parents, and peer networks and the influence these interrelationships have on the early adolescent's emerging sense of self. Therapists help parents to be open to discussions with their teen about how they feel about themselves and their lives. Frequently, parents find new information in these discussions that help them to understand what their adolescent is experiencing. The following segment illustrates ways therapists facilitate these discussions.

THERAPIST: You're talking about Tony's older brother—he wants to know who is more handsome? What do you think is going through his mind? You have some ideas.

MOM: I don't know—I guess he wants to know if he can talk to girls like Marcus does. Because Marcus is just the opposite of him. He's thin—real thin. He's skinny. Some girls are more attracted to a thinner person, and I guess he wonders about that.

TH: You think he wonders if he's going to be as attractive to women as his older brother?

M: Yeah. His brother has the charm, you know. But everybody's different in their own way. People see different things in people. You know.

TH: What do you think some of the things are that girls and other people see in Tony?

M: Some people think Tony's cute because he's pudgy—girls say that—or his eyes, his eyelashes are attractive. But it's what you think of yourself that counts.

TH: Do you know what he thinks about himself?

M: No. No, I don't know. I'd like to know.

T: You mean how I think I look?

M: Well, yeah. How do you think you look? What do you think you need to improve on?

T: Nothing really.

M: So you think you look fine. Then why are you always asking me if you look better than Marcus? You always ask me that. At least once a month [*Adolescent laughs*].

TH: You had some concerns that maybe Tony felt bad about how heavy he was.

M: Yeah. I always ask him that and he always denies it. [*To adolescent*] Do you think you're overweight?

T: I know I'm overweight but I don't worry about it.

M: You don't worry about it? Would you like to be thinner?

T: Yeah, I'd rather be skinny.

M: I didn't know that. I never knew that. You always told me, "I'm fine. It don't bother me." I didn't know that you felt like you'd rather be thinner.

TH: It's hard to lose weight, and I think it's hard to feel a little heavy—in school especially—I don't know if you get teased, Tony, but that's something that kids can be tough on.

In the remainder of this session, the therapist allows the adolescent time to share his feelings in greater depth, and helps the adolescent's mother follow up with sensitive, appropriate questions and support. By guiding their interaction, the therapist builds a foundation for future discussions in which the teen can feel safe to come to his mother with concerns and doubts with regard to his sense of self. Establishing the foundation of a close and responsive parent-adolescent relationship is critical in the formation of a healthy sense of identity and self-efficacy (Jackson, Dunham, and Kidwell, 1990). In fact, Resnick et al. (1997) report that the main threats to adolescent health stem from risk behaviors, and that close relationships with parents protect adolescents from almost every risk behavior examined, including substance use, emotional distress, and violence.

PEER RELATIONSHIPS IN EARLY ADOLESCENCE AND CLINICAL IMPLICATIONS

Peers become a significant source of support and intimacy in early adolescence. During and shortly after puberty, youths begin spending more time with friends and less time at home (Berndt and Perry, 1990). Whereas younger children select friends based on common interests and activities, adolescents tend to form peer relationships based on psychological or attitudinal similarities (Steinberg, 1991). Research has consistently shown that young adolescents with positive life styles are apt to select prosocial peers, whereas young adolescents oriented toward antisocial or problem behavior are likely to select similarly deviant peers.

Association with drug abusing peers is a primary risk factor for drug abuse (Brook, Kessler, and Cohen, 1999) and early adolescents are particularly susceptible to the influences of antisocial peers and crowds, more so than middle and late adolescents (Bush, Weinfurt, and Iannotti, 1994). However, negative peer influences do not operate in isolation. Youth with other risk factors for deviance are most vulnerable to negative peer association (Scheier and Newcomb, 1991). Steinberg and other researchers (Steinberg, Fletcher, and Darling, 1994; Dishion, Reid, and Patterson, 1988) have demonstrated that family and parenting risk factors such as poor monitoring and rejection create an environment in which adolescents have easy access to and relate more easily to deviant peers. Children raised in supportive, nurturing, and constructively challenging home environments tend to associate with positive peers, whereas children raised in neglectful or conflict-ridden homes tend to seek out other aggressive and peer-rejected friends (Barrera, Castro, and Biglan, 1999). Adolescents who have established a healthy balance of independence and connectedness with their parents are likely to do the same with their peers.

On the positive side, peer-related protective factors can buffer the young adolescent from drug abuse (Wentzel and McNamara, 1999). For example, peer crowds oriented toward positive behavior (e.g., sports, academics) may actively disapprove of drug use (Youniss, McLellan, and Strouse, 1994). Furthermore, intimacy in peer relationships allows young adolescents to express emotions (Berndt and Perry, 1990) and thus to prevent the buildup of negative affect that may contribute to drug abuse (Diamond and Liddle, 1996). Positive peers provide a safe outlet for expressing feelings and represent an important source of support and validation. An obvious clinical implication of these findings is to link drug abusing peers to more positive influences.

Because of the power of peer relationships in influencing the adolescent's developmental trajectory, intervening with the peer system is critical in MDFT. Several levels of intervention are possible when considering changes that need to occur in the adolescent's peer network. Therapists have important discussions with adolescents one-on-one to uncover the nature of these relationships and how these friends can support or interfere with the adolescent's goals. Therapists also motivate parents to learn more about their adolescent's friends, the places they hang out, and the things they do in their time together. In addition to these types of discussions, therapists look for opportunities to bring peers into therapy when appropriate. These interventions are delivered simultaneously, as the work in different therapeutic and developmental domains occurs concurrently in MDFT. Just as drug abuse and other problems develop in the context of multiple systems interacting and meshing (or failing to mesh) over time, MDFT interventions parallel this process of simultaneous influence. Our objective is to create a positive synergy that was not present in the adolescent's life before coming to therapy, wherein changes in one domain (e.g., a teen's new and competent self-expression) inspire changes in other important realms (e.g., a parent's renewed sense of hope and commitment; a teacher's change in attitude toward the adolescent).

The following segment is typical of the kinds of conversations therapists have with young adolescents one-on-one in the early stage of therapy. These discussions are part of hearing adolescents' stories, what life is like during this transitional period, how things have changed since they were younger, who their friends are now, and what they want for themselves in the future.

THERAPIST: So what kind of path are you on? I hear that Melvin's on this path of gambling and getting in trouble from time to time, and he's locked up now, right? And Justin's on this path of getting straight As and playing hoops, right? And Tyrell's kind of in between the two of them. It sounds like you've got a lot of different kinds of friends.

TONY: I don't even hang with them. I used to hang with them a lot, like last year, but not now.

TH: How come? What happened?

T: I just don't hang with them. I don't know. I'm trying to stay out of trouble and not get locked up or nothin'.

TH: Was that hard to do? Did you just make a decision and say, "I'm not going down that road, I don't want to hang with them?"

T: It wasn't hard or nothin'. I just don't hang with them. I ain't gonna be with a crowd of them, knowin' I'm standin' on the corner with them and they're selling drugs, and then I might get locked up.

TH: Right. When you're with those guys, you could get locked up for something you weren't even part of.

In this situation, the therapist is reinforcing the adolescent's decision not to be with the drug selling crowd. Again, the therapist is exploring the adolescent's "possible selves" (Oyserman and Markus, 1990), this time in the context of peer relationships, and establishing concrete building blocks toward positive goals. The MDFT therapist's goal is to encourage Tony to form friendships with those who have similar attitudes to his. As noted previously, simultaneous work with the adolescent and parent is also critical in eliciting the parent's reactions to, participation in, and reinforcement of this process of the "new" adolescent emerging.

Therapeutic work in the peer realm involves searching for and reinforcing prosocial activities and interactions. For early adolescents, it is often older peers who have influenced them to initiate drug use and engage in other antisocial behaviors. Yet older peers who have learned from their mistakes, who are straightening out their lives and becoming positive young adults, can have a significant positive influence as role models for early adolescents. In MDFT, resources that exist in the environment but may not be obvious are sought out by the therapist and included in the treatment. In the following case example, the therapist has worked with Mark and his mother for a few weeks and learned that Mark's older cousin plays an important role in his life and is interested in coming to therapy. In session they examine what life is like for these two young African-American men on the inner-city streets. The therapist learns that as an older peer, Trent has been part of the socialization process contributing to Mark's drug use, delinquency, and school truancy. Trent is now trying to live a "better" life and while he is concerned about the path his younger cousin has taken, he has not been able to express his concern to Mark.

THERAPIST: So, do you talk to your cousin about those kinds of things? About what it's like in the detention center, how it was for you there?

TRENT: [*Shakes his head no*] Not really. I talked about what I did, not "Hey, yo man, you don't want to go there." I don't tell him nothing like that.

TH: Why? You don't want him there 'cause you're protecting him. You look out for him, right? [*Trent nods*]. Then why wouldn't you tell him "Listen, you don't want to go there"?

T: I don't know. I just don't think about saying that, "Oh yeah, I did this, I been there, you gotta do this."

TH: All right. Well, I want you to start thinking about telling him things about where you've been and how you got there. I mean you sound like somebody who's a couple of years older than your cousin, and I think you want to try and keep him straight. So in order to do that it sounds like you need to start telling him things— reasons why he shouldn't be going there. You know what things pull y'all out in the street and keep y'all from going to school.

The therapist intervenes in this early adolescent's peer subsystem by assessing the unique "big brother" role that Trent plays, asking him to take his role seriously, as well as acknowledging Trent's negative influence on Mark's life in the past. Toward the end of the session, the therapist asks Trent to think about the positive influence he could be on Mark as his "big brother." In this way, therapists in MDFT initiate changes in the peer subsystem, one of the many areas of the adolescent's life that impact him in positive and negative ways.

THERAPIST: All right, I just want you to think a little bit about your role as big brother. If you're trying to protect him and keep him safe—certainly you want to keep him safe from the streets. You want to see him do some of the things you haven't done. I mean, that's what older brothers do, okay? I want you to just think about those things Trent. It's important.

RELATIONSHIPS WITH PARENTS DURING EARLY ADOLESCENCE AND CLINICAL IMPLICATIONS

Young adolescents' relationships with their parents necessarily undergo a process of change and transformation (Steinberg, 1991). While this transformation does not meet the predictions of chaos and rebellion that traditional psychodynamic theorists envisioned (e.g., Blos, 1962), it does involve a reformulation of parent and adolescent roles within the family (Steinberg, 1991). Developments in cognitive skills, emotional experiences, and social roles change the ways young adolescents relate to parents, and parents of young adolescents experience life transitions of their own that impact the nature of the parent-adolescent relationship (Silverberg, 1996). The relatively minor increase in parent-child distance and conflict during the early adolescent transition does not preclude the desire for acceptance from and attachment to parents. Research demonstrates that an early adolescent's well-being is closely connected to parental acceptance, involvement, and support (Lieberman, Doyle, and Markeiwicz, 1999). Minor increases in parent-adolescent conflict, which generally surround trivial matters, tend to decline during middle and late adolescence after peaking during and after puberty (Laursen, Coy, and Collins, 1998). Serious conflict and turmoil in families of young adolescents is indicative of more severe family problems (Steinberg, 1991) and tends to be a function of earlier difficulties within the family (Conger and Ge, 1999).

Poor parental monitoring is perhaps the most critical family factor in the initiation of early adolescent substance use (Steinberg, Fletcher, and Darling, 1994), as much of early adolescent drug use occurs in the adolescent's own home, in the absence of adult supervision (Steinberg, 1991). Protective factors within the family can help to insulate early adolescents from risk factors for drug abuse, including strong identification with parents (Brook, Kessler, and Cohen, 1999), a responsive and involved parent-adolescent relationship (Eccles, 1999), and parental limit setting and effective communication (Fletcher and Jefferies, 1999). Authoritative parenting, which combines warmth with challenge and supervision, is associated with the most favorable adolescent outcomes, including school achievement, prosocial peer affiliations, low levels of drug use, and a coherent sense of identity (Eccles, 1999; Steinberg, 1991; Fletcher and Jefferies, 1999). Conversely, permissive-neglectful parenting is associated with pervasive difficulties (Brook, Kessler, and Cohen, 1999). Perhaps most important, protective factors such as consistent discipline and monitoring within the family limit access to and attraction to drug using, deviant peers (Steinberg, Fletcher, and Darling, 1994).

The MDFT model specifies an array of interventions with parents designed to accomplish several interrelated goals. As in all therapeutic work in MDFT, change occurs in phases, following organized steps that build on one another and lead to increasingly more challenging work. First, therapists engage with parents, seeking to understand and elicit underlying feelings of hurt, disappointment, and despair blocked by anger and resentment. They use these accessed feelings to help parents understand that they are and can still be influential with the adolescent, and that the adolescent needs them to be. They use these more vulnerable emotions and specific "parenting relationship interventions" (Liddle et al., 1998) to help the parent to reconnect with the adolescent. This important work leads to the establishment of a commitment from parents that they are willing to try again. Once recommitted, therapists intervene to increase the effectiveness of parents' strategies with the adolescent by making realistic and concrete requests for change and then coaching, shaping, and providing feedback consistently. Throughout this process, therapists look for and prompt behaviors from the adolescent that will provide new evidence for the parents of the adolescent's motivation and ability to change. These opportunities are used with the parent to continue the softening process, and to motivate them further. The interventions used to accomplish these goals are described in more detail in other sources (Diamond and Liddle, 1996, 1999; Liddle et al., 1998; Schmidt, Liddle, and Dakof, 1996). Here, we highlight parenting interventions particularly important in our work with younger adolescents.

With parents of early adolescents, some of the most important work involves addressing parents' expectations and beliefs about what adolescence is all about. Parents may need to work through their own feelings of anxiety and insecurity, with therapists helping them to acknowledge that this is indeed a period of change for the whole family. In all of these conversations, therapists provide positive feedback about the parents' strengths, inspire hope for changing less effective strategies, and give encouragement that they are not going to be on this journey alone. In the following case example, the therapist confronts the teenager's mother, who has had difficulty making the adjustment to parenting Tony as a young adolescent.

THERAPIST: I'm concerned, because something I see you doing is you tease him. You chide him. I see you looking at him and it seems to me that you're thinking, "You're fourteen! I'm not ready for you to grow up." Do you know what I mean?

MOM: Yeah. I still think of him as little Tony that, you know, my baby. He's always just been my baby. He's not supposed to be interested in girls. I'm thinking, all he needs to do is eat and play with his little GI Joe men.

TH: Do you think it's going to be hard for you to help him through this change?

M: If I know where he's coming from, I can deal with it.

TH: And the more you can take him seriously—even though sometimes he doesn't look serious, you know, because he's fourteen— but the more you can take him seriously and help him grow, the more he's going to share with you and feel comfortable.

Therapists talk to parents about how the young adolescent is changing, as well as addressing parents' expectations about what parenting adolescents involves. MDFT therapists describe how authoritative parenting works in ways that parents can understand. Later in the same session, the therapist summarized the approach to Tony's mother in the following way:

TH: I think there are two things that a parent really needs to do. One is to be there—to find a way to help him feel comfortable talking to you about what he's going through. It means talking about girls, maybe about why school is so hard, all different kinds of things. And then the other half is even when Tony is going to tell you some of these things and share them with you, you still have the responsibility of a parent who cares to decide what's acceptable and what's not, and set the rules, and be firm and be consistent with them. And that's the second part that we were talking about now—how you're going to respond when you feel like Tony's not taking responsibility. So it's really both things together, and they complement each other. Both getting closer and helping Tony tell you the story of his life and you being able to not jump on him but to decide, "Well, here I'm not going to get crazy, but over here I am going to take a stand. And here's how I'm going to take a stand effectively." And we're going to do both things here, together.

MDFT interventions with parents of early adolescents are based on the known parenting factors associated with drug use during this developmental phase. As in the previous example, therapists convey that a close and supportive parent-adolescent relationship during early adolescence is critical because it is one of the only stable forces in the adolescent's life during this transitional period (Steinberg, 1991). Therapists in MDFT take the stand that early adolescents who are already in trouble with drugs, having problems in school, and involved with deviant peers are at an exceptionally vulnerable point in their lives, and they emphasize to parents that they (the parents) are probably the adolescent's only hope for turning things around. Parents may believe that the adolescent does not want or need their input or attention given the young adolescent's relatively new investment in peer relationships, yet therapists actively attack this misperception. Therapists also provide hope to parents who believe their adolescent is beyond their help, insisting that it is not too late.

The following segment illustrates a discussion with a mother of a twelve-year-old girl referred to drug abuse treatment for multiple problems, including shoplifting, drug abuse, school truancy and failure, and behavior problems. The therapist in this case instills hope by insisting that things can change for her adolescent, while conveying the urgency of the situation with her daughter and the importance of repairing the mother-daughter relationship in helping her daughter change.

MOM: At her age, I don't think she wants my time.

THERAPIST: I don't mean so much the way she did when she was a toddler, but I think yes, she wants your attention certainly, your interest in her and what she thinks, how she sees things, the things that happen to her. I don't mean prying. What we're talking about, what you're asking about, is how to be a parent to a kid this age. Yes, certainly you respect her privacy; there are some things she doesn't want to talk about, but I think you need to be more in her world, or know about her and how she sees things. I think she thinks a lot. She's thoughtful and smart and there's a lot going on in there. And I think that you're the person—the one person—the most important person—who has to know her. However you can make that time for the two of you. And what I would want you to do wouldn't be so much to focus on the problem things—there's always time for that—but to talk, to ask her to express interest in whatever's going on with her, and to talk about yourself if that's relevant. Let her know some things about you, and have more of an experience that the two of you would come away from that wouldn't be about the same old problems and bad feelings.

M: I've asked her to talk with me, but she doesn't want to. When I ask her things she doesn't say anything. It's frustrating. . .

TH: I know. I see how frustrated you get. But I want to tell you something. *You're going to have to do a lot of reaching out before she's gonna reach back.* There's just no question. I think that's maybe the hardest thing for me to help parents with.

Later in the session, after exploring what some of these particular difficulties might be given this parent's unique life circumstances and history, the therapist comes back to her main point concerning the importance of the mother-daughter relationship.

TH: She's kind of drifted off—she's sort of in her own world.

M: It's her self-protection role that she learned to cope with things.

TH: Well, it's not working so well, is it? Because the stuff she does to cope—like the smoking marijuana, staying out all night, not talking to people about what's bothering her—this is not good coping.

You know that. And so what's happened is there is some sort of a gulf between the two of you where it seems like you don't know her anymore.

M: I'll tell you the truth. I *don't* know her. I just don't know her. I don't know if it's this dysfunctional family or if I just can't do it, or if it's too late. . .

TH: No. You can do this. What I'm trying to say to you is you *can* do this stuff. She's still at an age where things can get turned around. You really have an opportunity here, but I think it's really at a critical point. And you're the key. You're the key there. She's kind of out there getting farther and farther away and it's going to be harder and harder to reach her. I think that's a scary thing, and as a parent I wouldn't want you to get so out of touch with her that by the time she's sixteen or seventeen she's just out there going on drugs, doing what she wants, getting pregnant, whatever. And I really think there are ways now that you could bring her back in, but it would really mean a different way of being with her.

M: I know what you're trying to say. But she doesn't want it. She won't let me in.

TH: You know, that's something we're going to do together. I want to help you have a different relationship with her, but it will take a lot of work from you. When you're talking with her and she's shutting down, don't get pushed away. She can do that. I've seen her do that in here with you—she just gets quiet and silent, and you think she doesn't care.

M: I ask her all sorts of things, about school, her friends, and I get nowhere.

TH: And sometimes she just doesn't deal well with those direct questions. But there are ways of being interested, of saying that you want to get to know her, of hanging in there—and hanging in there also might mean just making sure that you don't get turned off. As you reach out to her, whatever that takes, she'll know that you're going to keep trying to get in there with her. I don't think she really wants to push you away, and I know that wouldn't be good for her. I think you have an opportunity here at a time that's really critical for her. Because if she feels really cut off, and that keeps going on, she's going to find other connections that aren't going to be good for her. She's young enough to respond to you. It's not at all too late. She's at an age where things can go either way for her. She's struggling with a lot of things, and she needs you in there with her to sort things out.

The therapist in this segment is building a foundation for productive work in the parenting subsystem by resurrecting positive feelings of being together, generating hope that she can impact her daughter's life and that it is not too late for her daughter's life to turn around, while at the same time communicating the urgency of making changes in the relationship before things spiral out of control. These are all important first steps in ultimately changing the mother's approach to parenting. Future work in therapy with the mother and adolescent will focus on actively improving the nature of the relationship and increasing the effectiveness of the mother's parenting strategies.

Therapists also make it clear to parents that a close relationship is only one part of the complex equation that determines the development and maintenance of drug use and other problems. MDFT therapists insist that parents learn more about the young adolescent's life, who the adolescent spends time with, what school is like, where the adolescent goes with friends, and what he or she does during unsupervised time. With parents of young adolescents, therapists emphasize the continued importance of limit setting, firm and consistent discipline, and clear communication, despite the adolescent's desire for increased independence. The clinician helps parents and adolescents negotiate the parameters of their changing and evolving relationship. In the next example, the therapist insists that the young adolescent's mother provide more structure and limits.

THERAPIST: She's still at an age where she definitely needs you, and she needs somebody to push her—you know, not to let her go down that path she's going down. You know parents sometimes have to pull out all the stops. It's one thing to say to your kids, "We're not going to let you destroy yourself. You know we're not going to let you get into this kind of trouble. We're not going to stand by while you do that." It's easy to say that, but actively to stop them means something else. They may be angry at you for giving them a curfew, or for insisting that you know where they're going, and not letting them go places or be with people that you don't like. If you're saying to a kid, "I don't want you to do dangerous things. I don't like this path you're going down. I think you're doing things that are gonna get you in trouble," then you have to stand by that and not allow certain things if you think they're not good for her. You can't afford to have her take lightly when you tell her that she has to do something.

Therapists in MDFT stand by such statements with a clear commitment to do whatever it takes to help parents and adolescents find new ways of communicating, being together, working through problems, and managing obstacles to reaching goals. Therapists know what it takes to turn a young life around, and they understand the ramifications of failing to do so. Parents need to learn new parenting strategies and implement them consistently and effectively. Adolescents and parents need to learn how to talk to one another in new ways to establish open lines of communication. They are asked to take risks to reach one another, frequently confronting past disappointments and conflicts, becoming vulnerable and open to a positive, caring relationship. A clear sense of responsibility rests with the MDFT therapist to help parents and adolescents do the work needed to change the adolescent's life.

CONCLUSIONS

Young adolescents are at a point of heightened vulnerability to a range of negative outcomes, particularly those who have had a history of problems in childhood and lack positive relationships with parents and peers. The significant changes that occur during this stage also make it a time of great opportunity and a period in which positive transformations can take place given the right intervention. Research affirms that developmental factors have important implications for treatment with substance abusing adolescents (Deas et al., 2000). Family-based models that target risk factors in multiple domains are promising approaches for these youth (Liddle and Dakof, 1995). The data on certain family-based treatments are strong. Some recent reviews designate family therapy as the treatment of choice for adolescent substance abuse problems (Stanton and Shadish, 1997; Williams and Chang, 2000). In this chapter, we have highlighted relevant research findings and their clinical implications in the domains of the self, peers, and parents in order to present the most important interventions in MDFT with early adolescents. However, significant and complex work lies ahead. Issues of comorbidity (Rowe, Liddle, and Dakof, in press) and gender (Dakof, 2000) are of particular interest to us as we continue to refine and test the MDFT approach using our clinical and research experience and knowledge of how particular factors, such as client characteristics, predict treatment response (Dakof, Tejeda, and Liddle, 2001).

REFERENCES

Adams, G.R. (1985). Family correlates of female adolescents' ego-identity development. *Journal of Adolescence, 8,* 69-82.

Adams, G.R., Dyk, P.A.H., and Bennion, L.D. (1987). Parent-adolescent relationships and identity formation. *Family Perspective, 21,* 249-260.

Akers, J.F., Jones, R.M., and Coyl, D.D. (1998). Adolescent friendship pairs: Similarities in identity status development, behaviors, attitudes, and intentions. *Journal of Adolescent Research, 13,* 178-201.

Archer, S.L. (1982). The lower age boundaries of identity development. *Child Development, 52,* 1551-1556.

Barrera, M., Jr., Castro, F.G., and Biglan, A. (1999). Ethnicity, substance use, and development: Exemplars for exploring group differences and similarities. *Development and Psychopathology, 11,* 805-822.

Berndt, T.J. and Perry, T.B. (1990). Distinctive features and effects of early adolescent friendships. In R. Montemayor, G.R. Adams, and T.P. Gullotta (Eds.), *From childhood to adolescence: A transitional period?* (pp. 269-287). Newbury Park, CA: Sage.

Blos, P. (1962). *On adolescence: A psychoanalytic interpretation.* New York: Free Press.

Brook, J.S., Kessler, R.C., and Cohen, P. (1999). The onset of marijuana use from preadolescence and early adolescence to young adulthood. *Development and Psychopathology, 11,* 901-914.

Bush, P.J., Weinfurt, K.P., and Iannotti, R.J. (1994). Families versus peers: Developmental influences on drug use from grade 4-5 to grade 7-8. *Journal of Applied Developmental Psychology, 15,* 437-456.

Center for Substance Abuse Prevention (CSAP) (2000). *Strengthening America's families: Model family programs for substance abuse and delinquency prevention* [Brochure]. Salt Lake City, UT: University of Utah.

Center for Substance Abuse Treatment (CSAT) (1999). *Adolescent substance abuse: Assessment and treatment (Treatment Improvement Protocol Series [TIPS]).* Rockville, MD: Author.

Cicchetti, D. and Richters, J.E. (1993). Developmental considerations in the investigation of conduct disorder. *Development and Psychopathology, 5,* 331-344.

Cicchetti, D. and Toth, S.L. (1992). The role of developmental theory in prevention and intervention. *Development and Psychopathology, 4,* 489-493.

Conger, R.D. and Ge, X. (1999). Conflict and cohesion in parent-adolescent relations: Changes in emotional expression from early to midadolescence. In M.J. Cox and J. Brooks-Gunn (Eds.), *Conflict and cohesion in families: Causes and consequences* (pp. 185-206). Mahwah, NJ: Lawrence Erlbaum Associates.

Dakof, G.A. (2000). Understanding gender differences in adolescent drug abuse: Issues of comorbidity and family functioning. *Journal of Psychoactive Drugs, 32,* 25-32.

Dakof, G.A., Tejeda, M., and Liddle, H.A. (2001). Predictors of engagement into adolescent drug abuse treatment. *Journal of the American Academy of Child and Adolescent Psychiatry, 40,* 274-281.

Deas, D., Riggs, P., Langenbucher, J., Goldman, M., Brown, S. (2000). Adolescents are not adults: Developmental considerations in alcohol users. *Alcoholism: Clinical and Experimental Research, 24*(2), 232-237.

Diamond, G.M., Liddle, H.A., Hogue, A., and Dakof, G.A. (1999). Alliance building interventions with adolescents in family therapy: A process study. *Psychotherapy: Theory, Research, Practice, and Training, 36*(4), 355-368.

Diamond, G.S. and Liddle, H.A. (1996). Resolving therapeutic impasses between parents and adolescents in multidimensional family therapy. *Journal of Consulting and Clinical Psychology, 64,* 481-488.

Diamond, G.S. and Liddle, H.A. (1999). Transforming negative parent-adolescent interactions: From impasse to dialogue. *Family Process, 38*(1), 5-26.

Dishion, T.J., Reid, J.B., and Patterson, G.R. (1988). Empirical guidelines for a family intervention for adolescent drug use. *Journal of Chemical Dependency Treatment, 1,* 189-224.

Dunham, R.M., Kidwell, J.S., and Wilson, S.M. (1986). Rites of passage at adolescence: A ritual process paradigm. *Journal of Adolescent Research, 1,* 139-154.

Eccles, J. S. (1999). The development of children ages 6 to 14. *Future of Children, 9*(2), 30-44.

Fletcher, A.C. and Jefferies, B.C. (1999). Parental mediators of associations between perceived authoritative parenting and early adolescent substance use. *Journal of Early Adolescence, 19,* 465-487.

Hogue, A. and Liddle, H.A. (1999). Family-based preventive intervention: An approach to preventing substance abuse and antisocial behavior. *American Journal of Orthopsychiatry, 69,* 275-293.

Institute of Medicine (1998). *Bridging the gap between practice and research: Forging partnerships with community-based drug and alcohol treatment.* Washington, DC: National Academy Press.

Jackson, E.P., Dunham, R.M., and Kidwell, J.S. (1990). The effect of family cohesion and adaptability on identity status. *Journal of Adolescent Research, 5,* 161-174.

Jackson-Gilfort, A. and Liddle, H.A. (in press). Development of a culturally specific engagement/intervention with acting out, African-American male adolescents in family therapy. *Journal of Black Psychology.*

Jones, R.M. (1992). Ego identity and adolescent problem behavior. In G.R. Adams, T.P. Gullotta, and R. Montemayor (Eds.), *Adolescent identity formation: Advances in adolescent development* (pp. 216-233). Newbury Park, CA: Sage.

Jones, R.M. (1994). Curricula focused on behavioral deviance. In S.L. Archer (Ed.), *Interventions for adolescent identity development* (pp. 174-190). Newbury Park, CA: Sage.

Laursen, B., Coy, K.C., and Collins, W.A. (1998). Reconsidering changes in parent-child conflict across adolescence: A meta-analysis. *Child Development, 69,* 817-832.

Liddle, H.A. (1992). Family psychology: Progress and prospects of a maturing discipline. *Journal of Family Psychology, 5*(3/45), 249-236.

Liddle, H.A. (1995). Conceptual and clinical dimensions of a multidimensional, multisystems engagement strategy in family-based adolescent treatment. *Psychotherapy, 32,* 39-58.

Liddle, H.A. (1999). Theory development in a family-based therapy for adolescent drug abuse. *Journal of Clinical Child Psychology, 28*(4), 521-532.

Liddle, H.A. (2000). *Multidimensional family therapy treatment (MDFT) for Adolescent Cannabis Users* (Volume 5 of the Cannabis youth treatment (CYT) manual series). Rockville, MD: Center for Substance Abuse Treatment, Substance Abuse and Mental Health Services Administration (<http://www.samsa.gov/csat/csat.htm>).

Liddle, H.A. (in press). *Troubled teens: Multidimensional family therapy.* New York: Norton Professional Books.

Liddle, H.A. and Dakof, G.A. (1995). Family-based treatments for adolescent drug use: State of the science. In E. Rahdert and D. Czechowicz (Eds.), *Adolescent drug abuse: Clinical assessment and therapeutic interventions* (NIDA Research Monograph No. 156, NIH Publication No. 95-3908, pp. 218-254). Rockville, MD: National Institute on Drug Abuse.

Liddle, H.A., Dakof, G.A., and Diamond, G. (1991). Adolescent substance abuse: Multidimensional family therapy in action. In E. Kaufman and P. Kaufman (Eds.), *Family therapy of drug and alcohol abuse* (Second Edition) (pp. 120-171). Needham Heights, MA: Allyn & Bacon.

Liddle, H.A. and Hogue, A. (2001). Multidimensional family therapy: Pursuing empirical support through planned treatment development. In E. Wagner and H. Waldron (Eds.), *Adolescent substance abuse* (pp. 227-259). Needham Heights, MA: Allyn & Bacon.

Liddle, H.A., Rowe, C., Dakof, G., and Lyke, J. (1998). Translating parenting research into clinical interventions for families of adolescents. *Clinical Child Psychology and Psychiatry, 3,* 419-443.

Liddle, H.A., Rowe, C., Diamond, G.M., Sessa, F., Schmidt, S., and Ettinger, D. (2000). Towards a developmental family therapy: The clinical utility of adolescent development research. *Journal of Marital and Family Therapy, 26,* 491-506.

Lieberman, M., Doyle, A.-B., and Markeiwicz, D. (1999). Developmental patterns in security of attachment to mother and father in late childhood and early adolescence: Associations with peer relations. *Child Development, 70,* 202-213.

Loeber, R. (1989). Natural histories of conduct problems, delinquency, and associated substance use: Evidence for developmental progressions. In B.B. Lahey and A.E. Kazdin (Eds.) *Advances in clinical child psychology* (pp. 73-124). New York: Plenum Press.

Mendel, R. (2000). Less hype, more help: Reducing juvenile crime, what works—what doesn't. Washington, DC: American Youth Policy Forum.

National Institute on Drug Abuse (NIDA) (1999). *Principles of drug addiction treatment: A research-based guide.* Rockville, MD: Author.

Oyserman, D. and Markus, H.R. (1990). Possible selves and delinquency. *Journal of Personality and Social Psychology, 59*(1), 112-125.

Paikoff, R.L. and Brooks-Gunn, J. (1990). Physiological processes: What role do they play during the transition to adolescence? In R. Montemayor, G.R. Adams, and T.P. Gullotta (Eds.), *From childhood to adolescence: A transitional period?* (pp. 63-83). Newbury Park, CA: Sage.

Patterson, G.R., Bank, L., and Stoolmiller, M. (1990). The preadolescent's contributions to disrupted family process. In R. Montemayor, G.R. Adams, and T.P. Gullotta (Eds.), *From childhood to adolescence: A transitional period?* (pp. 107-133). Newbury Park, CA: Sage.

Pugh, M.V. and Hart, D. (1999). The role of peer groups in adolescent social identity: Exploring the importance of stability and change. In J.A. McClellan, M.V. Pugh et al., (Eds.), *New directions for child and adolescent development* (pp. 55-70). San Francisco, CA: Jossey-Bass, Inc.

Resnick, M.D., Bearman, P.S., Blum, R., Bauman, K.E., Harris, K.M., Jones, J., Tabor, J., Beuhring, T., Sieving, R.E., Shew, M., Ireland, M., Bearinger, L.H., and Udry, R. (1997). Protecting adolescents from harm. *Journal of the American Medical Association, 278*(10), 823-832.

Rowe, C.L., Liddle, H.A., and Dakof, G.D. (in press). Classifying adolescent substance abusers by level of externalizing and internalizing symptoms. *Journal of Child and Adolescent Substance Abuse.*

Scheier, L.M. and Newcomb, M.D. (1991). Differentiation of early adolescent predictors of drug use versus abuse: A developmental risk-factor model. *Journal of Substance Abuse, 3,* 277-299.

Schmidt, S.E., Liddle, H.A., and Dakof, G.A. (1996). Changes in parental practices and adolescent drug abuse during multidimensional family therapy. *Journal of Family Psychology, 10,* 12-27.

Silverberg, S.B. (1996). Parents' well-being at their children's transition to adolescence. In C.D. Ryff and M.M. Seltzer (Eds.), *The parental experience at midlife* (pp. 215-254). Chicago: University of Chicago Press.

Stanton, M.D. and Shadish, W.R. (1997). Outcome, attrition, and family-couples treatment for drug abuse: A meta-analysis and review of the controlled, comparative studies. *Psychological Bulletin, 122*(2), 170-191.

Steinberg, L. (1991). Adolescent transitions and alcohol and other drug use prevention. In E.N. Goplerud (Ed.), *Preventing adolescent drug use: From theory to practice* (OSAP Prevention Monograph No. 8, pp. 13-51). Rockville, MD: U.S. Department of Health and Human Services, Office for Substance Use Prevention.

Steinberg, L., Fletcher, A., and Darling, N. (1994). Parental monitoring and peer influences on adolescent substance use. *Pediatrics, 93*(6), 1060-1064.

Tarter, R., Vanyukov, M., Giancola, P., Dawes, M., Blackson, T., Mezzich, A., and Clark, D.B. (1999). Etiology of early age onset substance use disorder: A maturational perspective. *Development and Psychopathology, 11,* 657-683.

Wentzel, K.R. and McNamara, C.C. (1999). Interpersonal relationships, emotional distress, and prosocial behavior in middle school. *Journal of Early Adolescence, 19,* 114-125.

Williams, R.J., Chang, S.Y., and Addiction Centre Adolescent Research Group (2000). A comprehensive and comparative review of adolescent substance abuse treatment outcome. *Clinical Psychology: Science and Practice, 7,* 138-166.

Youniss, J., McLellan, J.A., and Strouse, D. (1994). "We're popular, but we're not snobs": Adolescents describe their crowds. In R. Montemayor, G.R. Adams, and T.P. Gullotta (Eds.), *Personal relationships during adolescence* (pp. 101-122). Thousand Oaks, CA: Sage.

SECTION IV:
RESIDENTIAL TREATMENT MODELS

Chapter 6

Mountain Manor Treatment Center: Residential Adolescent Addictions Treatment Program

Marc Fishman
Philip Clemmey
Hoover Adger

OVERVIEW

Mountain Manor Treatment Center (MMTC) is a community treatment provider in urban Baltimore, which is part of a larger system of behavioral health care programs for adults and adolescents in Maryland. The program described here is MMTC's residential treatment program for adolescents with substance abuse disorders. This program is part of the MMTC continuum of care for drug-involved and dual diagnosis adolescents, which also includes outpatient, intensive outpatient, day treatment, special education day school, and a mental health clinic. MMTC's programs are accredited by the Joint Commission on Accreditation of Healthcare Organizations (JCAHO).

The program is located on the campus of a nineteenth-century monastery with open fields and wooded grounds that provide a re-

This work was supported by a grant from the Center for Substance Abuse Treatment (CSAT), KD1 TI11424, to Marc Fishman, MD, Principal Investigator. The views expressed herein reflect those of the authors and do not necessarily reflect the opinion of SAMHSA/CSAT.

Correspondence should be sent to Dr. Marc Fishman, Assistant Professor, Department of Psychiatry, Johns Hopkins University School of Medicine, 3800 Frederick Ave., Baltimore, MD 21229.

spite from the surrounding urban setting. The program was founded in 1989, with an initial mission to serve inner-city Baltimore, public sector, agency involved (juvenile justice and social services), and impoverished youth who characteristically have been underserved by inadequate and scarce treatment resources. In particular, MMTC's residential program has become known for the care of the "toughest" patients. These are patients with a very high severity of substance use, often found to be refractory to previous treatment interventions. In addition, this target population is characterized by high rates of emotional/behavioral symptoms, comorbid psychiatric disorders, social and economic deprivation, and significant functional impairment across several psychosocial domains.

On admission all patients undergo a comprehensive multidimensional biopsychosocial assessment to determine a level of severity and to confirm appropriateness of placement utilizing the adolescent section of the American Society of Addiction Medicine Patient Placement Criteria for the Treatment of Substance-Related Disorders (Mee-Lee et al., 2001). In addition, this assessment is used to facilitate development of an individualized care plan. MMTC is probably best categorized as short- to medium-term residential treatment, with average length of stay of about thirty days (range: ten to sixty). It provides levels of residential care that span both Levels III.7 (medically monitored high-intensity inpatient/residential) and III.5 (clinically managed medium-intensity residential) of the ASAM criteria. The specific treatment approach (discussed in this chapter) is based on a milieu therapy approach, utilizing both medical model elements and therapeutic community (TC) elements. Patients are referred from the juvenile justice system, other government agencies, outpatient treatment providers, schools, parents, and a variety of other sources. More than half (54 percent) of the participants in the ATM study were referred to treatment by the courts, and two-thirds (66 percent) have been in detention or jail within the ninety days prior to admission. The primary funding source is Medicaid, followed by commercial insurance, state agencies (such as juvenile justice) for adolescents in their care and custody, and a small state program that provides supplemental funding for uninsured or underinsured "gray area" adolescents.

PATIENT CHARACTERISTICS

The patients are primarily local, with about half coming from Baltimore City. Because of the scarcity of adolescent treatment services in the area, the geographic catchment area extends to the broader region surrounding Baltimore and nearby metropolitan Washington, DC. Patients are also drawn from the various counties throughout Maryland, and the adjoining states of Delaware and Virginia. The age range is eleven to twenty, with an average age of sixteen. A separate young adult track is provided for ages eighteen to twenty. The average program size is about sixty patients. The program is mixed gender, approximately 75 percent boys and 25 percent girls. The racial composition of the program roughly reflects the demographics of the greater Baltimore metropolitan area: approximately 35 percent African American, and 65 percent Caucasian.

Marijuana is the most prevalent drug of abuse. As shown in Table 6.1, the high severity of drug involvement in the population is indicated by 29 percent reporting heroin and 16 percent reporting cocaine as one of the primary drugs for which treatment was sought. Most of the patients are high frequency users, and many are daily users. Approximately 96 percent have used substances on fifteen or more days out of the past ninety days prior to admission, a categorical threshold criterion that we have used as an index of severity. Another indicator of severity is that 91 percent met criteria for the full syndrome of substance dependence. As is typical of adolescents, most are polysubstance users (see Table 6.2, which shows the overlapping distribution of drugs used within the most recent ninety days prior to admission). Many patients have polydrug dependence, even if not meeting criteria for dependence on any single drug. As would be expected for this intensity of care, even those who do not meet criteria for dependence have had very severe degrees of impairment associated with their drug use. Most of the patients (71 percent) have had one or more prior treatment episodes, and nearly half (46 percent) have had prior residential treatment. Many of the patients present with co-occurring mental and behavioral disorders. Fifty-six percent have had prior psychiatric treatment, and 80 percent report being significantly disturbed by nerve, mental, or psychological problems during the past year.

TABLE 6.1. Cross Site Variables (N = 153)

Item	N	%
Number of cases	153	100
Gender		
Male	120	78
Female	33	22
Age		
11-12	0	0
13-14	14	9
15-16	54	35
17-18	75	49
19 and over	10	7
Ethnicity		
American Indian/Alaskan Native	3	2
Asian or Pacific Islander	0	0
Black	43	28
White	100	65
Hispanic (Puerto Rican, Mexican, Cuban, other)	2	1
Mixed/some other group	5	3
Current living situation		
A house or apartment (yours or parents)	81	53
A foster home or public housing	1	1
A friend's or relative's house or apartment	12	8
A nursing home, hospital, inpatient or residential	4	3
Jail, detention center, or other correctional institution	48	31
Temporary or emergency shelter	1	1
Vacant buildings	4	3
Any other housing situation	2	1
Present work or school situation		
Working full time	17	11
Working part time	6	4
Unemployed or laid off	66	43
Have a job but not working because of treatment, illness, seasonal	15	10
In school or training only (even if not in session now)	45	29

Item	N	%
In school or training at all in past 90 days	85	56
In jail or prison	4	3
Some other work situation	0	0
Substance severity measure		
No use	0	0
Use	1	1
Abuse	13	8
Dependence	139	91
Substance treatment needed for		
Any kind of alcohol	40	26
Marijuana, hashish, etc.	99	65
Crack, freebase cocaine, other cocaine	25	16
Amphetamine/methamphetamine	0	0
Inhalants	0	0
Heroin	45	29
"Acid" or other hallucinogens	10	7
Some other drug	10	7
No drug	3	2
Age when first got drunk or used any drugs		
Below 15	132	86
15-18	20	13
Over 18	0	0
Last grade or year completed in school		
< 6	1	1
6-8	52	34
9-10	64	42
11-12	35	23
> 12	1	1
Legal custody		
Parents together	27	18
Parents separated	14	9
Single parent	60	39
Other family	8	5

TABLE 6.1 *(continued)*

Item	N	%
County/state	3	2
Juvenile or correctional facility	4	3
Other	5	3
Times in life arrested, charged with a crime, and booked		
0	14	9
1-2	42	27
3+	97	63
Times in life admitted to drug treatment or counseling		
0	44	29
1-2	59	39
3+	49	32
	Mean	SD
Times in life arrested, charged with a crime, and booked	5.1	5.5
Times in life admitted to drug treatment or counseling	2.2	2.6
Substance use—last 90 days		
Days used alcohol, marijuana, or other drugs	59.6	23.9
Days drunk or high for most of the day	45.6	27.8
Days in jail (or other place) where you could not use drugs	17.7	20.0

TABLE 6.2. Percent Reporting Use in 90 Days Prior to Admission (N = 153)

Substance	%	N
Alcohol	84	128
Marijuana	90	138
Crack	35	23
Cocaine	35	23
Inhalants	4	3
Heroin	32	49
Analgesics	33	50
PCP	7	11
Hallucinogens	31	48
Tranquilizers	21	32
Downers	16	25
Uppers	10	16

TREATMENT APPROACH

MMTC provides a high intensity, twenty-four-hour treatment program that utilizes a milieu therapy approach. This approach draws heavily from the medical model, which uses individualized monitoring, evaluation, and treatment interventions, directed by professional clinicians, emphasizing individualized assessment- and diagnosis-based therapies. The program also incorporates some features of the TC model, which uses programmatic techniques, emphasizing the group milieu as the locus of recovery. The attempt to strike a balance between these two models is an inherent tension that drives the program. On the one hand, each patient receives a comprehensive individualized assessment and a treatment plan with individualized goals based on his/her unique matrix of needs. On the other hand, each patient is expected to meet certain common program goals as a member of the community that shares a set of common needs. Specific goals from the TC repertoire include: normalizing of peer and other interpersonal relations, practicing developmentally appropriate social roles, social skills acquisition, learning peer support and confrontation skills, learning peaceful assertiveness and conflict resolution skills, etc., all based on the community group as the agent of change. One of the most important goals of the therapeutic milieu is induction into a more healthy peer group that is struggling with the initial formation of a positive group identity that emphasizes recovery and overcoming adversity.

Detoxification

The program provides detoxification as one of its treatment services for those adolescents who suffer from substance withdrawal. Some adolescents require fairly intensive medical management of their withdrawal, with frequent monitoring of signs and symptoms. Pharmacological treatments are used for symptomatic relief during acute heroin withdrawal. Occasionally, substitute agonist tapers are used for heroin withdrawal or for alcohol withdrawal. Mild hypnotics are sometimes used for the severe sleep disturbance that often accompanies withdrawal from many substances. Nurses are available on the premises around the clock and physicians are always available on call when not on the premises. Special detoxification rooms are available to provide decreased stimulation through separation from the rest of the patient population. Special emphasis is placed on supportive care and comfort. The expectations of treatment participation and compliance are greatly diminished during detoxification in recognition of the clinical status and level of severity of debilitating symptoms.

The process of detoxification includes not only the attenuation of the physiological and psychological features of withdrawal syndromes, but also the process of interrupting the momentum of habitual compulsive use in adolescents with substance dependence. Because of the force of this momentum, and the inherent difficulties in overcoming it, the first week or so of treatment is often taken up by an initial phase establishing preliminary abstinence, which is required even when there is no clear physiological withdrawal syndrome requiring medical management or monitoring. This stabilization phase of treatment frequently entails a greater intensity of monitoring and feedback in order to initiate treatment engagement and patient role induction. Contrary to the principles of managed care, much of the productive work of active rehabilitative treatment does not begin until after this phase has been successfully completed.

Initial and ongoing abstinence by confinement provides substance dependent adolescents with a much needed reality orientation and reintroduction to their own patterns of emotional and cognitive experience without the nearly constant cloud of intoxication that was previously present for many. One of the key goals of detoxification in this more extended sense is simply to orient adolescents to the structure of daily life according to organizing principles other than getting high and being high.

Methods and Modalities

A mixture of therapeutic methods, techniques, and modalities are utilized in the program. Many of the modalities utilized in the core therapeutic programming are standard: group therapy, individual counseling, therapeutic milieu, community meetings, family therapy, and multifamily groups. Patients are organized into groups of six to nine, assigned to an individual counselor/case manager who leads group therapy daily, and individual therapy for each of them several times per week. In addition to the primary group therapy, other group therapy sessions are conducted in different groupings throughout the day. These additional group therapy sessions are organized around thematic content, including gender group, dealer's group, HIV/STD education group, step-work group, etc. Other program components include a daily recreation therapy program, art therapy, special off-premises excursions (such as trips to a local prison), an intensive psychoeducational school program, and outside guest speakers who present on a variety of topics.

In its inception, the program drew mostly from the methods of twelve-step facilitation. This remains a central theme, with close ties to the twelve-step fellowship, a strong emphasis on induction into NA/AA participation, incorporation of on-premises and off-premises NA meetings, and a clinical staff of whom approximately 50 percent are individuals in recovery. As the program has evolved, twelve-step facilitation has been necessarily adapted to the developmental and cognitive levels of our adolescent patients. The program has been successful in establishing a connection to a network of community NA meetings and potential sponsors that specialize in engaging young people. Furthermore, the traditional twelve-step approach is condensed into a more developmentally appropriate translation of the core concepts contained in the first three steps: (1) acknowledgment of a substance problem and unmanageability; (2) acknowledgment of the need for help; (3) recognition and acceptance of useful sources of help—such as treatment, family, school, mentorship, and a network of sober and supportive friends and acquaintances.

Over time, other elements have been added, including motivational enhancement techniques, and multisystemic techniques. Motivational enhancement techniques are especially emphasized in light of the population's typical precontemplative stage of readiness to change. Explorations leading up to problem identification and the discovery of unmanageability are emphasized. The therapeutic milieu, with its developmentally natural and very powerful peer group influences, is one of the program's most important discovery tools.

The program also incorporates one of the underlying principles of multisystemic therapy—that it is insufficient and unrealistic to expect change to be completely internal within the adolescent, and that the multiple external systems that are active in the adolescent's life (school, family, juvenile justice system, etc.) *must* be a significant locus and agent of change. This emphasis on integrating interventions across systems is also evident in the program's implementation of the centralized linkage concept.

CENTRALIZED LINKAGE

One of the key features that characterize the program model is the integration of several key adjunctive treatment components utilizing a strategy of centralized linkage. We have called this a centralized linkage model because it links the core substance abuse therapies with adjunctive treatment components in several closely related psychosocial domains that are delivered on a centralized, or "one stop shopping" basis (CSAT, 1994). These psychosocial domains are

1. emotional/psychiatric status,
2. medical status,
3. educational/cognitive status,
4. legal/behavioral status, and
5. family/recovery environment status.

This model is based on the concept that adolescent addiction is embedded in the developmentally dictated major functional domains of adolescent daily life. Functional deficits in these major domains act as critical sustaining factors for addiction, with continued deficits contributing to a cycle of progressive severity and impairment.

Because of the critical role of these sustaining factors, the model targets these psychosocial domains as crucial arenas for functional rehabilitation, with rehabilitative (or habilitative) therapeutic interventions aimed specifically at each of these domains. The treatment services in this centralized linkage model are built into the program and emphasized as central to the purposes of the program as a whole. Based on the identified psychosocial domains, these components include:

1. psychiatric evaluation and treatment,
2. primary care medical assessment and treatment,
3. educational/cognitive remediation,
4. delinquency/behavioral rehabilitation, and
5. family support services.

Psychiatric Evaluation and Treatment

It is well documented that adolescents with substance use disorders are at considerable risk of having comorbid psychiatric disorders (Kandel et al., 1999). Indeed, the program's target population includes a high proportion of patients with severe emotional disturbances and/or psychiatric disorders. Some patients have been previously diagnosed and treated prior to admission; many more of them are diagnosed and treated while in the program. With most patients, it is difficult to tease out the symptoms of various autonomous disorders from substance-related symptoms, and with most a broad overlap occurs.

One of the core program components is psychiatric evaluation and treatment provided by specialists in adolescent addiction psychiatry, and the program is designed to manage a considerable level of psychiatric acuity. This centralized linkage delivery of integrated substance abuse and mental health services follows the recommendations of the 1998 multi-agency White Paper: "National Dialogue on Co-Occurring Mental Health and Substance Use Disorders" (SAMHSA, 1998). Counselors are cross-trained in recognition of symptoms and syndromes, and make referrals to in-house psychiatrists as needed. Psychiatrists provide evaluation and treatment, and participate in the interdisciplinary treatment team. Psychologists are available to perform cognitive and other testing procedures. A concerted effort is made to observe the course of symptoms over time with enforced abstinence by confinement, before initiating pharmacotherapy. Approximately one-third of the patients receive pharmacotherapy for psychiatric disorders, the most common category being depressive disorders, followed by ADHD and bipolar disorder. The psychiatric treatment also includes various psychotherapeutic strategies implemented by or supervised by psychiatrists and/or psychologists.

Staffing includes twenty-four-hour nursing, which allows the administration of medications, skilled round-the-clock observation and monitoring of symptoms and treatment response. Another critical treatment element is the staff training, supervision, and culture that creates a therapeutic milieu that can tolerate and manage severe psychiatric symptoms, for example, disorganized and agitated behaviors, self-injurious behaviors, suicidal threats, etc. Specialized training and procedures are utilized for behavior management as needed, including deescalation techniques, specialized risk-assessments, specialized observation precautions, emergency medications as needed, and, rarely, brief physical restraints (referred to as therapeutic holds).

This program component emphasizes post-discharge linkages to further mental health care, including expedited referrals to outpatient treatment. Given the relative high psychiatric acuity of many of the patients, some need transfer to ongoing residential specialty psychiatric treatment, and the treatment team has developed close working relations with a variety of other community providers.

Educational Assessment and Rehabilitation

The target population includes a large proportion of patients with severe cognitive and educational disturbances. Many of them have dropped out of school, or have been expelled from school because of their drug use or related behavioral difficulties. Many of them, though not formally disenrolled, have simply stopped attending, or are sporadic attenders, with truancy steadily increasing as the preoccupation with drug-related activities increases. Even when they do attend school they are often intoxicated or recovering from using such that their educational participation and performance is severely impaired. Many of them also suffer from persisting substance-related cognitive impairment, usually reversible, but sometimes long lasting. These matters are even further compounded by their drug-related or -exacerbated emotional/behavioral difficulties.

One of the core program components is educational assessment and rehabilitation. The program includes a full school with 3.5 hours of programming daily, which is more extensive than most short-term residential placements provide under typical "home and hospital" teaching requirements. The school is certified by the Maryland State Department of Education and directed by a specialist in adolescent treatment and special education. The certification and staffing allow the school to transfer credits and grant degrees. Each patient undergoes a full educational evaluation including a battery of testing, review of school records, and review of an individualized educational plan (IEP) if previously identified as a special education student.

An important function of this program component is to reinforce the role of school as one of the developmentally appropriate main activities of an adolescent's daily life, and to model the role of school participation and achievement as having a critical value for recovery. The content of the school curriculum is carefully linked to the overall treatment program, including: recovery-oriented materials such as biology and health sciences of drug use, reading skills using NA and other recovery materials, writing skills using life-story essays and step-work, etc. Another major curriculum focus is prevocational and life skills development, including: interview training, money management, role-playing, etc. A large number of patients have cognitive limitations and/or learning disabilities, many unrecognized. Careful consideration is given to individual capacities so that the in-treatment educational experience can be a help to self-esteem and a positive re-inforcement for the role of student. Coordinating with each patient's home school is emphasized so that they can earn credits for their work in treatment (and often even catch up on credits missed). Extensive materials and coaching is offered to parents to assist them with the admission, review, and dismissal (ARD) process to obtain special education services as needed. A GED track is also available to patients for whom school is untenable.

Legal/Conduct Remediation

The program's target population includes a high proportion of patients with histories of delinquent behaviors, juvenile justice system involvement, and many meet criteria for disruptive behavior disorders. The majority have been involved extensively in illegal behaviors beyond simple drug use (including theft, assault, trafficking, etc.), whether or not they have been involved in the juvenile justice system. Many have been in detention; many have active legal involvement including probation or pending charges; many are actually court ordered to treatment.

Another core program component is remediation of legal and conduct problems. Each patient receives a thorough legal evaluation. For those patients with current legal involvement, their legal status becomes a crucial treatment tool. For example, the probation officer becomes an important member of the team, and the treatment team as a whole utilizes the prospect of its influence on potential legal sanctions as both a carrot and stick to shape treatment engagement and response. Detailed reporting to judges is the norm, and counselors sometimes accompany patients to court. Significant effort is expended on active coordination of an aftercare plan with the courts, e.g., through probationary mandate.

A key feature of conduct remediation is the staff training that creates a therapeutic milieu that can both tolerate and manage some degree of behavioral disturbance (as opposed to many treatment centers that discharge for insubordination or disruption) but also control and transform it. The patterns of severe behavioral disturbance that are reflected in the patients' histories are frequently expressed as disruptive behavior in treatment. Some patients may display behaviors such as oppositionality, aggression, threatening, fighting, excessive horseplay, tantrums, inappropriate sexual activity, theft, etc. Such behaviors are inextricably connected to patients' drug use and to their capacity for treatment response, so that as they occur, they become critical target symptoms for the treatment program. On the one hand, the maintenance of a safe, orderly treatment environment models the expectation of mutually cooperative and prosocial behavior. On the other hand, tolerance of some degree of disruption and developmentally appropriate adolescent frenetic energy sets a more "real world" atmosphere and acknowledges that longstanding patterns of behavior do not change overnight.

A system of behavioral contingency is used, with rewards, consequences, and frequent feedback. As part of the system, patients practice self-assessments of their own behavior. Based on integrated ratings of both behavior and recovery assignments, patients earn various "levels" of achievement, which are in turn linked to privileges. Patients must, themselves, seek out and obtain formal feedback and approval from numerous staff members and peers in order to earn changes in level status. Individualized behavior contracts are sometimes used for patients with particular difficulties. Patients also participate in a variety of conduct-focused specialty groups, such as dealer's group, values clarification, and peer conflict mediation.

Although MMTC's length of stay is not long enough to accomplish some of the more ambitious goals of longer programs that are more fully based on TC approaches, the program's therapeutic milieu *is* able to introduce some of these approaches effectively in the short term. In addition to managing behavior, the therapeutic milieu transmits the notion that appropriate behavior, respect, and mutual support are community values. It is a recurrent theme in the discussions at regularly scheduled and impromptu community meetings that the community as a whole must take responsibility for individual behavior, and that everyone shares responsibility for his/her brothers and sisters. This aspect of the program borrows heavily from the TC approach, with its philosophy of "right living." Important goals include an introduction to: acquisition of group living and conflict resolution skills, rehabilitation/habilitation of activities of daily living, and an articulation or clarification of values. The therapeutic milieu itself serves as an agent of change, gradually allowing adolescents with unregulated behavior and emotions to begin the process of internal self-regulation using the milieu's intensive external structure as a tool. This structured milieu furthermore models aspects of external structure and features of a recovery environment that the adolescents will utilize in their home, school, and other systems following discharge.

Family Evaluation and Therapy

The program's target population includes a high proportion of patients with disrupted or impaired families. Many patients have home environments that are not conducive to recovery, because of parents or other family members who are absent, who are not supportive, who are not effective at setting limits, who engage in active substance abuse, or who live in neighborhoods that are drug infested.

One of the core program components is family evaluation and therapy. Each patient receives a thorough family evaluation. Supervised visiting occurs each weekend, preceded by a mandatory multifamily group session with both didactic and interactive components. In addition, each family is expected to participate in family therapy sessions, both with and without the patient. These sessions are conducted by the patient's primary counselor/case manager throughout the week. The counselors also rotate through the weekend schedule, to have greater access to families who work during the week or live far away. One of the key goals of this program component is to bring families together and reinforce the role of parental attitudes, monitoring, and supervision in controling adolescent drug use (and other problem behaviors). In addition to identifying a family's impairment and offering training to parents (and surrogate parents), it is also crucial to recognize and emphasize each family's assets so that active treatment participation is encouraged, including acceptance of new approaches. The process of reintegration into the community is another key goal of the family component, with planning for discharge beginning as soon after admission as possible. The family home treatment contract is an important, frequently used tool for the reinforcement of structure, continuation of the model of behavioral contingency begun in treatment, and reinforcement of commitment to ongoing outpatient treatment.

Unfortunately some patients do not have viable home situations despite our attempts at family interventions. For these patients, the focus of family therapy shifts to finding alternative recovery environments. Efforts to identify and involve alternative resources within the extended family are significant. It is also considered part of the scope of family therapy to help extended families with planning in such difficult processes as custody and securing public benefits. Sometimes therapeutic mediation among adversarial family members is necessary. Sometimes evaluation and referral of impaired family members is necessary. And more often than one would like, patients require placement in other residential treatment settings, such as group homes, foster care, extended treatment or sheltered care programs, and residential treatment centers. The protracted arrangements for such placements, even if not in direct transfer, are a major component of this program, including financial arrangements, preparation of referral materials, and coordination among involved parties (e.g., families, agencies, payors, therapists).

Medical Evaluation and Treatment

The program's target population includes a high proportion of patients with a variety of health problems and health risk behaviors. As a result of the chaotic lives they have led as addicts and because many of them come from chaotic families, most patients have not had adequate primary health care screening and treatment. Those that have had care for chronic or episodic medical conditions have usually engaged in health care services in a haphazard fashion, not coordinated through a stable provider that appreciates the context of drug-involvement.

Another core program component is medical evaluation, treatment, and referral. Every patient receives a complete medical history and physical examination, along with a health needs target checklist. The medical staff (nurses, physician assistant, physicians) attempts to identify and coordinate with any prior community sources of care. All patients undergo STD screening (including syphilis, HIV, and Hepatitis B and C), immunization updates, and gynecologic screening for girls. Comprehensive medical and skilled nursing care is provided for all residents in the program. A team of physicians, physician assistants, and licensed nurses provide twenty-four-hour assessment, monitoring, and treatment for most common health conditions and access to emergency and specialty care as needed. A key purpose of this program component is to promote health awareness among the patients and reinforce the role of participation in primary health care. All patients participate in a series of "health recovery" groups aimed at health and risk-behavior topics, including: STDs/HIV, sexual abstinence and safety, injury prevention, nutrition, etc. Special topics are arranged intermittently for pregnant or parenting teenagers when appropriate. Finally, each family receives assistance in identifying a regular source of primary health care as part of discharge planning, and every patient receives a referral appointment to the identified primary care provider soon after discharge.

YOUNG ADULTS

A separate track exists for young adults ages eighteen to twenty, with seventeen-year-olds sometimes included based on level of maturity. In this track, ten to twenty young adults are separated from the younger patients for most of the day, and receive programming that is more suited to their developmental level. This allows a specialized emphasis on issues related to the transition to adulthood and independent living. It also reinforces their group identity, and gives them a kind of special status as being different from the "little kids." Whenever possible the young adults are encouraged to have a special community leadership role, including peer mentorship for the younger patients. A physically separate young adult area serves as the living quarters for the male young adults and provides program space for both males and females, who are allowed more inter-gender contact than the younger patients. They are also generally afforded a greater degree of freedom, with periods of less intensive structure, with an overall emphasis on learning self-regulation skills. For many of the young adults, the educational programming is less prominent, focusing on GED and/or pre-vocational instruction.

MANAGED CARE

The program also has a small short-stay track, designed specifically to meet the needs of patients with managed care benefits. This track has an average length of stay of ten days. In general less emphasis is placed on the TC elements of the program, and more emphasis in placed on the medical model elements, with increased intensity of individualized treatment and discharge planning. These patients do not receive the full psychoeducational school component. In keeping with the mandate of managed care, emphasis is placed on discharging patients as quickly as possible to less intensive levels of care.

DISCHARGE

It is the expectation that the treatment that begins in the residential program will continue as part of a longitudinal process of ongoing treatment. For most patients this means outpatient treatment. For most patients, discharge means a return to their homes and families. A significant minority, however, are discharged to other institutional placements. All patients who are discharged to the community are referred to outpatient substance abuse counseling; many are also referred to additional specialty outpatient treatments such as family counseling, mental health counseling, or psychiatric care. Building from the centralized linkage model, linkages to community services in each of the adjunctive treatment domains are emphasized, with referrals, communication of treatment goals, and sharing of treatment records. In particular, this means: referral to outpatient psychiatric treatment for those who need it, referral to primary care medical providers, coordination of return to or reenrollment in community schools, coordination of involvement by probation officers and the courts in mandated treatment plans, and explicit expectations for family participation in ongoing treatment, supervision, and monitoring. The program endeavors to connect adolescents to the culture of NA, with the hopeful expectation that they will continue to attend meetings after discharge. A substantial portion of these patients remain in the

Mountain Manor system (based primarily on geographical proximity) through the day program, intensive outpatient program, and integrated psychiatric outpatient treatment.

CONCLUSION

Mountain Manor Treatment Center is a short- to medium-term residential addictions and "dual diagnosis" treatment program for adolescents. The treatment model that is used is based on a milieu therapy approach, utilizing both medical model elements and therapeutic community (TC) elements. Program elements that are particularly emphasized include: psychiatric assessment and treatment, primary care medical assessment and treatment, intensive educational remediation, delinquency/conduct rehabilitation, and family support services. These components enable the program to care for a wide spectrum of youth, especially those with high severity of drug-involvement, those with a variety of comorbid psychosocial and psychiatric impairments, and those who have been refractory to previous interventions. Another strength of the program is its operation within a broad and integrated continuum of care, which provides ongoing treatment at various levels of care for many of its patients, enabling them to sustain and build on therapeutic gains begun in the residential program.

Future work under the CSAT-ATM project will include the development of a program manual that articulates the program model in more detail. In addition, compilation of data from patient follow-up interviews will allow an examination of outcomes following discharge from the residential treatment program (see Dennis et al., 2003).

REFERENCES

Center for Substance Abuse Treatment (CSAT) (1994). Assessment and Treatment of Patients with Co-Existing Mental Illness and Alcohol and Other Drug Abuse, Treatment Improvement Protocol (TIP) Series, Number 9, DHHS Publication No. (SMA) 95-3061.

Dennis, M.L., Dowud-Norusi, S., Muck, R., and McDermeit, M. (2003). The need for developing and evaluating adolescent treatment models. In S.J. Stevens and A.R. Morral (Eds.), *Adolescent Substance Abuse Treatment in the United States:*

Exemplary Models from a National Evaluation Study (pp. 3-26). Binghamton, NY: The Haworth Press, Inc.

Kandel, D.B., Johnson, J.G., Bird, H.R., Weismann, M.M., Goodman, S.H., Lahey, B.B., Regier, D.A., and Schwab-Stone, M.E. (1999). Psychiatric co-morbidity among adolescents with substance use disorders: Findings from the Methods for the Epidemiology of Child and Adolescent Mental Disorders (MECA) study. *Journal of the American Academy of Child and Adolescent Psychiatry,* 38:6, 693-699.

Mee-Lee, D., Shulman, G.D., Fishman, M., Gastfriend, D., and Griffith, J.H., Eds. (2001). *ASAM Patient Placement Criteria for the Treatment of Substance Related Disorders,* Second Edition-Revised (ASAM PPC-2R). Chevy Chase, MD: American Society of Addiction Medicine, Inc.

Substance Abuse and Mental Health Services Administration (SAMHSA) (1998). *National Dialogue on Co-Occurring Mental and Substance Abuse Disorders,* proceedings of a joint meeting of the National Association of State Mental Health Program Directors and the National Association of State Alcohol and Drug Abuse Directors, sponsored by SAMHSA, June 16-17.

Chapter 7

Culturally Competent Substance Abuse Treatment for American Indian and Alaska Native Youths

Candice Stewart-Sabin
Mark Chaffin

PREVALENCE OF ALCOHOL AND OTHER DRUG ABUSE AMONG AMERICAN INDIAN YOUTHS

The problem of alcohol and other drug (AOD) abuse is significant to the American Indian and Alaska Native (AI/AN) community. Alcohol disorders, although not as rampant as stereotypes might suggest, are disproportionately prevalent in the AI/AN population, and are associated with a variety of social problems. Although tribes differ in their rates of general alcohol *use,* with overall rates less than the overall U.S. population, the general prevalence of *problem drinking* in AI/AN populations is substantially higher than overall U.S. rates, often by a factor of two or three times (see May, 1994, for a detailed review). Brian McCaffrey (2000), the drug control adviser for the Clinton administration, reports that 19.6 percent of teenage American Indians used illicit drugs, the highest rate of any group in the country. The national average for adolescents ages twelve through seventeen is 9 percent. While Indians as a whole drink alcohol at a lower rate then the general population, the alcohol-related deaths

---

Electronic mail may be sent to Dr. C. Sabin at drugfree@cyberport.com.

among Indian adolescents ages fifteen to twenty-four are seventeen times higher than the national average. For example, in the National Household Survey of Drug Use, the Substance Abuse and Mental Health Services Administration (SAMHSA, 1998), reported that the rate of *any* alcohol use in AI/AN populations was similar to overall population rates; however the rate of alcohol dependence was 60 percent higher. Because general population surveys often focus on sustained heavy drinking or dependence, they may underestimate AI/AN rates of alcohol-related problems due to drinking style differences in AI/AN populations, where binge drinking is more common (May, 1994; Weisner, Weibel-Orlando, and Long, 1984).

The toll taken by alcohol-related problems on the AI/AN community in which 70 percent of the population lives off the reservation, is particularly staggering. For example, the death rate due to cirrhosis is 2.7 times that of the overall population rate, and the rates of alcohol-related hospital admissions, suicides, and automobile accidents are significantly elevated (Hisnanick, 1994; Lincoln, 1999). Overall alcohol-related mortality for AI/AN populations has been found to be almost four times that of Caucasians, although the rates vary from tribe to tribe (Christian, Dufour, and Bertolucci, 1989). In addition, several of the leading causes of death for AI/AN people between the ages of fifteen and forty-four years involve behaviors that are often AOD abuse related, such as suicide, homicide, or motor vehicle accidents. Although the AI/AN death rate due to alcoholism has declined 17 percent since 1980, this trend has shifted in recent years. Since 1990, the proportional rate has risen to seven times that of all races in the United States (Lincoln, 1999).

Most Indian adolescents by the age of fifteen have tried alcohol and other drugs and the average age of first experimentation appears to be dropping (Taylor, 2000; Moncher, Holden, and Trimble, 1990). Beauvais (1996) reports that 74 percent of reservation Indian adolescents between seventh and twelfth grade have tried alcohol and 51 percent have become intoxicated. Other studies have reported rates of Indian adolescent alcohol use (lifetime prevalence) from 56 percent to 89 percent (May, 1982). Moncher, Holden, and Trimble (1990) reported that 50 percent of nonreservation AI/AN adolescents and 80 percent of reservation AI/AN adolescents used alcohol on a moderate level compared to 23 percent of urban, non-Indian adolescents. AI/AN adolescents report higher rates of marijuana use ranging from 41 to

62 percent versus the U.S. general adolescent population of 28 to 50 percent. Inhalant abuse for the AI/AN adolescent is 17 to 22 percent versus 9 to 11 percent of adolescents in the geneal population. However, there is a wide variation that occurs among tribes.

IMPACT OF AOD ABUSE ON AI/AN YOUTHS

The potential adverse consequences of AOD abuse on Indian adolescents include higher involvement with the juvenile justice system, increased mental health problems, and lower educational achievement. In addition, parental AOD abuse may lead to increased levels of child maltreatment and family problems that can potentially compound the risk for juvenile system involvement, mental health or educational problems, and youth involvement in AOD abuse.

Juvenile Justice System Involvement

LaFromboise (1988) reported that Indian people in urban areas are taken into custody for violations committed under the influence of drugs or alcohol four times as often as blacks and ten times as often as whites. Indian adolescents are overrepresented in the juvenile justice system and have the second highest rate of juvenile correctional incarceration of any racial group (Duclos et al., 1998). Poupart (1995) examined juvenile court records from 1985 to 1989 in a rural Wisconsin county with a substantial (7.14 percent) Native American population. Four decision points were analyzed: intake, detention, filing of a petition, and final disposition. At intake, 62.7 percent of Native American youths were referred to the prosecutor compared with 38.7 percent of white youths. At each additional step in the process, native youths were more likely to experience the more severe outcome. Although AOD abuse is not the sole factor resulting in disproportionate juvenile justice system involvement among AI/AN youths, it is a prevalent factor in crimes occurring in Indian country. AOD use has been found to be a factor reported in 55 percent of violent crimes committed by American Indians, compared to 44 percent for whites and 35 percent for blacks (Bureau of Justice Statistics, 1993).

Mental Health

Comorbid emotional and behavioral disorders are prevalent among Indian adolescents (Duclos et al., 1998), and Indian adolescents who receive substance abuse treatment have a higher prevalence of co-morbid psychiatric disorders than their non-Indian counterparts. Comorbid disorders may be associated with a complex and interrelated group of risk factors: trauma or abuse, chronic environmental stress, poverty, social isolation, family problems, or parental psychopathology. Windle (1990) reports that familial influences (e.g., harsh disciplinary practices, marital discord, and parental psychopathology) have been consistently related to antisocial behavior and substance use in childhood and adolescence in general.

Abuse, Trauma, and Victimization

In the Indian Child Welfare Act of 1978 it has been reported that the risk that AI/AN children have of experiencing child maltreatment is twice as high as for children in the general population. In a survey administered to 297 Indian adolescents attending a high school (grades nine through twelve) in a large southwestern Indian community, 51 percent of the students reported that they had experienced a traumatic event, with 37 percent experiencing more than one such event, and 16 percent reporting four or more events (NCAIANMHR, 1999). Child neglect has been reported to be especially prevalent among AI/AN families, although prior to passage of the Indian Child Welfare Act of 1978 (that recognized sovereign status to the tribes), concerns were raised that Native cultural practices were often mislabeled as neglectful behavior. More recent studies suggest that AI/AN child neglect cases are far more likely to be alcohol involved than among other populations (DeBruyn, Lujan, and May, 1992). In a survey of 2,037 AI/AN cases served by federally funded programs, substance abuse was reported to be present in 76 percent of neglecting fathers and 78 percent of neglecting mothers, and was more likely to be associated with neglect than with either physical or sexual abuse (National Indian Justice Center, 1992).

When combined with a history of parental AOD problems, histories of abuse or maltreatment are associated with an increased risk of adolescent AOD problems. In a recent study of 4,023 adolescents (139 Indian adolescents) twelve to seventeen years of age, victimization and witnessed violence were found to double the risk of past-year alcohol and other substance abuse/dependence (Kilpatrick et al., 2000). In addition, this study found that witnessing violence tripled the risk of abuse/dependence for all substances after the effects of demographics, familial substance use, and victimization were statistically controlled. The direct or indirect impact of witnessed violence on children and adolescents has been well documented (Bean, 1992; Ireland and Widom, 1994; Fitzpatrick and Boldizar, 1993; Groves, 1997; Kilpatrick et al., 2000; Ollendick, 1996; Swaim et al., 1989), and prevalence rates of domestic violence among AI/AN populations have been reported ranging from 52 to 91 percent (Fairchild, Fairchild, and Stoner, 1998; Robin, Chester, and Rasmussen, 1998). Substance use may be used as a strategy to cope with the stress produced by experiencing or being exposed to interpersonal aggression. Kilpatrick et al. (1997) suggest that the use or abuse of substances following assault may be an effective, but maladaptive, strategy to reduce negative feelings. However, after controlling for the effects of demographics, familial substance use, and abuse or other forms of direct victimization, it was found that witnessing violence was among the most powerful risk factors for substance use disorders and negative affective states.

Suicide

Suicide is a complex behavior usually caused by a combination of factors. The majority of people who complete suicide have a diagnosable mental or substance abuse disorder or both, with the majority having a depressive illness (Surgeon General, 1999). From 1979 to 1992, suicide rates for Native Americans (including both American Indians and Alaska Natives) were about 1.5 times the rate for the general population (Surgeon General, 1999), with a disproportionate number occurring among young male Native Americans (ages fifteen to twenty-four). This group accounted for 64 percent of all suicides by Native Americans. During the twelve months preceding the 1999 Youth Risk Behavior Surveillance Survey (YRBS), one of five AI/AN adolescents (20.7 percent) seriously considered suicide with 17.6 percent making a suicide plan, 13.6 percent attempting suicide, and 4.4 percent requiring medical attention as a result of a suicide attempt.

Educational

A significant number of AI/AN students continue to attend Bureau of Indian Affairs (BIA) funded schools (U.S. Department of the Interior, 1988). Approximately 13,400 Indian adolescents currently attend boarding school, constituting about 14 percent of the AI/AN high school population. This percentage of students in BIA boarding schools is expected to increase as Federal and tribal educators continue their struggle to strike a reasonable balance between local access to schools and educational quality, resulting in a recentralization of some instructional resources (Development Associates, 1983). Indian boarding schools have been criticized for providing substandard education and fostering an unsafe environment for Indian adolescents.

All adolescents need knowledge and skills to compete in today's employment market. It is not enough to merely get by in school; one must excel in order to ensure a productive adulthood. Many AI/AN students who are indifferent toward school skip classes and drop out at high rates. Chavers (1991) estimates the dropout rate for Indian adolescents at 50 percent. In some Indian communities the dropout rate is 100 percent after the ninth grade. Traditional Western educational approaches may be incongruent with AI/AN learning styles or culture, potentially contributing to school disengagement.

Cultural Issues

Cultural competence has no single definition on which all scholars can agree (Segall, 1986). However, for the purposes of this review cultural competence is defined as a combination of cultural knowledge, social skills, and personal attitudes. This includes possessing:

1. a knowledge of cultural beliefs and values,
2. positive attitudes towards majority and minority groups,
3. bicultural social efficacy,
4. bicultural communication ability,
5. a diverse role repertoire, and
6. a sense of being grounded in the culture (LaFromboise, Coleman, and Gerton, 1993).

Five patterns of cultural adaptation have been proposed for understanding bicultural functioning: assimilation, acculturation, alternation, multiculturalism, and fusion (see LaFromboise, Coleman, and Gerton, 1993). The alternation pattern appears to be the most fluid and supportive pattern for attaining cultural competence. In this pattern, it is possible for an individual to know and understand two different cultures, and have the ability to alter behavior to fit the particular social or cultural context. Ogbu and Matute-Bianchi (1986) have noted, "it is possible and acceptable to participate in two different cultures or to use two different languages, perhaps for different purposes, by alternating one's behavior according to the situation" (p. 89).

Many AI/AN people function in this bicultural pattern. McFee (1968), studying individuals on the Blackfeet reservation, found that many Indians were knowledgeable about both Blackfeet and Anglo-American cultures and were able to interact easily with members of each group, providing they were not perceived by the minority group as being overly identified with the majority group. Boyce and Boyce (1983) studied the relationship between reported illness among Navajo students and cultural background. This study was conducted on first-year students at a reservation boarding school (the primary mechanism for acculturating Indian people until the 1970s). It found a significant positive association between the number of clinical visits, referrals for health or psychosocial problems, and the degree of cultural incongruity (dissonance between family and community cultural identities). This suggests that imposed acculturation, as opposed to bicultural alternation, might have a deleterious impact on health related behaviors, possibly including alcohol and other drug abuse.

The literature suggests that cultural minorities can become biculturally competent without experiencing psychological problems, totally assimilating, or retreating from contact with the majority culture, and that bicultural alternation may be a particularly adaptive pattern for AI/AN youth. This is supported through the educational performance, where bicultural Indian college students have been found to be better adjusted, specifically in the academic and cultural domains, than their nonbicultural counterparts. A higher degree of participation in cultural activities, enrollment in American-Indian-oriented college courses, and perception of their Indian heritage as an advantage resulted in higher grade point averages, more effective study habits, and better utilization of resources to support academic success (Schiller, 1987). Individuals who have the ability to effectively alternate their use of culturally appropriate behavior also have been reported to demonstrate higher cognitive functioning and mental health status than individuals who are monocultural, assimilated, or acculturated (Garcia, 1983; Rashid, 1984; Rogler, Cortes, and Malgady, 1991). One study of Navajo children from five elementary schools in Arizona (Beuke, 1978) revealed that students in the high-Indian/high-Anglo cultural identification category had significantly higher self-esteem scores than those in the low-Indian/low-Anglo category.

A number of authors stress the importance of focusing on bicultural social skills of individuals in a cultural minority group who are experiencing difficulties within the majority culture. They have specifically suggested that bicultural skills are appropriate for helping Indian youth combat substance abuse and other mental health issues (LaFromboise, 1983; Schinke et al., 1988). The ability to develop bicultural competence is based on one's level of ethnic socialization. Ethnic socialization is the cultural transmission of values and beliefs that is a part of effective individual and family functioning (Stevenson, 1996). Ethnic socialization consists of protective factors that promote the youth's ethnic heritage (e.g. history, cultural values, and teachings), and provide positive ethnic role models, exposure to cultural activities, and strategies for effectively negotiating oppressive circumstances within a multicultural society (Stevenson, 1996). Many AI/AN adolescents have limited ethnic socialization and remain without a sense of grounding within their own Native American culture. Native Americans in general have experienced generations of pressure to abandon native culture and assimilate into the majority culture.

The native people in the past were forced, and now seduced, into believing residential/boarding schools were the best way to educate and promote productivity in their children's lives. This has led to one of the main historical issues that our American Indian and Alaska Native adolescents face today. Many of today's AI/AN adolescent's parents and elders did not learn how to parent, and subsequently passed on the cultural loss, shame, and severe psychic pain of the cultural genocide they experienced. This cultural loss may have led to violence, domestic violence, severe child maltreatment (i.e., emotional, physical, and/or sexual abuse) and the use of alcohol and other substances to manage their lives. This genocide and the lack of assimilation has resulted in severing of their ancestral heritage and many of the AI/AN adolescents are culturally "adrift," lacking a firm Native American identity and continuing the proliferation of poverty and other social problems.

Approximately 61 percent of Our Youth Our Future, Inc., adolescents have attended residential/boarding schools. In light of the severity of AOD abuse and family problems in the lives of these adolescents, one could postulate that the core of these issues might stem from intergenerational transmission as a result of residential/boarding school experiences. In current residential/boarding schools little or no parenting exists and many times the children/adolescents learn from their peers. A large deviant peer relationship to AOD abuse occurs and little parental/adult guidance is offered. Developmentally, the age that a child is placed in a residential setting (sometimes as early as age four) can be devastating to the child. Many of the children live in substance using and violence prone homes, making a difficult adjustment for the child without some negative developmental impact.

Unfortunately, minimal scientific study looking at the impact of these experiences on lifetime AI/AN adolescent development has occurred. More attention needs to be focused on the historical relationship of residential/boarding school attendance and today's AI/AN substance use and severe family problems.

Treatment and Outcome Studies

Native American and Alaska Native adolescents are an understudied population and limited literature exists on the treatment population, or on their response to common treatment approaches. Some evaluation studies have been conducted on AI/AN *adult* populations and have found disappointingly low rates of success in existing alcohol rehabilitation programs (Kline and Roberts, 1973; Lang, 1974; Snake, Hawkins, and LaBoueff 1977; Towle, 1975; Weibel-Orlando, 1984). May (1986) reviewed Indian alcoholism programs and reported that they were inadequate to meet the needs of the Indian communities, both in terms of accessibility and cultural competency. Traditional alcohol services have been described as a poor fit with native cultures, and the treatment approaches themselves may create unique barriers to service delivery. For example, confrontational techniques, confession-like disclosure of personal problems, or a complete emphasis on nonnative religious precepts may be perceived as unhelpful or culturally incongruent for many Native Americans. Also, programs in which staff is largely or exclusively nonnative, or located well outside Native American communities may also present cultural barriers. Alcohol treatment programs incorporating native cultural approaches such as traditional healing methods and concepts have begun to appear in AI/AN communities. A number of these approaches have been described in the adult substance abuse treatment literature (see Abbot, 1998 for a review of many of these programs). Most represent a blend of Native American and Western approaches, consistent with the fact that many Indian people use two health care systems—the mainstream medical system and traditional healers or. medicine people (Coulehan, 1980; Stewart, May, and Muneta, 1980).

Although currently no published randomized clinical trials exist that compare alcohol treatment programs incorporating traditional AI/AN cultural components with purely majority culture-based approaches, limited data suggest that incorporating Native American cultural elements may improve service access and retention, and possibly outcomes. First, affiliation with American Indian and Alaska Native culture in general may be associated with improved outcomes. Westermeyer and Neider (1984) examined ten-year follow-up data for adult AI/AN alcoholics exiting treatment. Clients having predominantly AI/AN friends and higher affiliation with AI/AN culture were found to have better outcomes at follow-up. Walker et al. (1989) reported on a small sample quasi-experimental comparison of an Indian-specific program with a more general treatment program. No differences were found in outcomes for service completers, but service utilization and retention was better in the Indian-specific program. Gutierres and Todd (1997) reported that Native American men and women stayed in treatment longer than their cohorts if they had participated in a culturally sensitive residential program. Fisher, Lankford, and Galea (1996) compared retention rates before and after changing to an approach emphasizing native lifestyles and beliefs in an Alaskan program. Retention rates for native clients, which had lagged behind rates for other racial groups, improved after changing to a more native culture-based approach, and subsequently approximated retention rates similar to other racial groups. Our experience has echoed these findings. Prior to instituting a bicultural model for youth in our residential AOD treatment program, retention rates through treatment completion were less than 54 percent. In the year after changing to a bicultural program model incorporating native cultural practices and personnel, retention rates increased to 83 percent.

Among Western treatment approaches, cognitive/behavioral and motivational interviewing techniques may be a potentially better fit with many native cultures. Mariano et al. (1989) examined cognitive behavioral techniques and other social skills training approaches among Native American problem drinkers, noting that these techniques may be more easily adapted to AI/AN populations. This is due to the focus on specific patterns of behavior rather than a focus on changing philosophical, religious, or social belief systems. Motivational interviewing approaches also may be good choices because they explicitly avoid heavy confrontation, confessionals, or imposed problem definitions.

BICULTURALLY COMPETENT TREATMENT MODEL

Treatment Philosophy and Purpose

Our Youth Our Future, Inc. (OYOF) is a nonprofit organization providing services for AI/AN adolescents and has been in existence since 1989. It is a twenty-four-bed residential facility that has treated over 1,200 Indian adolescents ages twelve to nineteen. The program serves a large rural area populated by six major tribes from both reservation areas and reservation border towns. Over the past three years the program has evolved from a twelve-step program and adventure-based or recreational model of treatment into a bicultural treatment model. The bicultural treatment model combines cognitive-behavioral and biopsychosocial treatment approaches with an integrated program of culturally relevant practices and activities that compliment the rehabilitative effort of each youth.

The model takes as its premise that the acculturation of many AI/AN adolescents into their ancestral heritage has been incomplete or disrupted. Minority stress, exposure to child maltreatment, violence, intergenerational trauma, and/or lack of parenting may have contributed to both their substance abuse problem and a range of possible comorbid mental health problems. The model is designed to promote the successful development of bicultural skills that will allow the individual to alternate behavior according to the cultural situation, and to develop a firm identity in their native culture. The native culture-focused spiritual program provides cultural teachings, activities, sweat lodge, and other traditional ceremonies fostering cultural pride, identity and values, and supporting a harmonious lifestyle. The model assumes that sobriety and the ability to develop bicultural competence may depend upon the adolescent's level of ethnic socialization and cultural identity. High ethnic socialization and strong cultural identity may serve as protective factors against minority and environmental stress. In addition, cultural ceremonies serve as an opportunity to develop and reinforce competencies designed to promote cultural identity, self-esteem, and a peer support system. Finally, the model supports both abstinence principles and harm reduction principles when abstinence is not feasible. The overall model allows adolescents' to begin developing a framework for becoming interdependent within all cultures in which they may interact.

Evaluation Process

OYOF provides a battery of assessments, both general and culturally specific, before admission as part of a triage process to determine the appropriate level of care and appropriateness for different treatment tracks within the overall program. A variety of assessment instruments are used during the initial evaluation process, including:

- The Native American version of the addiction severity index (Accurate Assessments, n.d.) is conducted to determine the level of severity and treatment priority in the seven domains (medical, academic, legal, substance abuse, family/social, psychological, and cultural). The Native American ASI consists of the standard ASI plus additional items with cultural content. The ASI is given at admission and one week prior to discharge in order to determine change over the course of treatment.
- The Millon Adolescent Clinical Inventory (MACI) (Millon, 1993) is conducted at admission and one week prior to discharge with each adolescent in order to support mental health

diagnosis, identify substance abuse proneness, and comorbid emotional or behavioral issues.

- At admission and discharge the adolescent and family are given a cultural assessment developed by OYOF. This instrument is considered an essential element of the program and is administered by Native American Healing Practitioners (NAHP) affiliated with the program. The instrument is intended to measure the client's cultural self-image, beliefs, activities, and taboos along with cultural identification within their tribe and within the Anglo-American culture. It specifically inquires into any culturally unique explanations (e.g., violation of cultural prohibitions) the adolescent and his/her family may believe are related to the adolescent's problems (currently the psychometrics are being conducted).

- The Northwest Educational Achievement (NWEA) test series is a norm-referenced test in the areas of reading, literature, and math, that is used to determine the level of academic attainment and specialized educational needs. The adolescent is given the NWEA at admission and one week prior to discharge.

- The Trauma Symptom Checklist for Children (TSCC) (Briere, 1995) is a self-report measure of trauma-related symptoms, including post-traumatic stress disorder, disassociation, anxiety, anger, and other common symptoms that may be trauma sequelae (currently being normed for cultural relevance). The adolescent is given the TSCC at admission and one week prior to discharge.

- The Kaufman Brief Intelligence Test (Kaufman and Kaufman, 1990) is conducted when other tests or clinical presentation indicate possible impairment. If the test suggests neurological problems, the adolescent is referred for a full neurological assessment.

Treatment Tracks

Given the diversity of the client population and their individualized needs, youth are assigned to one of three treatment tracks that best fit their level of severity (i.e., polysubstance usage, comorbidity, learning style, trauma, and/or violence exposure history. The tracks are briefly described as follows:

- *The adventure base-counseling track (Air Group)* is for adolescents who typically have a major substance abuse problem and often a comorbid behavior disorder diagnosis (i.e., inhalant usage, fetal alcohol syndrome (FAS), ADHD, impulsive disorders). These youth typically have problems managing their behaviors and are often highly impulsive. Their learning styles may be less verbal and involve more holistic and less conventionally linear forms of thinking and reasoning. This treatment track uses a primarily behavioral or reinforcement based model. In addition, adventure-based counseling and other interactive interventions are used.
- *The emotional management track (Water Group)* is designed for adolescents who have experienced serious emotional, physical, or sexual abuse along with neglect, and may have difficulty in mood regulation to the extent that this becomes a barrier to their treatment. This track uses cognitive-behavioral therapy approaches to develop coping strategies and stress reduction skills, and expressive therapy approaches (e.g., role-playing, play therapy, drama therapy, etc.) are used to teach affect-regulation skills, reduce mood swings, and develop productive ways to manage dysphoria and other types of internal distress.
- *The general management track (Earth Group)* is a more traditional substance abuse treatment approach, with much less emphasis on dual-diagnosis or comorbid problems. These adolescents generally have a primary diagnosis of substance abuse; although anger management and related relationship problems may be issues for many youth in this track.

Native cultural themes are common to all three tracks. Adolescents in all tracks participate in the overall cultural-spiritual treatment and have multiple cultural-spiritual teachings, activities, and ceremonies (i.e., sweat lodges, talking circles, drumming and singing, early morning runs, meditation, medicine wheel, Native American current events and storytelling). For example, the sweat lodge teaches the individual the art of prayer utilizing four doors or rounds with drumming, singing, and prayers honoring the four directions. Each round or direction provides different viewpoints for the purpose of purifying and healing oneself. The sweat lodge provides a culturally appropriate environment to express and share one's emotions that may not be expressed in a clinical setting. The talking circle is a group process that provides a safe environment for individuals to share openly and honestly, and respects opposing viewpoints. The talking circle utilizes an eagle feature, and/or the talking stick is the conduit through which the individual is allowed to speak and is listened to until finished. The most important clinical aspect of the talking circle is giving the adolescent an opportunity, maybe for the first time, to be hard and understood. The medicine wheel is a univeral concept that is utilized in many different cultures including the European cultures. The medicine wheel concept is the Navajo concept of the four directions and relates them to the different components of treatment. One such teaching is that the gifts of thinking, planning, living, and resiliency were given from the Holy People within the Four Sacred directions. These gifts are provided as a means for affecting how we use our mental being for a productive and fulfilling life during our journey on Mother Earth. The medicine wheel teaching demonstrates to the adolescent that substance usage has a negative impact on one's ability to successfully use the "sacred gifts" and subsequently make healthy decisions.

All tracks receive group-based stress management skills training based upon the Heart Power Program and emotional freedom therapy models (Childre, Martin, and Beech, 1999; Craig, 1999). In addition, adventure-based counseling (ABC), psychotherapy, smoking cessation groups, behavior modification groups, substance abuse groups, child maltreatment groups, domestic violence exposure groups, and violence prevention training are offered. All adolescents receive individual, group, and family therapy along with academic services.

Cultural-Spiritual Program

The cultural-spiritual program provides cultural teachings and activities that foster cultural pride, identity, and values, and enhance the effort for sobriety and recovery. The program strives to support balance in the adolescent's spiritual, emotional, mental, and physical dimensions for continued well-being and harmony. The native cultural-spiritual program is based upon the Navajo belief that each creation begins with "Emergence" or progression through Four Worlds: the "Black World" to the "Blue World" into the "Yellow World," and finally into the "White World." Each adolescent is seen as a four-dimensional Being whose dimensions must be in balance, resulting in "Harmony" or "Walking in Beauty." These concepts are integrated into a traditional level system within the residential center by incorporating the Emergence concept with the teachings of the four dimensional Beings into program levels. Upon successful completion of the program and preparation for emergence into the "Glittering World," the adolescent are given the teachings of the four Gifts, that are not viewed as positive experiences. The teachings of the Glittering World are to remind us that the world has not changed and that we will have to adjust to the Gifts by utilizing their knowledge while in treatment. The four Gifts are *The Gift of Prejudice and Resentment, The Gift of Suffering and Sacrifice, The Gift of Loneliness,* and *The Gift of Hardship.* Finally, positive thinking and searching for purpose in life leads to a better way of life, self-balance, and self-harmony.

The staff members that provide the cultural-spiritual services are Native American Healing Practitioners (NAHP). These individuals have been under the apprentice of trained and respected native healing practitioners in the community and received the approval by the OYOF cultural team to conduct ceremonies and other relevant Native American practices. The NAHP must be granted clinical privileges from the cultural and ethics team and receive approval from this team to conduct certain ceremonies (i.e., herbs and individual ceremonies). They deliver all of the cultural lectures, conduct the sweat lodge ceremonies, talking circles, drumming, singing, smudging, meditation, early morning runs, Native American current events and storytelling, medicine wheel, tribal identification (i.e., clanship) and Native American history. NAHP's also conduct each adolescent's and family's initial cultural assessment to determine the level of identification, ethnic socialization, specific spiritual disruptions or taboo violations, that may have occurred.

It must be noted that all families are oriented to the type of program at the point of triage and given the option to be referred to other programs if the cultural/spiritual aspects are significantly inconsistent with their own beliefs. We explain that the cultural/spiritual aspects of the program are core tenets and would compromise the treatment success if the adolescent did not participate on some level. In addition, we serve multiple tribes and support and encourage the option of each tribe to have its own medicine people or elders perform needed ceremonies.

Alcohol and Other Substance Program

Philosophy

OYOF believes that adolescents must be approached in alcohol and other drug treatment from developmental factors such as differences in their value and belief systems, gender specific issues, stage of readiness to change, and level of family support. It is important to determine the cognitive and social-emotional development and level of severity of AOD usage to appropriately individualize treatment. In addition, family and social issues that appear to impede their ability to maintain sobriety are emphasized. The AOD program places no pressure on adolescents to accept that they have a disease. The program strives for abstinence; however, due to the high rate of comorbidity, a harm reduction philosophy is implemented when needed. Finally, the AOD program utilizes the cultural/spiritual aspects woven throughout, to enhance the understanding, from their culture, of the impact that AOD has on their spiritual life.

Education

The alcohol and other drug education begins by identifying the health consequences of the AOD use by the adolescent. Motivational techniques help the adolescent to assess, understand, and accept that their AOD usage has become a problem and is negatively impacting their life. A majority of the adolescents who attend OYOF engage in the use of marijuana, alcohol, inhalants, and cocaine. All adolescents receive education on the effects of cigarette smoking, marijuana, alcohol, inhalant, methamphetamines, cocaine, and other drugs when use is identified.

AOD Groups

All adolescents identify patterns of use, cues that lead to usage (i.e., emotional, peers, family), relapse patterns, and refusal skills. The groups focus specifically on the socializing ability of each adolescent in the groups. In addition, each adolescent receives relapse prevention training and has a written relapse plan that is presented at discharge to the community consisting of family, aftercare counselors, probation officers, and OYOF staff.

Individual Treatment

All adolescents receive individual therapy according to their ability to manage individual treatment. The individual sessions serve to aid the adolescent to develop a deeper understanding of their AOD usage and other individualized issues (child abuse, gender identity, and mental health) that serve as barriers to their successful sobriety. In addition, the sessions support the adolescent in identifying their strengths, and practicing their interpersonal skills.

The Twelve-Step Program

The adolescents are introduced to the twelve steps and work these steps throughout their treatment. The twelve steps are processed in the individual sessions. Big book studies and speaker meetings occur on site. At discharge the adolescent identifies an AA/NA community they will be attending, when appropriate.

Outside Networks

The adolescent is educated in the need to have support on all levels in the community. They are assisted in identifying different means of support that will enhance their success after discharge. At discharge, the adolescent identifies a cultural/spiritual community they plan to access (i.e., medicine man, sweat lodges).

Skill-Building Program

The skill-building program is based upon more traditional Western treatment approaches and focuses on both substance abuse and identified comorbidity, with the particular combination of approaches determined by the treatment track combined with individual need. The program consists of various skill-building groups:

- *The Cognitive-Behavioral Skill-Building Group* (CBSB) is based on dialectical behavior therapy (Linehan et al., 1991; Linehan, Heard, and Armstrong, 1993). The CBSB group is utilized with adolescents who display emotional vulnerability to support them in modulating emotions.
- *The Behavior Modification Skills Group (BMSG)* is based on behavioral intervention that helps the adolescent identify thoughts, feelings, and triggers associated with their impulsive behaviors. The emphasis is on teaching youth how to monitor their behaviors and manage them successfully.
- *The Anger Management Skills Group (AMSG)* teaches adolescents to understand and identify their anger triggers and patterns, as well as interpersonal conflict avoidance and nonviolent conflict resolution techniques. These skills focus on adolescents managing themselves in school, home, and community situations.
- *The Coping and Problem Solving Skills Group (CPSSG)* teaches stress and coping strategies along with establishing boundaries. Education on family roles discusses the dysfunctional family's tendency to exhibit blurred boundaries and role confusion. The adolescent identifies healthy physical, emotional, and spiritual boundaries. This awareness of boundaries helps the adolescent develop a sense of responsibility, self-esteem, resiliency, and subsequent empowerment.
- *The Heart Power Skills Group's (HPSG)* main goal is to teach adolescents how to develop empathy for self and others. Many adolescents feel unloved, confused, afraid, and stressed. The physical heart responds to love, and this can be measured in the electrocardiogram and in heart rate variability rhythms. When a youth or adult feels frustrated, angry, worried, fearful, or stressed, his or her heart rhythms become unbalanced and disordered. By learning to generate loving and appreciative feelings, heart rhythms come back into balance and regain their natural harmony. Harmonizing heart and brain through love can establish a complete intelligence and complete self, whereby each youth can look at life and realize there are no dead ends, but always possibilities. The heart power skill teaches the adolescent to develop *deep heart listening* that results in intuitive listening (*Teaching Children to Love,* HeartMath Series, Doc Lew Childre).

Family Program

The family therapy program is based on the same bicultural philosophy and the family experiences the same cultural teachings, activities, and ceremonies as the adolescent experiences. All families receive training in heart power skills, communication, and parenting techniques. These skills are introduced immediately due to the vulnerability of our families. The family is provided didactics on substance abuse and relapse, mental health issues, child maltreatment, domestic violence, and other community violence. In addition, they receive support to renew or develop trust within the family through the use of adventure-based counseling. The families receive the didactics together and in the afternoon break into individualized tracks to process the materials. During the sessions each family is rated on the level of effort it takes the team to engage them in treatment. Families receive individual family counseling when the treatment team determines the appropriateness of this intervention. Families that have experienced child maltreatment receive individualized treatment according to the level of the family's ability to be empathic and appropriate with the adolescent.

The family program has been very successful. In 1997 the family participation was 33 percent, however, following the implementation of the bicultural model the participation rate increased to 91 percent in 2000. Two main factors play a role in this success; one is in the shifting of the message from a shame-based issue to one of a family experiencing long-term stress and lack of support. Second, the increase of cultural/spiritual activities serves to strengthen the family's ethnic foundation. Finally, many of the families leave with new skills and a renewed motivation toward change.

Academic Program

OYOF is an accredited school through the North Central Association (NCA). The program utilizes innovative teaching approaches to support motivation and academic success. The classroom size is limited to ten adolescents who receive individualized attention. If adolescents become disruptive or are unable to manage themselves in the school, a counselor provides immediate intervention which gives the adolescent instant feedback on behavior and supports the successful return to the classroom.

CLIENT PROFILE AND PROGRAM ENVIRONMENT

Client Profile

Our Youth Our Future serves Native American adolescents ages twelve to nineteen and 80 percent of the youths are from area reservations and border towns while 20 percent are from other tribes across the country. The referrals are received from court (35 percent), AOD youth programs (22 percent), Indian Health Services (18 percent), tribal programs (12 percent), school programs (6 percent), social services (5 percent), self-referral (1 percent) and hospital transfers (1 percent). The average length of stay is fifty-one days with 77 percent to 83 percent successful completion rate.

Biopsychosocial-Spiritual Status

Legal history. The majority of the adolescents have been on probation during their lifetime (male 82 percent; female 67 percent), have been court ordered to treatment (male 56 percent; female 43 percent), and on an average have been in detention (male 4.5 times; female 2.5 times). The average first time in detention is age twelve for males and age thirteen for females. Eighty-nine percent of them have been arrested, booked, or charged with a crime.

Family environment. The home environment is perceived stressful (male 85 percent; female 80 percent) and the majority live in single-parent homes (male 64 percent; female 70 percent). The home environment in many cases is not able to support the adolescent in sobriety due to significant dysfunctional family relationships and active alcohol and drug use within the family.

Traumatic experiences. A significant number of adolescents in the program have experienced neglect and either physical and/or sexual abuse. Many times their use of AOD coincides with their abuse event. The program has a track of treatment that focuses on providing education and specialized therapy for these adolescents and their families.

Psychiatric comorbidity. The majority of the adolescents admitted have a mental health disorder (male 73 percent; female 88 percent). Most adolescents report that the mental health issues occurred before the use of substances or in close proximity to the first usage. Substance-induced mood is not as prevalent (male 1 percent; female 9 percent) as one would suspect. Post-traumatic stress disorder (PTSD) is difficult to diagnose due to the acute and chronic stress that is experienced by the adolescents. All diagnosis is according to the DSM-IV criteria and is provided by a psychologist and/or psychiatrist.

Inclusion/Exclusion Criteria

All adolescents admitted must be between the ages of twelve to nineteen with a certificate of Indian blood. Admission requires a primary diagnosis of alcohol and other substance abuse, and mental health issues are allowed, if stabilized. No adolescent with a major untreated psychiatric personality disorder or with pending felony adjudication is admitted. In addition, the adolescent must be free of infectious disease and have no gross to mild retardation affecting treatment participation. A pregnant adolescent may be accepted in her first trimester with physician's approval.

Program Environment

Milieu

A majority of the adolescents admitted to OYOF have significant behavioral disruption and emotional vulnerability, therefore the milieu is one of low stimulation and is very structured. A behavioral log is utilized to provide the needed intervention, and the program supports a positive reinforcement model with no punishment. The staff does not use confrontation but rather a "care-frontation" model. Care-frontation is used to allow the adolescent to have choices and learn respect through the modeling of the staff. If an adolescent becomes aggressive, and/or will not participate, the team discusses the choices with the adolescent.

Staff Training

Ninety percent of the staff consists of American Indians who have various levels of education and licensure. All staff members including Native-American healing practitioners are licensed alcohol and drug abuse counselors or are licensed alcohol and drug abuse interns. A majority of the staff has limited college experience and are considered paraprofessionals. The staff also includes one PhD clinical psychologist, one master level art therapist, and one registered, certified alcohol and drug nurse. Medical, psychiatric, and emergency services are provided through the Indian Health Medical Center.

OUTCOME SURVEY

Our Youth Our Future provides follow-up for one year after discharge to determine the level of functioning of the adolescent once they have returned to their community. This information is utilized to modify the treatment that supports the improvement of the standard of care. The adolescents, aftercare counselors, probation officers, and referral agents are sent the same survey every ninety days for one year. The survey consists of questions on relapse status, new mental health issues, legal issues, school attendance, family problems, and aftercare attendance. In addition, an exit survey is conducted at the day of discharge with the family and the adolescent. In 1997 the exit survey reported that the family attendance was 33 percent and with the implementation of the culturally competent treatment model the family attendance (81 percent) has significantly increased over the past three years. This suggests that the bicultural emphasis may have influenced the increase participation of the families with their adolescents.

CONCLUSION

It is clearly demonstrated that AI/AN youth have substance abuse usage that is disproportionately higher than the general population. It is also clear that a limited appropriate continuum of care is offered to the AI/AN on the reservation and border towns. The follow-up survey suggests that six months after discharge the treatment effect begins to dissolve and at twelve months has disappeared. The reason for this could be that minimal to no appropriate aftercare services are available to the discharged adolescents in their communities. A majority of the adolescents and their families receive AA/NA support, but no individual or family treatment. There is a great need to fill this service gap on the reservation and in border towns, and should the appropriate treatment be available, the follow-up rates may reflect a more positive outcome. Some major barriers that American Indian and Alaska Native youths face are substandard education, continuation of the use of boarding schools, a heritage of traumatic parenting, violent communities, and the prevalence of alcohol and other substance use. Our Youth Our Future has found that the implementation of a bicultural competent treatment approach supports the successful completion of treatment, improves family participation in treatment, increases the cultural identity, and subsequently provides an environment that fosters long-term sobriety and improved productivity.

REFERENCES

Abbott, P.J. (1998). Traditional and Western healing practices for alcoholism in American Indian and Alaska Natives. *Substance Use and Misuse 33*(13), 2605-2646.

Accurate Assessments (n.d.). Native American Software. Omaha, Nebraska. Catalog available online: <http://www.accurateassessments.com/native.htm>.

Bean, N.M. (1992). Elucidating the path toward alcohol and substance abuse by adolescent victims of sexual abuse. *The Journal of Applied Social Sciences, 17,* 57-94.

Beauvais, F. (1996). Trends in drug use among American Indian students and dropouts, 1975 to 1994. *American Journal of Public Health, 86,* 1594-1598.

Beuke, V.L. (1978). The relationship of cultural identification to personal adjustments of American Indian children in segregation and integrated schools. *(Dissertation Abstracts International, 38,* 7203A. (University of Microfilms No. 7809310).)

Boyce, W. and Boyce, T. (1983). Acculturation and changes in health among Navajo boarding school students. *Social Science and Medicine, 17,* 219-226.

Briere, J. (1995). *The trauma symptom checklist for children (TSCC): Professional manual.* Psychological Assessment Resources, Inc., Odessa, Florida.

Bureau of Justice Statistics (1993). Bureau of Justice Statistics Fiscal Year 1993. Office of Justice Programs in the U.S. Department of Justice, Washington, DC.

Centers for Disease Control and Prevention. CDC Surveillance Summaries, June 9, 2000. *Youth risk behavior surveillance—United States, 1999.* (Morbidity and Mortality Weekly Report 2000; 49 No. SS-5). Atlanta, GA: U.S. Department of Health and Human Services.

Chavers, D. (1991). Indian education: Dealing with a disaster. *Principal, 70,* 28-29.

Childre, D., Martin, H., and Beech, D. (1999). *The HeartMath solution.* New York: HarperCollins.

Christian, C.M., Dufour, M., and Bertolucci, D. (1989). Differential alcohol-related mortality among American Indian tribes in Oklahoma, 1968-1978. *Social Sciences and Medicine, 28*(3), 275-284.

Coulehan, J.L. (1980). Navajo Indian medicine: Implications for healing. *Journal of Family Practice, 10,* 55-61.

Craig, G. (1999). *Emotional freedom therapy manual.* (Version 3). Available on-line: <www.emofree.com/eftmanl.pdf>.

DeBruyn, L.M., Lujan, C.C., and May, P.A. (1992). A comparative study of abused and neglected American Indian children in the Southwest. *Social Science and Medicine, 35,* 305-315.

Development Associates (1983). *Final report: The evaluation of the impact in the Part A Entitlement Program funded under Title IV of the Indian Education Act.* Arlington, VA: Author.

Duclos, C.W., Beals, J., Novins, D.K., Martin, C., Jewett, C.S., and Manson, S. M. (1998). Prevalence of common psychiatric disorders among American Indian adolescent detainees. *Journal of the American Academy of Child Adolescent Psychiatry, 37*(8), 866-873.

Fairchild, D.G., Fairchild, M., and Stoner, S. (1998). Prevalence of adult domestic violence among women seeking routine care in a Native American health care facility. *American Journal of Public Health, 88*(10), 1515-1517.

Fisher, D.G., Lankford, B.A., Galea, R.P. (1996). Therapeutic community retention among Alaska Natives: Akeela House. *Journal of Substance Abuse Treatment, 13*(3), 265-271.

Fitzpatrick, K.M. and Boldizar, J.P.(1993). The prevalence and consequences of exposure to violence among African-American youth. *Journal of the American Academy of Child and Adolescent Psychiatry, 32,* 424-430.

Garcia, H.S. (1983). Bilingualism, biculturalism and the educational system. *Journal of Non-White Concerns in Personnel and Guidance, 11,* 67-74.

Groves, B.M. (1997). Growing up in a violent world: The impact of family and community violence on young children and their families. *Topics in Early Childhood Special Education, 17,* 74-102.

Gutierres, S.E. and Todd, M. (1997). The impact of childhood abuse on treatment outcomes of substance users. *Professional Psychology: Research and Practice, 28,* 348-354.

Hisnanick, J.J. (1994). Comparative analysis of violent deaths in American Indians and Alaska Natives. *Social Biology, 41,* 96-109.

Ireland, T. and Widom, C.S. (1994). Childhood victimization and risk for alcohol and drug arrests. *The International Journal of the Addictions, 29,* 235-274.

Kaufman, A. S. and Kaufman, N. L. (1990). *Kaufman Brief Intelligence Test: Manual.* Circle Pines, MN: American Guidance Science.

Kilpatrick, D.G., Acierno, R., Resnick, H.S., Saunders, B.E., and Best, C.L. (1997). A 2-year longitudinal analysis of the relationships between violent assault and substance use in women. *Journal of Consulting and Clinical Psychology, 65,* 834-847.

Kilpatrick, D.G., Acierno, R., Saunders, B., Resnick, H.S., Best, C.L., and Schnurr, P.P. (2000). Risk factors for adolescent substance abuse and dependence data from a national sample. *Journal of Consulting and Clinical Psychology, 68*(1), 19-30.

Kline, J.A. and Roberts, A.C. (1973). A residential alcoholism treatment program for American Indians. *Quarterly Journal of Studies of Alcohol, 34,* 860-868.

LaFromboise, T.D. (1983). *Assertion training with American Indians.* Los Cruces, NM: Eric Clearinghouse on Rural Education.

LaFromboise, T.D. (1988). American Indian mental health policy. *American Psychologist, 43,* 388-397.

LaFromboise, T.D., Coleman, H.L.K., and Gerton, J. (1993). Psychological impact of biculturalism evidence and theory. *Psychological Bulletin, 3,* 395-412.

Lang, G.M.C. (1974). Adaptive strategies of urban Indian drinkers. Unpublished doctoral dissertation, University of Missouri, Columbia, MO.

Lincoln, M.E. (1999). Native American Alcohol and Substance Abuse Program Consolidation Act. Senate Committee on Indian Affairs, Hearing on S. 1507.

Linehan, M.M., Armstrong, H.E., Suarez, A., Allmon, D., and Heard, H.L. (1991). Cognitive-behavioral treatment of chronically parasuicidal borderline patients. *Archives of General Psychiatry, 48,* 1060-1064.

Linehan, M.M., Heard, H.L., and Armstrong, H.E. (1993). Naturalistic follow-up of a behavioral treatment for chronically parasuicidal borderline patients. *Archives of General Psychiatry, 50,* 971-974.

Mariano, A.J., Donovan, D.M., Walker, P.S., Mariano, M.J., and Walker, D. (1989). Drinking-related locus of control and the drinking status of urban Native Americans. *Journal of Studies on Alcohol, 50,* 331-338.

May, P.A. (1982). Substance abuse and American Indians: Prevalence and susceptibility. *International Journal of the Addictions, 17*(7), 1185-1209.

May, P.A. (1986). Alcohol and drug misuse prevention programs for American Indians: Needs and opportunities. *Journal of Studies on Alcohol, 47,* 187-195.

May, P.A. (1994). The epidemiology of alcohol abuse among American Indians: The mythical and real properties. *American Indians Culture and Research Journal, 18,* 121-143.

McCaffrey, B. (2000). U.S. aims anti-drug ads at Indians. White House Conference of Tribal Leaders and substance abuse experts.

McFee, M. (1968). The 150 percent man, a product of Blackfeet acculturation. *American Anthropologist, 70,* 1096.

Millon, T. (1993). The Millon Adolescent Clinical Inventory. Description available online: <http://assessments.ncs.com/assessments/tests/maci.htm> (MACI).

Moncher, M.S., Holden, G.W., and Trimble, J.E. (1990). Substance abuse among Native-American youth. *Journal of Consulting and Clinical Psychology, 58*(4), 408-415.

National Center for American Indian and Alaska Native Mental Health Research (NCAIANMHR) (1999). *Foundations of Indian teens.* Denver, CO: University of Colorado Health Sciences Center.

National Indian Justice Center (1992). Child abuse and neglect in American Indian and Alaska Native communities and the role of the Indian Health Service. Phase III, final report, Petaluma, California.

Ogbu, J.U. and Matute-Bianchi, M.A. (1986). Understanding sociocultural factors: Knowledge, identity, and social adjustment. In California State Department of Education, Bilingual Education Office, *Beyond language: Social and cultural factors in schooling* (pp. 73-142). Sacramento: CA: California State University-Los Angeles, Evaluation, Dissemination and Assessment Center.

Ollendick, T.H. (1996). Violence in youth: Where do we go from here? Behavior therapy's response. *Behavior Therapy, 27,* 485-514.

Poupart, L.M. (1995). Juvenile justice processing of American Indian youths: Disparity in one rural county. In Leonard, K.K., Pope, C.E., Feyerherm, W.H. (Eds.), *Minorities in Juvenile Justice* (pp. 179-200). Thousand Oaks, CA: Sage.

Rashid, H.M. (1984). Promoting biculturalism in young African-American children. *Young Children, 39*, 13-23.

Robin, R.W., Chester, B., and Rasmussen, J.K. (1998). Intimate violence in a Southwestern American Indian tribal community. *Cultural Diversity and Mental Health, 4*(4), 335-344.

Rogler, L.H., Cortes, D.E., and Malgady, R.G. (1991). Acculturation and mental health status among Hispanics. *American Psychologist, 46*, 585-597.

Schiller, P.M. (1987). Biculturalism and psychosocial adjustment among Native American university students. *Dissertation Abstracts International, 48*, 1542A. (University Microfilms No. DA8720632).

Schinke, S.P., Botvin, G.J., Trimble, J.E., Orlandi, M.A., Gilchrist, L.D., and Locklear, V.S. (1988). Preventing substance abuse among American Indian adolescents: A bicultural competence skill approach. *Journal of Counseling Psychology, 35*, 87-90.

Segall, M.M. (1986). Culture and behavior: Psychology in global perspective. *Annual Review of Psychology, 37*, 523-564.

Snake, R., Hawkins, G., and LaBoueff, S. (1977*). Report on alcohol and drug abuse Task Force Eleven: Alcohol and drug abuse.* Final report to the American Indian Policy Review Commission. Washington, DC: Author.

Stevenson, H.C. (1996). Theoretical considerations in measuring racial identity and socialization: Extending the self further. In R. Jones (Ed.), *Theoretical advances in Black psychology* (pp. 498-508). Hampton, VA: Cobb and Henry.

Stewart, T., May, P., and Muneta, A. (1980). A Navajo health consumer survey. *Medical Care, 18*, 1183-1195.

Substance Abuse and Mental Health Services Administration (SAMHSA) (1998). National Household Survey of Drug Use. Rockville, Maryland.

Surgeon General (1999). The Surgeon General's call to action to prevent suicide, 1999. Office of the Assistant Secretary of Health/Surgeon General.

Swaim, R.C., Oetting, E.R., Edwards, R.W., and Beauvais, F. (1989). Links from emotional distress to adolescent drug use: A path model. *Journal of Consulting and Clinical Psychology, 57*, 227-231.

Taylor, M.J. (2000). The influence of self-efficacy on alcohol use among American Indians. *Cultural Diversity and Ethnic Minority Psychology, 6*(2), 152-167.

Towle, L.H. (1975). Alcoholism treatment outcomes in different populations. In Chafetz, M.E. (Ed.). *Research treatment and prevention: Proceedings of the Fourth Annual Alcoholism Conference of the National Institute on Alcohol Abuse and Alcoholism.* Washington, DC: NIAAA (SUDICS No. HE 20.8314.974).

U.S. Department of the Interior (1988). *Report of BIA education: Excellence in Indian education through effective schools process.* Washington, DC: U.S. Government Printing Office.

Walker, R.D., Benjamin, G.A.H., Kiviahan, D.R., and Walker, P.S. (1989). *American Indian alcohol misuse and treatment outcome: Epidemiology of alcohol use and abuse among U.S. minorities.* Research Monograph No. 18, DHHS Publication No. (ADM) 87-1435, Washington, DC: Government Printing Office.

Weibel-Orlando, J. (1984) Indian alcoholism treatment programs as flawed rites of passage. *Medical Anthropology Quarterly, 15*(3), 62-67.

Weisner, T., Weibel-Orlando, J., and Long, J. (1984) Serious drinking, white man's drinking and teetotaling: Predictors of drinking level differences in an urban Indian population. *Journal of Studies on Alcohol, 45*(3), 237.

Westermeyer, J. and Neider, J. (1984). Predicting treatment outcome after ten years among American Indian alcoholics. *Alcoholism: Clinical and Experimental Research 8*(2), 179-184.

Windle, M. (1990). A longitudinal study of antisocial behaviors in early adolescence as predictors of late adolescent use: Gender and ethnic group differences. *Journal of Abnormal Psychology, 99*(1), 86-91.

Chapter 8

La Cañada Adolescent Treatment Program: Addressing Issues of Drug Use, Gender, and Trauma

Sally J. Stevens
Joseph Hasler
Bridget S. Murphy
Rebekah Taylor
Mark Senior
Martha Barron
Patricia Garcia
Zöe Powis

INTRODUCTION

Although the number of high school students who use illicit substances is somewhat lower than it was in the 1970s, adolescent use of illicit drugs continues to be of significant concern (see Dennis et al., 2003). Increasingly alarming is the fact that the purity and potency of drugs used by teens today has increased 19 to 49 percent, while prices have decreased dramatically (White House Office of National Drug Control Policy, 1998). In addition, only 1 percent of teens who have used illicit drugs report having received substance abuse

This study was funded by the Substance Abuse Mental Health Service Administration-Center for Substance Abuse Treatment (SAMHSA-CSAT) grant # KD1 TI11422. The opinions expressed in this paper are those of the authors and do not reflect the official position of SAMHSA-CSAT.

For reprints and information contact: Sally J. Stevens, PhD, Services Research Office, University of Arizona, 3912 S. 6th Avenue, Tucson, AZ 85714; e-mail: <sstevens@dakotacom.net>; phone: (520) 434-0334.

treatment (McGeary et al., 1998). Drug trends in Tucson, Arizona, are higher for some drugs compared to national trends. In 1995, 17 percent of Arizona's high school seniors reported using methamphetamines, which is four times the national average. In a one year period, amphetamine use among Arizona's teens rose 34 percent (Drug Strategies, 1996). Besides the use of methamphetamines, the use of alcohol, marijuana, tobacco, LSD, cocaine, and Rohypnol (a powerful sedative known as the "date-rape" drug) are popular drugs among drug-involved youth living in Tucson (Henry, 1998). Because the issues that surround drug use are many and complex, it is difficult to provide clear-cut answers as to why drug use among teens in Tucson is so prevalent. Southern Arizona presents many problems to adolescents and their families that add to the complexity of drug use and treatment. A large percentage of youth who use drugs come from homes in which parents or guardians use drugs, and many families in Tucson are first generation families who lack extended family support (CODAC, 1996). It has been suggested that the high rate of drug use in southern Arizona is also related to its proximity to Mexico; residents of Tucson have easy availability to a wide array of drugs coming from south of the U.S.-Mexico border.

Arizona ranks as the forty-sixth state in the national Kids Count survey, a survey which examines both positive and negative factors related to child and adolescent well-being. According to the survey, Arizona's children experience 30 percent more poverty today than in the 1980s, with family poverty up 27 percent (Sanders and Henry, 1999). Arizona's poverty rate is 46 percent for those under six years old, compared with 12 percent for the national average (Wabnik, 1998). Arizona's large immigrant population contributes to this factor, as immigrants tend to have a lower income level than nonimmigrants. Despite its large indigent population, however, Arizona ranks thirtieth in the nation in providing services for the poor (Wabnik, 1998).

Poverty in Arizona is unlikely to diminish soon due to the increasing high school dropout rate, which, at 16 percent, is the highest in the nation. Arizona's Native American and Hispanic populations have dropout rates of 18.8 percent and 17 percent, respectively. High school dropouts are predicted to earn 30 percent less in wages than those who earn their high school diplomas (Sanders and Henry, 1999), and unless something is done to reduce the dropout rate, it seems likely that the current poverty trends in Arizona will continue. Notably, adolescents who live in poverty are more likely to have children than adolescents in other economic groups, and lack the emotional and financial support necessary to effectively raise children. Arizona's teen pregnancy rate of 35 percent, compared to the national rate 32.6 percent, is the second highest in the nation.

Many other negative factors have been linked to substance abuse, including suicidal ideation, abuse, and neglect. Arizona's adolescent suicide rate is twice the national average at 24 suicides per 100,000 teens (Sanders and Henry, 1999). In nearly 90 percent of child abuse and neglect cases substance abuse is a primary factor, and an increasing number of babies are being born with drug-related problems (McKinnon, 1997). From 1990 to 1995, child abuse-related deaths tripled in Arizona (Volante, 1996).

Harper and McLanahan (1998) demonstrated that adolescents in nonintact families (without a mother and father in the home) are twice as likely to use drugs and be involved in the juvenile justice system. Nonintact families are common in Arizona as are juvenile arrests. Juvenile arrests for drug violations have more than tripled in Arizona from just over 1,000 in 1990 to approximately 5,000 in 1995 (Arizona Department of Juvenile Corrections, 2000). Arizona has an exceptionally high crime rate, second only to the District of Columbia (Collins and Keith, 1998). With 8,214 crimes per 100,000 population, Arizona's crime rate rose 4.1 percent from 1990, while the national average dropped 9.3 percent. For Tucson, the crime rate of 9,785 per 100,000 population exceeded that of the overall state, and was even higher than that of the Phoenix area of 8,790 per 100,000 (Collins and Keith, 1998). Many Tucson teens have witnessed and/or been involved in violent crimes, contributing to a high level of experienced trauma (Stevens and Murphy, 1999).

In summary, Arizona ranks higher than the national average in poverty, high school dropout, teen pregnancy, teen suicide, child abuse and neglect, violent crimes, and juvenile arrests. These factors are not only strongly related to substance abuse among adolescents living in Arizona, but also add to the difficulties of providing appropriate, diverse, and culturally competent drug treatment services. To address these issues along with the problem of substance abuse among adolescents living in southern Arizona, a residential step-down program, La Cañada, was developed to meet the needs of this population.

LA CAÑADA TREATMENT PROGRAM

Overview

In response to the need for adolescent substance abuse treatment services in Tucson, Arizona, two not-for-profit social service agencies, Arizona's Children Association (AzCA) and CODAC Behavioral Health Services (CODAC), proposed to provide a residential step-down program for adolescent substance users. In 1996, the La Cañada Adolescent Treatment Program (La Cañada) was established, with AzCA providing the housing component of the residential phase, and CODAC providing the substance abuse treatment curriculum for both the residential phase and the intensive and nonintensive aftercare phases.

AzCA is the largest private, nonprofit, nonsectarian organization in Arizona, providing child welfare and behavioral health services to children and families. AzCA was founded in 1912 as an orphanage. Today, AzCA is a statewide, full-service agency providing a comprehensive array of services to severely abused or troubled children and their families. The focus of AzCA is protecting children and preserving families.

CODAC Behavioral Health Services, Inc. was established in 1970, and is a community-based, private, nonprofit agency that provides a full continuum of managed behavioral health care either directly or through subcontracts. CODAC has thirty years experience in providing behavioral health and prevention services in southern Arizona. CODAC has extensive specialized services for juveniles, specifically adjudicated youth.

In 1998, AzCA and CODAC officials approached the University of Arizona's Services Research Office (UofA-SRO) about the possibility of conducting an extensive process and outcome evaluation of the La Cañada program, as their preliminary data indicated that the program was successful in intervening with drug-involved youth. The UofA-SRO is part of the Southwest Institute for Research on Women (SIROW), and is well known for its evaluation studies on social and health issues, particularly issues involving substance use and health consequences of drug use. Together, AzCA, CODAC, and UofA-SRO were awarded the Adolescent Treatment Model evaluation grant sponsored by the Substance Abuse and Mental Health Service Administration's (SAMHSA) Center for Substance Abuse Treatment (CSAT) (see Dennis et al., 2003).

The La Cañada program is funded by tobacco tax dollars from the state of Arizona. The program serves an ethnically diverse population of male and female adolescents age twelve to seventeen years. To be admitted into La Cañada, referred adolescents must have a DSM Axis I diagnosis of substance abuse and be from one of Arizona's five southern counties, two of which are on the U.S./Mexican border. Adolescents in need of detoxification services are referred to and must complete detoxification prior to entering La Cañada. There are three exclusionary criteria: (1) the client requires a lockdown facility or intensive supervision due to homicidal or suicidal ideation (based on a psychiatric evaluation); (2) the client's IQ is such that he or she would be unable to benefit from the program (based on school records and/or testing); and (3) the client is receiving any other state subsidy. The vast majority of adolescents enrolled in La Cañada are referred from the five juvenile county courts (87 percent). The other clients are referred to La Cañada by other behavioral health care agencies (7 percent), and by families and self-referral (6 percent). All youths enter the residential phase first and are "stepped-down" to the intensive aftercare and nonintensive aftercare phases.

Program Philosophy

The La Cañada program provides an integrated treatment model that combines traditional psychiatric and milieu approaches with systems theory. It is believed that the problems of chemical dependency, substance abuse, and antisocial behaviors are often indicative of larger family dysfunction. Since the family is viewed to be the cornerstone of successful treatment, family therapy and involvement are essential to the program. The La Cañada program provides a structured living environment for each resident which addresses and remediates problems and issues associated with daily living, personal care, social development, interpersonal behavior, and recreation. The therapeutic milieu is considered to be a critical factor in the treatment and rehabilitation of the adolescents placed in the La Cañada p gram. The milieu is designed to be a supportive environment that fosters growth, development, and the movement toward an adolescent's reintegration into the community. Abstinence from alcohol and drug use is the goal, however when youths report using drugs, the incident is reviewed and used as a learning experience for deeper understanding of why the adolescent engaged in drug use on that occasion. Community involvement opportunities provide healthy alternatives to the use and abuse of substances, and treatment encourages a high level of involvement in the milieu. Clinical services include family, individual, and group therapy. The treatment plan and criteria for successful treatment are negotiated with the adolescent and the family during the residential phase of the program and are carried out during residential and the two aftercare phases of treatment.

Intake Assessment

Prior to intake, adolescents undergo a physical examination to determine medical health status and stability for intake. This assessment is a Joint Commission on Accreditation of Healthcare Organizations (JCAHO) mandated assessment. Adolescents also undergo a nursing assessment twenty-four hours after intake as governed by AzCA regulations. Medical assessments are very useful tools, as they aid in determining the appropriateness for treatment and need for medical stabilization prior to intake. Medical assessments also demonstrate areas of need and possible barriers to treatment. For example, the medical assessment might reveal the presence of a sexually transmitted disease (STD), which then becomes an area of treatment focus.

At intake, a psychosocial assessment is conducted by a masters level or bachelor's level (with experience) case manager. The assessment obtains the adolescent's history in areas such as school, family, previous substance use, prenatal and child development, exposure to domestic violence, abuse, substance use, previous traumas, coping skills, and other areas of concern. If areas of psychiatric concern are identified the intake evaluator may recommend that a complete psychiatric assessment be conducted. The intake evaluator uses information from the psychosocial assessment (and in some cases the psychiatric assessment) to develop strategies for treatment, to aid in individualization of the treatment plan, and to identify barriers to stabilization within the treatment milieu. Clients are admitted to La Cañada in an ongoing basis (versus as a cohort) as openings occur.

Phase I: Residential

The Phase I residential component includes treatment slots for six males and three females. It is thirty days in duration, and occurs in an unlocked facility (i.e., house) located in a residential neighborhood in Tucson, Arizona. The house has three medium-sized bedrooms, each housing two adolescent boys. The three adolescent girls are housed at the AzCA main campus located approximately seventeen miles from the La Cañada house, and are transported to and from La Cañada every day for treatment. A large kitchen is available where meals are prepared and a dining room where the meals are served. Meetings and group counseling sessions take place in the large living room, which also is used for relaxation. A large garage was converted into a recreation room and a separate small office for the house manager and other house staff. A large fenced-in backyard contains a Jacuzzi, an in-ground swimming pool, a small garden area, and a porch with tables and chairs.

The staff that oversee the residential component work for AzCa while the substance abuse treatment staff who facilitate the curriculum work for CODAC. Both sets of staff have male and female employees most of whom are professionally trained without recovery in their background. However, both agencies attempt to have diversity (e.g., gender, ethnicity, Spanish speaking, individuals in recovery) within their staffing pattern. CODAC staff conducting therapy must have degrees and licensures to meet accreditation standards.

The Phase I residential component allows the adolescents to take a "time out" from the pressures of their family, school, and community life, enabling the youth to engage in self-examination in a highly structured, drug-free environment. This externally guarded sobriety offers the youth the opportunity to experience thirty days of clear thinking and increased physical, emotional, and social health while addressing family issues in a safe and protected milieu. This phase begins the process of developing a sense of pride and hope for the future, giving adolescents the motivation needed to continue their recovery in Phase II when they return home from the residential phase of treatment. The weekly therapeutic intervention during the residential phase includes

1. individual therapy,
2. family therapy,
3. group therapy,
4. psychoeducational groups, and
5. case management.

Individual Therapy (One Hour per Week)

Individual therapy is conducted by the primary therapist/substance abuse counselor at the La Cañada residence. The goal of individual therapy is to uncover previously unexplored issues that have contributed to the adolescent's dysfunction. Individual therapy offers the clients a private place to disclose issues and feelings that they might not feel comfortable sharing with the group, such as sexual abuse, other trauma, sexual orientation, and sensitive family concerns. Individual therapy is also a logical place to encourage a commitment to recovery, explore the consequences of substance abuse, and acknowledge the impact substance abuse has had in the adolescent's life.

Family Therapy (One Hour per Week)

While providing a "locus of stability" for youth, Phase I is a crucial time of preparation to cope with the damage substance abuse has inflicted upon the adolescent's family. Upon admission to La Cañada, the family therapist meets with parents or guardians at CODAC's central office to assess the need for family education and treatment rehabilitation. In many cases, the family system has enabled the youth's substance abuse and disruptive behaviors; consequently, this system must be addressed and restructured before the client can be expected to make major life changes and before he or she returns home. The family therapist assesses what work needs to be done with the family before, during, and after the youth's residential stay. The family therapist, in conjunction with the therapeutic team, negotiates a behavioral goal agreement between the youth and the family. The agreement forms the basis of recovery for both the client and the family, and sets the stage for ongoing family recovery once the youth returns home.

Group Therapy (Five Hours per Week)

Group therapy is held in the living room of the La Cañada house and is led by one of the La Cañada staff members (i.e., substance abuse counselor, psychologist). All of the adolescents (both boys and girls) participate in the group therapy sessions, although there may be some times when the sexes are separated to address gender-specific issues. Strategies are used to develop trust, empathy, and support within the group, as well as confront behaviors that are destructive and antisocial. Each of the four weeks during the residential phase of treatment focuses on a theme:

1. identity and self-esteem;
2. family and relationships;
3. emotions and feelings; and
4. life management skills.

Groups which occur during Phase 1 cover the topics of family roles, identification of feelings, and identity, and coincide with the four-week curriculum utilized by the residential team. Family roles group focuses on educating the clients about dysfunctional familial behavior patterns. The identification of feelings group focuses on clients' awareness of their own feelings. The identity groups have two themes; one group focuses on "self-concept," and the other group focuses on "self-worth." For the "self-concept" theme a compact disk (CD) exercise is facilitated in which clients create a CD cover that represents who they are. The clients express themselves pictorially through the CD cover and generate a list of song titles to be included on the CD. For the "self-worth" theme, an advertisement exercise is facilitated in which the clients draw an advertisement promoting themselves, and then identify and discuss their positive attributes. The clinical staff can use these two identity groups interchangeably; the self-concept theme is designed to be effective with adolescents who have little identity outside of drug usage, while the self-worth theme works well with adolescents whose self-worth is notably low.

The remaining groups are chosen depending on the client population and their therapeutic needs. For example, the Johari window/secrets group is routinely facilitated when the treatment team believes the group to be holding secrets that negatively impact upon the group dynamics. This group emphasizes the importance of seeing your own blind spots and sharing your secrets to enhance the treatment process. Secrets are written out by all participants, including the facilitator, and placed anonymously in a container. All secrets are then read by the facilitator to the group and discussed. A DSM-IV group is conducted when the majority of clients are new to treatment or appear untrusting of treatment. The DSM-IV group provides clients an introduction to the diagnostic procedures for substance abuse treatment; it provides an objective view of how diagnoses are made, and is aimed at relieving anxiety about having labels attached to clients arbitrarily. Process groups are helpful when residents lack communication skills or have open conflicts. Clients learn how to communicate more respectively with others through exercises which teach ownership of feelings and behavior, as well as ways to offer feedback in an appropriate, nonaggressive way.

Psychoeducational Groups (Three Hours per Week)

During the residential phase, weekly groups focus on the drug most commonly abused by these adolescents; each week a different class of drugs is presented. In addition, each week has a secondary focus, which covers topics related to the emotional and familial contributors to drug abuse, as well as skills needed to deal with stressful situations without the use of drugs. During week one, the educational focus is on cocaine and crystal methamphetamine. Education is provided on the history of the drugs, along with physical, psychological, and social effects of their use. The second focus during week one is on building self-esteem through daily activities, including trust building; team building; identity exploration; affirmation groups; the gaining and giving of respect; and defining goals and dreams. Examples of trust building exercises include a group on secrets or a trust walk. Adolescents gain team building skills through a day of indoor/outdoor challenge activities, such as separating into teams and building a tower out of paper. Identity exploration is facilitated through activities such as body mapping, ceramic mask making, group games, the ropes course, and constructing a family portrait. Affirmation groups involve the giving and receiving of positive messages. Respect is taught through acknowledging and admiring diversity, including diversity in areas such as family traditions, gender, ethnicity, and religion. Diversity is processed in the group to help clients learn about and gain respect for others. Goals and dreams are explored through activities such as nature hikes and autobiographic presentations.

During week two, adolescents learn about the history of alcohol use in the United States, as well as the physical, psychological, and social effects of alcohol. The second area of focus is family and relationships, which is addressed through discussion and activities, including communication; problem solving; prejudice and discrimination; sexual awareness; morals and values; and family history. Adolescents explore communication through charades/role-play, the telephone game, the "mad libbing" game, and through organized debates. Problem solving is explored through role-play, the indoor/ outdoor challenge, a mystery game, and other problem-solving activities. Prejudice and discrimination are explored through a segregation of privileges that take place throughout a day (with later processing), and discussions of experiences and individual prejudices. Adolescents explore sexual awareness through an HIV/STD prevention group, a "sex feud" game (concerning sexual facts), and group discussions and questions. The exploration of morals and values is accomplished through group discussion, a lifeboat ethics exercise, and creation of a family crest. Family history is explored through drawing, discussion of the family house, family visits, and the weekly wrap up/discussion of events.

The focus of week three includes education on the history of the use of hallucinogens, along with its physical, psychological, and social effects. Management skills are the second area of emphasis. Management skills include hygiene and manners; jobs and careers; money and budgeting; education; planning and organization; and hobbies and interests. Hygiene and manners are discussed and learned through educational groups, and through a game called "hygiene jeopardy." Jobs and careers are researched through quizzes, exploring resources, completing a job application, interview groups, discussions of work ethics, and possible Growth Activities and Self-Help (GASH) activities. Adolescents learn about money and budgeting through a daylong budgeting workshop, and in training sessions on shopping and banking (checking and savings accounts). Home skills are learned through educational groups, participation in meal preparation, and specific instruction (i.e., setting an alarm clock, house cleaning). The importance of education itself is explored through discussions of how one learns, the acquisition of study skills, and library field trips. Adolescents learn about planning and organization in several groups, as well as through the planning of the day's activities. Hobbies and interests are explored through discussions and GASH activities, which include recreational, volunteer, spiritual, or work activities to replace previous drug-involved activities.

Week four focuses on the history of marijuana use, as well as the physical, psychological, and social effects of the drug. The second focus of week four involves exploration, identification, expression, and management of emotions; anger management; grief and loss; love and commitment; and conflict resolution. Clients are encouraged to express emotions through discussion of previous experiences and conflicts. The skills of anger management, dealing with grief and loss, and love and commitment are explored through therapeutic groups and activities. Adolescents help one another through sharing their sensitive life experiences and their feelings about their experiences. Conflict resolution techniques are learned through exploration of house and family conflicts, and participation in self-fulfillment exercises. Every week ends with a wrap-up and discussion.

Case Management (Four Hours per Week)

Case management services begin at intake when the case manager conducts a face-to-face interview with the client and his or her parent/guardian. During this interview, the case manager completes all the required paperwork for the funding agency, and explains the role of case management in the adolescent's treatment. During Phase I, case management activities consists of telephone and/or face-to-face contact with the primary people in the adolescent's life, including parents, court officials, school personnel, and other community agency staff. These contacts made during Phase I are designed to assist clients with reintegration into the community after they are discharged from the residential component.

Phase II: Intensive Aftercare

After the thirty-day residential component, adolescents are moved into Phase II, the two-month intensive aftercare component. The intensive aftercare component is facilitated by CODAC staff and accommodates approximately eighteen adolescents. Youths from rural counties are referred to aftercare services in their own county. Given this and some inconsistency in aftercare attendance, enrollment in the intensive aftercare component at the Tucson CODAC facility typically ranges from twelve to fifteen clients at any given time. Intensive aftercare includes:

1. family and individual therapy,
2. therapeutic groups,
3. family activities, and
4. community activities.

These activities are facilitated by CODAC staff and are conducted at one of CODAC's outpatient treatment facilities or within the community (i.e., parks, family home). All of the intensive aftercare activities are designed to follow the therapeutic process and strategies developed and implemented during the residential phase.

Family and Individual Therapy (One and a Half Hours per Week)

These services are divided into four family sessions and two individual sessions per month. However, the La Cañada program allows for considerable flexibility, given that it is difficult to engage some families in the treatment process. Consequently, clients with no family involvement would receive six individual sessions per month while those with active family participation would receive more family sessions than individual sessions. Both the family and individual sessions last approximately one hour, and are facilitated by the substance abuse counselor or family therapist. Whether with individuals or with families, the goals and objectives developed during the residential phase are reviewed and adjusted as needed. Problems with the adolescent's reentry into the family system are discussed, and strategies for a successful return are articulated.

Aftercare Groups (One Hour per Week)

Aftercare groups are facilitated by the family therapist and primary counselors twice weekly; each group lasts one hour, and clients must attend one of the two groups. Topics of these groups include the adolescents reintegration into the family, discussion of events or situations that challenge the adolescents sobriety, and any relapses and the triggers that led to that relapse.

Family Activities (Three Hours per Week)

During the family therapy sessions, the family therapist negotiates with the family the structured family activities that are required during the intensive aftercare phase. These activities may include outings to a park or movie theater, family dinners, family projects or board games, or attending sporting events. For uninvolved families, the adolescent is encouraged to interact with siblings and/or other relatives, or to initiate activities with his or her parent/guardian. If family activities cannot be fulfilled, the adolescent is encouraged to become involved in additional community activities.

Community Activity (Five Hours per Week)

Community activities are designed to engage the youth in positive, prosocial activities which alleviate boredom and provide positive alternatives to using drugs and engaging in criminal behavior. Community activities may include volunteer work at local community agencies, recreation/sporting activities at community centers, church activities, and extra educational tutoring or classes. Adolescents discuss their community activity involvement during group and individual sessions.

Phase III: Nonintensive Aftercare

After participating in the two-month intensive aftercare phase, adolescents are moved into Phase III, a two-month nonintensive aftercare component. Again, CODAC staff facilitate the nonintensive aftercare component for Tucson-based youths with attendance consisting of twelve to fifteen youths at any given time. Phase III includes:

1. two hours of individual and/or family therapy per month,
2. one hour of therapeutic group per week,
3. two hours of family activities per week, and
4. two or three hours of community activities per week.

All of these activities are similar to those included in Phase II.

EVALUATION ACTIVITIES

Three types of evaluation activities have been implemented by the UofA-SRO research team. These include (1) a treatment outcome study; (2) a qualitative study; and (3) a cost study. Aggregated findings from each of the evaluation activities are shared with program staff on a regular and as-needed basis. During the intake process, the UofA-SRO evaluation activities are explained to the adolescents and their parents or guardians. If interested in participating in the evaluation component, two sets of consent forms are signed; one by the adolescent and the other by a parent or guardian. Of the adolescents enrolled in La Cañada, 95 percent participated in the evaluation component.

Treatment Outcome Study

The treatment outcome evaluation activities include a baseline assessment completed within seven days of intake, and follow-up assessments at three, six, nine, and twelve months from the date of intake. The baseline interview takes approximately 1.5 to 3 hours, while the follow-up assessments take 1 to 2.5 hours. Variation in the time of the assessment interview is typically due to (1) the client's experiences during the reference period (i.e., substance use, criminal activity, education, employment), (2) the client's ability to recall their activities during the reference period, (3) the client's command of the English language (some report Spanish as their first language), and (4) the client's ability to stay focused. Clients are not paid for the baseline interviews, but are paid $25.00 for each of the follow-up assessment interviews. The baseline and follow-up assessments include the following instruments:

- *Global Appraisal of Individual Needs—Initial (GAIN-I) and Follow-Up (GAIN-M-90).* (See Dennis et al., 2003, for description of assessment.)
- *Hispanic Acculturation Scale.* The scale consists of twelve questions assessing language use, nativity, and ethnic affiliation. This instrument was normed on 600 Mexican-American Hispanics in Arizona (Cronbach's alpha = .89), and has been

used in Tucson's COPASA project with Mexican-American injection drug users (Cronbach's alpha = .92).

- *HIV/AIDS Knowledge and Risk Assessment.* The HIV/AIDS Knowledge and Risk Assessment measures the adolescent's knowledge of HIV/AIDS transmission and their access to and use of contraception.

- *Environmental Stress Inventory.* The inventory measures environmental stress and trauma in the client's life, including grief and loss, gang affiliation, violence, sexual and dating relationships, parental involvement and behaviors, changes in primary settings (i.e., housing, school), and immediate family alcohol and drug use.

- *Adolescent Relapse Coping Questionnaire.* This questionnaire assesses an adolescent's coping skills in relation to substance abuse by providing her or him with hypothetical temptations and situations. Factor analysis conducted on this questionnaire indicates good internal consistency (alpha = .78 to .82).

Qualitative Study

The qualitative study component includes in-depth case studies of selected La Cañada participants; examination of the treatment process; and assessment of parent satisfaction with the treatment program. The case study component includes qualitative sessions with ten adolescents during residential treatment, aftercare, and up to six months after treatment discharge. During the residential phase of treatment, the UofA-SRO ethnographer meets with the adolescents approximately once a week. The qualitative sessions are reduced to approximately two times per month as the youth enters the aftercare phase of treatment. Sessions are continued on a monthly basis for approximately six months after discharge or until the ethnographer reaches redundancy with the participant. All of the case study data are transcribed verbatim from the audiotaped sessions. From the transcribed case study notes, the data are coded into ten categories:

1. Self
2. Family
3. Friends
4. Neighborhood

5. Legal involvement
6. Drug use
7. Drug treatment
8. Mainstream connections
9. Future expectations, and
10. Ethnographic notes

In addition, within the ten broad categories there are many subcategories. These qualitative data are used to illuminate the treatment process, as well as to help interpret findings from the quantitative component.

The UofA-SRO research staff also examine the treatment process by assessing each client's progress through treatment, as well as the client's perception of what treatment components have assisted her or him with the process of change. Parent satisfaction with the La Cañada program is also assessed. The following scales and assessments are used to obtain this information:

- *Counselor-Rated Progress Scale.* This scale is completed by the primary counselor and assesses the client's communication skills, self-esteem, social skills, conflict resolution, and social adjustment, as well as the client's primary caregiver(s)' parental skills. In addition, the primary counselor rates the client's level of participation, genuineness, and attitude during program activities. This scale is collected at two weeks, thirty days, and ninety days postintake.
- *Client-Rated Satisfaction Scale.* This scale asks the clients to rate how program activities have or have not assisted them with change. The client also self-reports the amount of alcohol or other drugs consumed, and whether the amount has increased, decreased, or not changed since being in the program. It is collected at two weeks, thirty days, and ninety days postintake.
- *Parent Satisfaction Questionnaire.* This questionnaire was modified from the Client Rated—Satisfaction Scale. This questionnaire asks the parents to rate how the program's activities have or have not assisted their adolescent with change. The questionnaire also asks the parents to report the amount of substances they believe their child is using or has used. Finally, the parents report how sat-

isfied they have been with La Cañada activities in assisting with personal change and/or other changes in their family.

Cost Study

A cost study examining the cost of treatment was conducted by Capital Consulting Corporation. Cost of treatment matched with treatment outcomes will be examined across the ten Adolescent Treatment Model funded programs (see Dennis et al., 2003, for description of the cost study).

POPULATION DESCRIPTION

As of August 2000, 140 baseline assessments, 113 three-month, 90 six-month, 69 nine-month, and 46 twelve-month follow-up assessments were completed. Completion rates for each of the follow-up assessment points are as follows: 98 percent three-month, 99 percent six-month, 96 percent nine-month, and 90 percent for the twelve-month follow-up assessments. These follow-up assessments are ongoing. For the purpose of this chapter only baseline data are presented, including: (1) client population description; (2) gender differences in drug use; and (3) experience of trauma and stress.

Client Population Description

As described in Table 8.1, the majority of La Cañada clients are male (72.5 percent), aged fifteen to sixteen years old (59.8 percent). Hispanics comprise 46.1 percent of the adolescents. Prior to enrollment, the majority of the youths (86.3 percent) were living in a house or an apartment. The majority of the youths (76.5 percent) reported that prior to enrollment into the La Cañada program, they were not going to school or working. Given this percentage, it is not surprising that average last grade completed in school was 8.6. Fifty-one percent of the youths reported that they needed substance abuse treatment for marijuana. The next largest percentage of substance necessitating treatment was alcohol (15.8 percent). Interestingly, 10.9 percent of the youths self-reported at intake that they did not need treatment for any substance. Almost all of the youths (97.1 percent) reported that the first time they got drunk or used any drugs was before the age

TABLE 8.1. Cross Site Variables (N = 102)

Item	N	%
Gender		
Male	74	72.5
Female	28	27.5
Age		
11-12	1	1.0
13-14	7	6.8
15-16	61	59.8
17-18	33	32.4
19 and over	0	0.
Ethnicity		
American Indian/Alaskan Native	0	0.
Asian or Pacific Islander	0	0.
Black	2	2.0
White	35	34.3
Hispanic (Puerto Rican, Mexican, Cuban, other)	47	46.1
Mixed/some other group	18	17.6
Current living situation		
A house or apartment (yours or parents)	88	86.3
A foster home or public housing	2	2.0
A friend's or relative's house or apartment	8	7.8
A nursing home, hospital, inpatient or residential	2	2.0
Jail, detention center, or other correctional institution	0	0.
Temporary or emergency shelter	1	1.0
Vacant buildings	0	0.
Any other housing situation	1	1.0
Present work or school situation		
Working full time	0	0.
Working part time	1	1.0
Unemployed or laid off	3	3.0
Have a job, but not working because of treatment, illness, seasonal	4	3.9
In school or training only (even if not in session now)	16	15.6

TABLE 8.1 *(continued)*

Item	N	%
In jail or prison	0	0.
Some other work situation (no school/no work)	78	76.5
Substance dependence (meeting criteria)	82	80.4
Substance treatment needed for		
Any kind of alcohol	16	15.8
Marijuana, hashish, etc.	51	50.5
Crack, freebase cocaine, other cocaine	11	10.9
Amphetamine/methamphetamine	9	8.9
Inhalants	0	0.
Heroin	0	0.
"Acid" or other hallucinogens	3	3.0
Some other drug	0	0.
Nothing	11	10.9
Age when first got drunk or used any drugs		
Below 15	99	97.1
15-18	3	2.9
Over 18	0	0.
Last grade or year completed in school		
< 6	0	0.
6-8	55	53.9
9-10	41	40.2
11-12	6	5.9
> 12	0	0.

	Mean	SD
Times in life arrested, charged with a crime, and booked (median = 7.0; mode = 2.0)	9.41	9.82
Substance use—last 90 days		
Days used alcohol, marijuana, or other drugs	46.6	29.8
Days drunk or high for most of the day	37.6	29.6
Days in a jail (or other place) where you could not use drugs	19.4	19.4
Times in life admitted to drug treatment or counseling	1.4	4.9

of fifteen years old. The average number of times in their life that they were arrested was 9.4; however, this statistic was highly variable (SD = 9.8).

Gender Differences in Drug Use

As described in Table 8.2, several gender differences in drug use were evident. Almost all of the boys and girls have used alcohol and

TABLE 8.2. Gender Differences in Drug Use (n = 102)

	Boys		Girls	
Item	**n**	**percent**	**n**	**percent**
Alcohol				
Ever used	74	99	28	100
Used 90 days prior to treatment	57	78	23	82
Marijuana				
Ever used	74	100	27	96*
Used 90 days prior to treatment	57	77	24	89
Cocaine				
Ever used	58	78	24	86
Used 90 days prior to treatment	28	48	15	63
Downers				
Ever used	48	65	17	61
Used 90 days prior to treatment	17	35	7	41
Hallucinogens				
Ever used	59	80	23	82
Used 90 days prior to treatment	27	46	16	70
Methamphetamine				
Ever used	40	54	23	82*
Used 90 days prior to treatment	11	28	16	70
Heroin				
Ever used	3	4	6	21*
Used 90 days prior to treatment	0	0	3	50

*$p < .05$

marijuana at least once during their lifetime, although significantly more boys than girls have ever used marijuana ($p < .05$). The majority of the girls reported using cocaine and methamphetamine (86 percent and 82 percent respectively), which was much higher than that reported by boys (78 percent and 54 percent respectively). A significant difference ($p < .05$) was also seen in the area of methamphetamine use, with girls reporting more "ever use" than boys. In addition, girls also reported ever using heroin significantly more often than boys, with 21 percent of the girls compared to 4 percent of the boys reporting heroin use. Downers, which include the drug Rohypnol which is very popular in Arizona, were used by approximately the same percent of boys (65 percent) and girls (61 percent), as were hallucinogens (boys = 80 percent; girls = 82 percent). Past ninety-day use was higher in every drug category for girls, with particular differences observed in the use of cocaine, hallucinogens, methamphetamine, and heroin.

Trauma and Stress

As described in Table 8.3, the La Cañada youths have experienced considerable environmental trauma and stress during their lifetimes. Adolescents were queried at intake about different types of stress (i.e., family, social, educational, criminal, and personal), the age that the stress first occurred or that they realized that it was occurring, and how upsetting the first occurrence of that stress was for them. Table 8.3 details the trauma and stress that was experienced by the adolescents, as well as whether or not they found that type of stress to be quite or very upsetting.

Results from the stress inventory indicate that a substantial percentage of adolescents experienced a wide range of stress, typically first occurring between the ages of ten and thirteen years. The percent of youths who reported being upset differed by type of stress. While some types of stress can be categorized in more than one area (i.e., social versus criminal), the data indicate that more stressful events were related to family stress than to any other category. The most common family stress reported was "someone in their family had AOD problems" (81.4 percent), of which 37.3 percent reported being quite or very upset the first time it occurred or they realized it was occurring (average age 9.9 years). In the area of social stress, the most fre-

TABLE 8.3. Stress Inventory (n = 102)

Type	n	%	% upset	Age	SD
Family					
Family member had AOD problems	83	81.4	37.3	9.9	3.9
Moved to a new neighborhood	80	78.4	36.3	10.2	4.0
Family member died (not including parent)	75	73.5	76.0	11.3	3.6
Had serious arguments with siblings	66	64.7	53.0	11.4	3.7
Family member had serious accident or injury that bothered you	63	61.8	81.0	12.2	3.6
Parents divorced or separated	59	57.8	39.0	7.0	0.5
Serious money problems at home	48	47.1	50.0	11.9	3.9
Bothered by a lack of affection and kindness by one or both parents	47	46.1	89.4	11.0	4.0
You physically hurt someone in your family	44	43.1	45.5	12.9	2.9
One or both of your parents remarried	44	43.1	27.3	9.5	4.9
Social: Peers and Partners					
Broke up with partner whom you were dating on a regular basis	77	75.5	57.1	13.5	1.8
An important friend moved away	62	60.8	29.4	11.4	3.6
A close friend died	58	56.9	96.6	13.6	0.5
One of your sexual partners "cheated" on you	57	55.9	64.9	14.1	1.3
You had friends who died violently	53	52.0	98.0	13.8	2.2
Education—Schooling					
Poor grades in school	97	95.1	32.0	11.9	2.7
Suspended or expelled from school	96	94.1	30.2	12.9	2.1
Changed schools	91	89.2	20.9	10.0	3.5
Problems at school	86	84.3	30.2	11.5	2.9
Criminal Behavior and Legal Trouble					
Got in trouble with the law	102	100.0	52.0	12.8	2.3
A family member went to jail/prison	66	64.7	53.0	10.4	4.8
You or your friends were shot at	62	60.8	48.4	13.8	2.1
You were "jumped" by other kids	48	47.1	46.3	13.0	2.3
You were a victim of crime	45	45.1	69.6	11.8	0.5

TABLE 8.3 *(continued)*

Type	n	%	% upset	Age	SD
Personal					
Animal died	75	73.5	65.3	10.3	3.6
You ran away from home	65	63.7	27.7	13.3	2.2
Placed in a new living situation (i.e., foster home, residential setting, or institution)	54	52.9	63.0	14.3	2.9
Had a serious accident or illness	48	47.1	55.3	10.8	4.7
Gained a lot of weight	44	43.1	38.6	14.4	0.5

quently reported stress was "broke up with partner whom they were dating on a regular basis" (75.5 percent), of which 57.1 percent reported being quite or very upset the first time it occurred (average age 13.5 years). With regard to education-related stress, the most common stress reported was "got poor grades in school" (95.1 percent), of which 32.0 percent reported being quite or very upset the first time it occurred (average age 11.9 years). The most frequently reported criminal related stress was "got in trouble with the law" (100 percent), of which 52.0 percent indicated being quite or very upset the first time it occurred (average age 12.8 years). Finally, in the area of personal stress, the most frequently reported stress, was "animal died" (73.5 percent) of which 65.3 percent said they were quite or very upset the first time it occurred (average age 10.3 years).

DISCUSSION

The La Cañada Adolescent Treatment Program addresses adolescent substance use and related problems by working with adolescents and their families through a "step-down" approach. As described in Table 8.1, substantial diversity exists among the clients enrolled in La Cañada. Consequently, the staff must be able to address ethnic/cultural and gender issues, and be able to work with youths from diverse backgrounds and diverse life situations. Ongoing staff training beyond that required by licensing and certification agencies is offered on topics such as gang activities, use and effects of club drugs, Hepatitis B and C, HIV and other sexually transmitted diseases, and culture and acculturation.

Gender differences in drug use among La Cañada participants are noteworthy. While boys and girls report close to the same percentage of downer (including Rohphynol) and hallucinogen use, girls report more cocaine, methamphetamine, and heroin use. This elevated use of harder drugs among girls compared to boys may be due to issues surrounding body image and weight control, as girls report using these drugs recreationally as well as for dieting. In addition, a higher percentage of girls report having been sexually molested as children, which has been noted in the literature as correlating with adolescent substance use. Moreover, La Cañada girls who report having boy-friends indicate that their boyfriends are older than them by an average of three years. These girls may have easier access and more opportunity to use harder drugs, including cocaine, methamphetamine and heroin, because of their relationship with an older male. Another possible reason for greater "hard drug" use among girls compared to boys is that substance using girls are typically more hidden than are boys. Not only do they stay more hidden by living with older men, they also have less contact with the criminal justice system and their contact typically involves offenses (i.e., shoplifting, runaway) that do not merit referral to substance abuse treatment. As with most adolescent programs, referrals to La Cañada were primarily from juvenile probation (87 percent). Consequently, fewer girls are identified, referred, and admitted to La Cañada, and by the time the girls are enrolled many have progressed to harder drug use. From these data, two treatment needs are identified, including the need for gender-specific outreach strategies to identify and enroll girls into treatment, and the need for gender-specific groups, curriculum, and counseling that focuses on body image, self-worth, self-esteem, sexuality, and intimate relationships.

Trauma and stress were experienced by a substantial percent of adolescents who entered the La Cañada program. The vast majority of these stressful events occurred just prior to the onset of substance use. Thought must be given to the impact that these stressful events have on adolescents, and how these events might lead adolescents to use drugs either as a coping strategy or a way of denying their occurrences. Treatment providers must address trauma and stress, and provide avenues for adolescents to not only emote, but to comprehend the link between traumatic life experiences and subsequent behavior. Examination of the data indicates that many of the adolescents already acknowledge how upsetting certain stressful life events have been. Perhaps even more interesting, however, is how many of the adolescents report that these events were *not* upsetting. Getting youths to acknowledge past pain or hurt is the first step to resolution, and should be a major component of any substance abuse treatment program.

In summary, the La Cañada treatment program serves an adolescent population whose substance abuse and criminal behaviors have resulted in criminal justice personnel, counselors, or parents enrolling them into treatment. La Cañada's step-down model allows a month in a residential placement to take "time out" for self-examination in a highly structured, drug-free environment. As reentry can be particularly difficult for these youths, a two-phase (intensive and nonintensive) aftercare system is provided. Although structured programming is utilized, significant focus is also given to the cultural and gender-specific needs of those in treatment. Moreover, attention on individual life experiences and how those experiences impact the adolescent's current behaviors are emphasized in the treatment milieu through assisting clients to effectively deal with emotional pain and environmental stress without the use of drugs and alcohol.

REFERENCES

Arizona Department of Juvenile Corrections (2000). <www.juvenile.state.az.us>.

CODAC (1996). La Cañada: Residential and Aftercare Treatment for Substance Abuse. Proposal prepared for the Community Partnership of Southern Arizona.

Collins, T. and Keith, L.D. (1998). Quality of life: Census data in Arizona are grim. *The Arizona Daily Star,* B-1, column 1-5, August 3.

Dennis, M., Dowud-Noursi, S., Muck, R., and McDermeit, M. (2003). The need for developing and evaluating adolescent treatment models. In S.J. Stevens and A. Morral (Eds.), *Adolescent Substance Abuse Treatment in the United States: Exemplary Models from a National Evaluation Study* (pp. 3-26). Binghamton, NY: The Haworth Press, Inc.

Drug Strategies (1996). *Arizona Profile.* Report prepared for the Robert Wood Johnson Foundation.

Harper, C. and McLanahan, S. (1998). Father absence and youth incarceration. Presented at the American Society Association. Available online: <http://www.preventingdivorce.com/life_without_father.htm>.

Henry, B. (1998). Mending hooked kids. *The Arizona Daily Star;* E-1, column 5, April 5.

McGeary, K.A., Dennis, M.L., French, M.T., and Titus, J.C. (1998). National estimates of marijuana and alcohol use among adolescents: Overlap in use and related consequences. Miami, FL: University of Miami.

McKinnon, S. (1997). Drug abuse soars among Arizona's youths: Far exceeds U.S. average. *The Arizona Daily Star,* A-1. January 28.

Sanders, R.B. and Henry, B. (1999). Sad statistics: Arizona's youth ill-served by stingy state. *The Arizona Daily Star,* A-1, May 18.

Stevens, S.J. and Murphy, B.S. (1999). General and reproductive health: strategies and resources. Presented at the Conference on Gender and Reproductive Health, Scottsdale, AZ, November 18, 1999.

Volante, E. (1996). Death toll from abuse has tripled. *The Arizona Daily Star,* June 27, pp. A-1, A-8.

Wabnik, A. (1998). Poor kids' ranks have soared in Arizona: Increase outpaces nationwide rate. *The Arizona Daily Star.* A-1, July 10.

White House Office of National Drug Control Policy (1998). ONDCP Drug Policy Clearinghouse Fact Sheet: Drug Data Summary. February.

SECTION V:
MODIFIED THERAPEUTIC COMMUNITY TREATMENT MODELS

Chapter 9

An Evaluation of Substance Abuse Treatment Services for Juvenile Probationers at Phoenix Academy of Los Angeles

Andrew R. Morral
Lisa H. Jaycox
William Smith
Kirsten Becker
Patricia Ebener

INTRODUCTION

In the United States, almost half of all adolescent admissions to publicly funded substance abuse treatment programs occur under pressure from the juvenile justice system (Substance Abuse and Mental Health Services Administration, 2001). By this time, however, many youths are extensively involved in truant and delinquent behavior, violence, and high-risk activities such as unprotected sex and driving under the influence of drugs and alcohol. They are often

This chapter was supported by funds from the Center for Substance Abuse Treatment (CSAT) of the Substance Abuse and Mental Health Services Administration, Department of Health and Human Services, grant number TI11433. The opinions expressed herein are those of the authors and do not reflect official positions of the government. We wish to acknowledge the important collaboration and assistance of the Los Angeles Department of Probation, the Superior Courts of Los Angeles, and the individual group homes that agreed to participate in this research as comparison programs.

Please address correspondence to Andrew Morral, Drug Policy Research Center, 1700 Main Street, Santa Monica, CA 90407; Phone: (310) 393-0411 x7791; Fax: (310) 393-4818; e-mail: <morral@rand.org>.

213

alienated from their families and other social institutions, and have adopted a set of attitudes, beliefs, and peers that support their dangerous patterns of behavior.

To address the typically severe and complex presenting problems, adolescent treatment services for youths in the juvenile justice system must do more than address problems specific to substance abuse. They must help youths to reconcile with their families whenever possible, recover from scholastic setbacks, and negotiate the difficult developmental challenges of adolescence using more prosocial strategies than those that, in many cases, brought them into the juvenile justice system. This is an extraordinary and broad set of challenges for providers of adolescent substance abuse treatment services. The difficulty of the task is compounded by a dearth of information concerning the specific needs of these youths and the treatment strategies that most effectively address these needs. Thus, a better understanding of adolescent probationers' treatment needs and outcomes is both an important goal for improving juvenile justice outcomes as well as an important public health research effort.

In Los Angeles County over 13,000 juveniles are arrested and processed each year. After an initial investigation by the Juvenile Services Bureau of the Probation Department, a disposition recommendation is made to the juvenile court. These recommendations can include, in order of restrictiveness, release with community supervision, placement in a "suitable" residential community setting, placement in a juvenile camp facility, or commitment to the California Youth Authority (state prison for youths).

More than 2,000 youths are annually referred to "suitable" placements, which are unlocked residential group homes, family homes, or psychiatric hospitals, designed to provide youths with rehabilitation services and opportunities greater than those available to them in their home environments. Typically these placements last from seven to fifteen months, during which youths may receive a variety of specialized services depending on their needs and the particular placement.

Phoenix Academy of Los Angeles is one of the principal "suitable" placements providing long-term residential substance abuse treatment services for the Los Angeles Probation Department. In the remainder of this chapter we describe the Phoenix Academy program, the design of RAND's Adolescent Treatment Models evaluation of the program, and characteristics of the 449 youths referred by Probation to Phoenix Academy or one of six other large group homes included in this evaluation.

THE PHOENIX ACADEMY OF LOS ANGELES AT LAKE VIEW TERRACE

Phoenix Academy of Los Angeles was established in 1987 by Phoenix House, currently the largest nonprofit substance abuse treatment provider in the United States. The program model, called a Phoenix Academy, is a modified therapeutic community for adolescents that integrates an on-site public school into the treatment milieu. Phoenix House operates Phoenix Academies in Rhode Island, New Hampshire, Vermont, New York, Texas, and in several other locations in California.

Facilities

Phoenix Academy of Los Angeles at Lake View Terrace (which we call Phoenix Academy here) is located on a fifteen-acre site at the foothills of the San Gabriel Mountains in Los Angeles. It is housed in a large, modern building surrounded by parking and recreational areas (pool, playing fields, basketball courts), in a middle-class residential neighborhood. The building has several wings broken up by courtyards filled with gardens and trees. The classrooms (including an art room and computer stations) are located in one part of the building, near large kitchen facilities and a cafeteria.

Four dormitory areas each contain a series of double-dorm rooms, a lounge area, and a meeting room. Together, these dormitory wings house up to 150 residents. A suite of staff offices is located in one section of the building, but staff offices are also interspersed throughout the building; some administrator and supervisor offices are located in dormitory areas to allow maximum contact with residents. Several large group rooms are used for activities such as family teas (an unstructured event during which residents may socialize with their families) and house-wide meetings.

The Therapeutic Model

Phoenix Academy offers a modified therapeutic community treatment. It shares with traditional therapeutic communities the view that substance abuse is the outward manifestation of a broad set of personal and developmental problems. Correspondingly, therapeutic change is seen as requiring thoroughgoing changes in virtually all aspects of an adolescent's life. This holistic view of substance abuse contrasts with other common approaches to treatment, which focus more narrowly on physiological dependence, behavior, or on identification of cognitive or emotional problems from which drug abuse may stem.

According to the therapeutic community perspective, therapeutic change requires a commitment to help oneself and others. Self-help in the therapeutic community is the process whereby people with a common problem help one another. In these and many other respects, Phoenix Academy adheres to the basic principles followed by most therapeutic community treatment programs, which have been documented elsewhere (De Leon, 1997), and will not be repeated here.

Although the adolescent therapeutic community model derives from adult therapeutic community approaches, modifications are made to accommodate the unique needs and circumstances of adolescents (Jainchill, 1997). The major modifications include an increased emphasis on recreation, a less confrontational stance than found in adult programs, more supervision and evaluation by staff members, assessment of psychological disorders (e.g., Attention Deficit Hyperactivity Disorder and learning disabilities), a greater role of family members in treatment, and more frequent use of psychotropic medication for emotional disorders. In addition, adolescents participate somewhat less than adults in certain daily operations of the Academy (e.g., driving). However, they are expected to assist in running departments and working with staff members to make decisions, and thus have influence in the management of the Academy, just as in adult programs. Finally, a key difference between the Phoenix Academy and adult therapeutic community treatment is the emphasis placed on education and the integration of the academic program with the treatment regimen.

Clinical Approach

Phoenix Academy is structured to offer an opportunity for the community of residents to provide each member with immediate consequences, both positive and negative, for his or her actions. A basic concept of the therapeutic community is that individual change can be facilitated by teaching the consequences of behavior. This concept holds that desirable behavior can be stimulated by providing positive consequences and removing negative ones. By contrast, unacceptable behavior can be discouraged by introducing negative consequences or removing positive ones. Compliance with the rules and expectations of the therapeutic community is rewarded with status promotions and other privileges. Behavior that deviates from accepted practices of the community is met with disciplinary consequences or "sanctions." Decisions regarding privileges and sanctions are made by staff members at weekly meetings, and are announced at house meetings when the entire community convenes. This public sharing of information regarding privileges and sanctions has an important function in the therapeutic community. Members learn desirable behavior not only through the consequences of their own behavior, but also through the observation of others' behaviors and the resulting consequences. This social learning process occurs as members adopt behavior they have observed to be effective in the attainment of rewards and avoid those that result in negative outcomes.

Within the therapeutic community, earned privileges are believed to instill pride and self-regard whereas unearned positive consequences are regarded as stimulating an unwarranted sense of entitlement. For this reason, no privileges are granted to a resident without being earned. Although basic entitlements such as sufficient food, sleep, clean clothing, hygiene, and educational opportunities are provided to members of the community, virtually all other resources are regarded as privileges and linked to engaging in specific behaviors.

As residents spend more time in the program and meet program goals, they advance through the phases of the program. With each phase advancement comes the opportunity to earn additional privileges. These include more frequent communication with persons outside of the therapeutic community, greater access to personal property (e.g., radios, jewelry), more free time, and enhancements to a resident's status within the community (for instance, promotion to a more responsible job, assignment to a more desirable room, invitation to lead seminars, and permission to take special trips).

The therapeutic community imposes sanctions on residents whose actions run counter to approved standards. Sanctions are intended to serve as a learning experience for the resident, stimulating individual growth. Sanctions are imposed in proportion to the severity of the infraction and length of time in the program. For violation of most house rules or regulations, relatively mild sanctions are imposed. If, for example, a resident refuses to accept authority or is late for a meeting, then the resident may be verbally reprimanded.

The most common form of sanction is termed a "learning experience." During the learning experience, a privilege that had been previously earned by the resident can be taken away. For example, the resident may be demoted from his or her current job to one of lesser status within the community. Other types of learning experiences include writing assignments, cleaning, or other assigned activities, and generally last from one to five days. During a learning experience, residents may also be excluded from participation in planned program activities that are not regarded as primarily educational or therapeutic in nature.

The Role of Community Participation

The community is structured into groups: within each of four dormitory units, the residents are further divided into "clans" or families. Each clan has six to fifteen residents and a clan leader who serves as the primary counselor for each clan member. Primary counselors are responsible for most aspects of the residents' day-to-day experiences, including privileges, personal needs, communication with family, outings, and one-on-one counseling sessions. Thus, the clan mimics a large family structure, with common meetings, meals, and one day a week spent together for all clan activities.

Residents are given pre-employment tasks and are expected to master specific vocational skills, such as routine household (facility) related chores. These tasks are expected to help the resident build up good work habits and a sense of responsibility, and to help counteract the maladaptive behaviors that often characterizes them before coming to Phoenix Academy. Residents begin with jobs that require little responsibility, more physical labor, few rewards, and little status. Advancement is based on good job performance as well as psychological growth and attainment of treatment goals.

Several different types of meetings are held, all serving a role in the recovery process. "Daily meetings" involve goals of taking attendance, assembling the community, assimilating new residents into the community, and affirming the community itself as the principal teacher and healer. These include community-wide morning meetings and daily house meetings ("family gatherings"). Second, "seminars" are regularly scheduled in which presentations concerning concepts central to the Phoenix Academy mission are made by residents, staff, or guest speakers. Third, "workshops" are offered to cover special topics relevant to treatment and/or recovery for many Phoenix Academy youths. "Tutorials" are extended experiential groups that focus on a particular life theme.

"Peer support groups" bring together residents who are in the same phase of the program (e.g., orientation) to support one another concerning typically phase-specific issues (e.g., feeling lonely, or not having trusted friends in the program). "Peer process groups" are convened to encourage discussion about feelings aroused by various program activities. For instance, after a seminar on sexual abuse, a peer process group would be scheduled to discuss feelings and other responses to the issues addressed in the seminar.

"Encounter groups," a hallmark of the therapeutic community, are held about three times a week and are seen as a primary mechanism of improving negative attitudes and behavior. They use confrontation by peers to increase individual self-awareness. The goals of the encounter are to

1. confront negative behaviors that need to be modified
2. help the confronted person admit responsibility for (or "own") the behavior
3. help the confronted person identify feelings that underlie the negative behavior
4. have the confronted person make a commitment to change the behavior in the future; and have the person accept support of the group in setting realistic goals for altering his or her attitude and/or behavior.

Finally, "marathons" are extended therapeutic groups that are held periodically (a few times a year) to work through adolescents' major issues. Typically residents have been in the program at least five months before participating in a marathon, and they are selected carefully to make sure that they are ready for what is often an intense emotional experience. Marathons are preceded by several months of preparation, and consist of a group process lasting from twenty-four to thirty-six hours. The schedule and plan for the marathon is submitted to the Community Care Licensing Board and the Department of Probation prior to implementation for approval. The schedule includes frequent food, drink, and bathroom breaks, and residents are permitted to attend to their personal needs and to sleep at night as needed. The goal of the marathon is to open a window of opportunity for effective treatment of participant resident's most entrenched problems. It is intended as a cathartic experience that demonstrates to residents that they are not alone in their personal struggles, but are members of a community of individuals with similar experiences that can offer support and a shared treatment process. Thus, the marathon experience is believed to increase commitment to treatment.

The Role of Counseling

Therapeutic work at the individual and family levels occurs chiefly through two mechanisms: one-on-one meetings with the primary counselor and individual or family sessions with the family therapist (case manager). One-on-one counseling with the primary counselor occurs frequently: at least once a week, always after residents have trial home visits, after encounter groups if the youth was confronted in group, following a crisis, and whenever the youth seeks it out.

Phoenix Academy counselors strive to combine honesty and consistency in their interactions with residents in order to build a trusting therapeutic relationship. Part of this honesty involves providing continuous and consistent feedback to residents about their behaviors. Whereas some aspects of the treatment are confrontational (e.g., the encounter groups), counselors maintain a supportive stance with youths.

In addition to a primary counselor, each resident is assigned a family therapist and a vocational counselor. Residents participate in at least one hour of family therapy per week—either in a family format when parents can be involved, or in an individual format if obstacles to family involvement exist. Family therapists maintain a traditional therapeutic role, but they too spend considerable time on the dormitory units with the residents.

Parents of residents are expected to participate in weekly family therapy sessions. In addition, family involvement includes a mandatory two-hour parent orientation meeting, a family assessment meeting with the family therapist, and parent education seminars, followed by a family tea or informal social hour for visiting with the youths in an unstructured format. A family recreation day is planned every six to eight weeks on a weekend day for about four hours. Residents are eligible to go home on passes once they have completed the orientation phase of their treatment (described in the following), but passes are contingent upon progress in the program and are earned as a privilege.

Each resident works with a vocational counselor who helps the resident identify higher educational goals and career aspirations. Pre-employment counseling is also offered, and residents over the age of sixteen are routinely registered with the State Department of Rehabilitation, which helps them develop a treatment plan (including work at Phoenix Academy and afterward) and pays for training and/or college costs.

All staff members work as a team to provide uniform feedback and consistency within the therapeutic community.

The Role of the Educational Program

Educational services fulfill several functions within the therapeutic community, as well as fulfilling the residents' educational needs. Phoenix Academy houses an on-site high school (eighth to twelfth grade) which is run by the Los Angeles County Office of Education—Court School Program. Special education services are also available to those in need, as determined by the educational assessment that occurs just after intake and in ongoing observation of residents' performance. In addition to junior high or high school education, Phoenix Academy operates an on-site culinary arts program sponsored by Mission College.

Behavior in the classroom is considered in determining privileges and sanctions in the therapeutic community and progress in the educational program is linked to treatment phase advancements. Educational staff and therapeutic staff communicate frequently and work together to integrate the educational process into the therapeutic experience. In addition to being a part of the therapy itself, the educational process accelerates adolescents' progress in school, preparing them for the transition back into the community after leaving Phoenix Academy.

Other Services

Medical and dental services are available from consulting professionals or through linkages with community clinics and medical centers. Residents receive routine care upon entrance into the program and then at specified intervals. Legal services are arranged on an as-needed basis, through legal aid or pro bono work through the Phoenix House Foundation legal department.

Community service is a requirement of probation for many residents, and is seen as important to recovery for all residents. Community service is arranged to fulfill probation requirements early in the program. As residents prepare for reentry, they begin to identify and participate in community service in their own neighborhoods.

Recreational activities are thought to help the adolescent develop healthy interests and abilities ("clean fun") to replace those related to substance abuse, and residents spend at least two hours a day involved in physical education, sports, singing, games, dramatic arts, arts and crafts, and religious activities.

Program Referrals and Assessments

Referrals to Phoenix Academy of Los Angeles generally come from four sources: Juvenile Probation (about 90 percent), Department of Children and Family Services (about 5 percent), the Department of Mental Health (DMH), self-referrals, or other county agencies (about 5 percent). A series of assessments occur, first over the telephone, then an in-person interview during which a decision on admissions is usually formed. Finally, a more detailed intake is conducted at the Academy to finalize the admission and gather information for treatment.

Criteria for admission include

1. age between 13 and 17.5 years;
2. able to function in the therapeutic community in a voluntary and open setting;

3. ability to speak English; and
4. have undergone detoxification (if necessary).

There are several different reasons for exclusion from the program, though no hard-and-fast rules are applied. Among the characteristics most likely to cause a youth to be denied program entry are: histories of fire-setting, suicide attempts, violence toward authority, sexual predatory behavior, active suicidal or homicidal ideation, self-mutilation, severe psychotic symptoms, severe impulse control problems, untreated tuberculosis or other infectious disease, some physical disabilities, or having an IQ below 70. Many of these factors may be mitigated by considerations of the context in which the behavior occurred, the youth's placement history, any remorse exhibited by the youth or other behaviors during the interview. During this phase, staff work with the resident to assess his or her needs and to develop a treatment plan.

Phases of Treatment

The treatment program at Phoenix Academy has four phases. Phase I consists of both an orientation and a stabilization component. The orientation phase, which typically lasts two to three months, is devoted to orienting participants to the basic philosophy, concepts, and rules of the therapeutic community. Over the next four months (months two through six), the residents begin to participate as fully integrated members of the community, engaging in a broadening range of community activities. The objective of Phase I is full engagement in the treatment process and compliance with program rules.

Phase II consists of the primary treatment during the residents' sixth through ninth month in the program. Internalization of values and intrinsic motivation for drug-free living and personal growth is accomplished in this phase.

Phase III is the reentry process and occurs during months nine through twelve of the program. The objective of this phase is to provide final preparation for residents to return to their communities. As residents near completion of the program, they are given a series of seminars that are specifically geared toward issues that arise as residents transition out of Phoenix Academy. After completing the residential portion of the program, arrangements are made for residents to begin Phase IV, the aftercare portion of treatment. These arrangements might include returning home, entering a less restrictive setting, such as a transitional living program, or entering one of the adult programs. During this phase, youths are encouraged to participate in the aftercare services at Phoenix Academy. These include continued case management, weekly group meetings, and an open invitation to visit or to stay overnight. These services continue for twelve months.

THE PHOENIX ACADEMY EVALUATION

The Center for Substance Abuse Treatment evaluation of the Phoenix Academy model is conducted by the Drug Policy Research Center at RAND, a nonprofit research institute, in collaboration with Phoenix House, the Los Angeles Superior Courts, the Los Angeles Department of Probation, and six Los Angeles area group homes. Prior to beginning the evaluation, RAND and Phoenix House entered a research partnership in which RAND serves as an independent evaluator. Several components of the CSAT evaluation are shared with other Adolescent Treatment Model sites, and will not, therefore, be discussed here (e.g., qualitative case study and cost study components).

Evaluation Design

The evaluation uses a two-group, quasi-experimental, longitudinal design that compares outcomes of youths entering treatment at Phoenix Academy (the PA condition) with those who enter other residential programs (COMP condition). Phoenix Academy is one of over seventy residential programs licensed by the state and authorized by the Probation Department to serve as "suitable" placements for juvenile probationers in Los Angeles. In collaboration with the Probation Department, focus groups were conducted with most probation officers responsible for referring youths to such placements, in order to identify which other programs received referrals of youths most like those referred to Phoenix Academy. Specifically, we asked probation officers to describe the typical characteristics they considered when referring youths to Phoenix Academy, and the other group homes to which they might send youths with similar characteristics. These focus groups generated a rank-ordered list of possible comparison group homes. Before using these sites as comparison group homes, we solicited agreements with the group homes to allow us to conduct follow-up interviews at their sites. All but one of the six most comparable group homes agreed to participate in this way, as did the seventh on our list.

Subjects and Recruitment Procedures

Study participants were recruited and interviewed at all three Juvenile Hall detention centers in Los Angeles County, using procedures approved by the Juvenile Courts and RAND's Human Subjects Protection Committee. Between February 1999 and December 1999, all juveniles meeting eligibility requirements were invited to participate in the study. In order to equalize the number of subjects in each condition (PA and COMP), juveniles sent to Phoenix Academy were oversampled during the final months of recruitment, between December 1999 and April 2000. To be eligible to participate in the study, youths had to

1. be referred by Probation to Phoenix Academy or one of the six comparison group homes,
2. be between thirteen and seventeen years old at the time of the initial interview,
3. provide written assent to participate in the research,
4. allow their parent or legal guardian to be notified of study participation.

RAND had a court order from the presiding judge of the Los Angeles Superior Courts, Juvenile Courts Division, granting permission to interview wards of the court meeting these eligibility criteria.

Administrative and Survey Data Collection

After agreeing to participate and signing an informed consent form, participants received the first of four interviews and a gift worth $15 in compensation for their time and effort. Follow-up interviews were scheduled to occur three, six, and twelve months later. The principal data collection instrument at each of the four assessments is a version of the GAIN (Dennis, 1999) adapted for local implementation. Participating group homes provided weekly updates on the status of each study participant. Administrative delinquency and placement records are collected from Probation's Juvenile Automated Index database upon completion of each participant's twelve-month interview. These data are not yet complete, and are not presented in this chapter.

Program Characteristics of Phoenix Academy and the Comparison Group Homes

Although each program included in this study is unique, guided by its own philosophy, *all* programs strive to work with juvenile probationers and to modify the delinquent behaviors that brought them into the juvenile justice system. Since it is beyond the scope of this chapter to describe the differences among programs in depth, we compared them here on some of the cardinal features that reflect their overall philosophies and emphases, their basic structures, populations served, and the type and level of services offered.

Phoenix Academy and each of the comparison sites serve an ethnically diverse community comprised primarily of adolescent probationers. Whereas approximately 90 percent of Phoenix Academy clients are referred by Probation, three comparison sites reported 90 percent or more, two reported 80 percent, and one reported 75 percent of their clients as referred by Probation. Whereas Phoenix Academy serves boys and girls, four of the six group homes serve only boys, two serve boys and girls. None of the programs accept youths over eighteen years old. Three comparison sites and Phoenix Academy accept youths as young as thirteen. The three other sites accept residents as young as twelve, eleven, and eight. All sites are used by Probation to place youths for nine to twelve months.

Phoenix Academy, with 150 beds, is the largest of the programs, though all have more than 70 beds, and three of the comparison programs have over 100 beds. At Phoenix Academy these beds are all in one facility, which is also true of two comparison sites. Two others have one large facility as well as several small six- to nine-bed group homes in other community settings. The sixth program is exclusively composed of nine six- to twelve-bed group homes located in various communities. Two comparison programs have on-site schools, as does Phoenix Academy, whereas two others provide limited on-site schooling. Sites with limited on-site schooling rely more on community school linkages for educational services.

Although only Phoenix Academy is explicitly designated as a substance abuse treatment program, all of the programs offer substance abuse treatment services. All, for instance, offer drug and alcohol counseling. Furthermore, one of the comparison programs has as one of its principal therapeutic goals, "intensive drug and alcohol rehabilitation services." Other therapeutic services offered include family therapy and vocational training (provided at every site); group therapy (provided at Phoenix Academy and five of six comparison sites); and individual therapy (provided at Phoenix Academy and four of six comparison sites). All sites are staffed by social workers, among other professionals. Three of six comparison sites have psychologists on staff, and four of six have a psychiatrist on staff. Both psychologists and psychiatrists are on staff at Phoenix Academy.

When asked about the philosophy or therapeutic strategy employed at each of the comparison sites, program representatives (usually program directors) emphasized a wide range of approaches. One program was described as following principles of cognitive-behavioral treatment, another indicated a reliance on reality therapy, a third referred to an emphasis on peer culture and consensual decision making, a fourth to group processes and self-governance, and two indicated no explicit philosophy. In addition, four programs emphasized emancipation preparation (i.e., assisting youths to achieve the means and the skills necessary to live on their own in the community), two mentioned a focus on gang interventions, and one emphasized family interventions.

Characteristics of Adolescents Entering Study Programs

A total of 449 juveniles were recruited for this study (78 percent of those eligible to participate). Among the 125 eligible youths who were not recruited, most (80 percent) were taken to a placement before they could be interviewed for the study, 2 percent refused to participate, 6 percent were unable to participate because of language barriers, 4 percent were taken to another detention center before they could be interviewed, and 7 percent were not interviewed for other reasons.

Characteristics at admission of juveniles assigned to the PA and COMP conditions are presented in Table 9.1. The majority of youths entering the study were male, ages fifteen to sixteen, Hispanic/Latino, and domiciled in a family-owned house or apartment prior to their detention. Ages ranged from thirteen to seventeen, with 43 percent of the sample fifteen years old or younger at the time of the interview. Youths entering PA were, on average, half a year older (M = 15.81, SD = .92) than those entering COMP (M = 15.31, SD = 1.23). Although the ethnicities of youths entering each condition were comparable, PA received a greater share of whites and Hispanic/Latino youths, and proportionately fewer blacks and youths indicating their ethnicity as "other."

Almost 80 percent of the sample met criteria for a lifetime substance use disorder, with the majority meeting criteria for dependence. Despite this high rate of problem substance use, the majority of youths indicated they were not in need of substance abuse treatment. As expected, a greater share of youths entering PA qualified for substance dependence disorders, and a disproportionate number of youths entering COMP denied any prior use of drugs or alcohol. However, a substantial proportion of youths entering COMP qualified for a diagnosis of substance abuse. As might be expected from these results, PA youths reported more prior substance abuse treatments than COMP youths, though more than 10 percent of the latter group reported multiple such treatments prior to the baseline interview.

Of those who acknowledged needing treatment, most indicated marijuana as the drug for which they most needed treatment. Youths entering COMP were more than twice as likely to deny needing substance abuse treatment as those entering PA. Similarly, more than 75 percent of youths who acknowledged a treatment need for their use of illicit drugs other than marijuana were admitted to PA.

Youths in this sample are young and experienced with drugs, so it is not surprising that most indicate first getting drunk or using an illicit drug when younger than fifteen. In fact, 20 percent of the sample reports age of first use before age eleven, and 25.7 percent report their first such experiences between the ages of eleven and twelve. Equivalent proportions of PA and COMP cases reported first using drugs or getting drunk during these earliest ages.

Table 9.1 describes the distribution of last grades completed for members of the sample. Since this is, in part, a function of age, it is

TABLE 9.1. Baseline Characteristics of Research Participants Entering Phoenix Academy (PA) (n = 449) versus Comparison Group Homes (COMP)

Item	Total		PA		COMP	
	n	%	n	%	n	%
Total Sample	449	100.0	176	100.0	273	100.0
Gender						
Male	392	87.3	144	81.8	248	90.8
Female	57	12.7	32	18.2	25	9.2
Age						
11-12	0	0.0	0	0.0	0	0.0
13-14	95	21.2	14	8.0	81	29.7
15-16	255	56.8	121	68.8	134	49.1
17-18	99	22.0	41	23.3	58	21.2
19 and over	0	0.0	0	0.0	0	0.0
Ethnicity						
American Indian/Alaskan Native	8	1.8	5	2.8	3	1.1
Asian or Pacific Islander	8	1.8	2	1.1	6	2.2
Black	66	14.7	15	8.5	51	18.7
White	72	16.0	36	20.5	36	13.2
Hispanic (Puerto Rican, Mexican, Cuban, other)	248	55.2	106	60.2	142	52.0
Mixed/some other group	47	10.5	12	6.8	35	12.8
Current living situation						
A house or apartment (yours or parents)	296	65.9	129	73.3	167	61.2
A foster home or public housing	11	2.4	1	0.6	10	3.7
A friend's or relative's house or apartment	63	14.0	22	12.5	41	15.0
A nursing home, hospital, inpatient or residential	20	4.5	2	1.1	18	6.6
Jail, detention center, or other correctional institution	37	8.2	13	7.4	24	8.8
Any other housing situation	6	1.3	1	0.6	5	1.8
Missing/refused	16	3.6	8	4.5	8	2.9
Substance Severity Measure						
Physiological dependence	203	45.2	105	59.7	98	35.9

TABLE 9.1 *(continued)*

Item	Total n	Total %	PA n	PA %	COMP n	COMP %
Dependence	37	8.2	18	10.2	19	7.0
Abuse	115	25.6	41	23.3	74	27.1
Use	0	0.0	0	0.0	0	0.0
No use	94	20.9	12	6.8	82	30.0
Substance treatment needed for						
Any kind of alcohol	23	5.1	8	4.5	15	5.5
Marijuana, hashish, etc.	82	18.3	49	27.8	33	12.1
Crack, freebase cocaine, other cocaine	33	7.3	28	15.9	4	1.5
Amphetamine/methamphetamine	32	7.1	28	15.9	4	1.5
Heroin	4	0.9	2	1.1	2	0.7
"Acid" or other hallucinogens	1	0.2	0	0.0	1	0.4
Some other drug	3	0.7	2	1.1	1	0.4
No need/missing/refused	270	60.1	63	35.8	207	75.8
Age when first got drunk or used any drugs						
Below 15	378	84.2	157	89.2	221	81.0
15-18	54	12.0	19	10.8	35	12.8
Over 18	0	0.0	0	0.0	0	0.0
Missing/refused	17	3.8	0	0.0	17	6.2
Last grade or year completed in school						
< 6	4	0.9	0	0.0	4	1.5
6-8	178	39.6	59	33.5	119	43.6
9-10	214	47.7	92	52.3	122	44.7
11-12	39	8.7	21	11.9	18	6.6
> 12	0	0.0	0	0.0	0	0.0
Missing	14	3.1	4	2.3	10	3.7
Times in life arrested, charged with a crime, and booked						
0	10	2.2	4	2.3	6	2.2
1	110	24.5	35	19.9	75	27.5
2-3	159	35.4	69	39.2	90	33.0
4-8	113	25.2	47	26.7	66	24.2
9+	51	11.4	17	9.7	34	12.5

Item	Total n	Total %	PA n	PA %	COMP n	COMP %
Missing/refused	6	1.3	4	2.3	2	0.7
Times in life admitted to drug treatment or counseling						
0	275	61.2	85	48.3	190	69.6
1	75	16.7	41	23.3	34	12.5
2-3	38	8.5	23	13.1	15	5.5
4-8	13	2.9	8	4.5	5	1.8
9+	30	6.7	15	8.5	15	5.5
Missing/refused	18	4.0	4	2.3	14	5.1
	Mean	SD	Mean	SD	Mean	SD
Substance use—last 90 days						
Days used alcohol, marijuana, or other drugs	35.87	34.95	48.4	33.58	27.80	33.46
Days drunk or high for most of the day	21.51	30.37	28.39	31.77	17.07	28.63
Days in jail (or other place) where you could not use drugs	18.24	29.25	13.9	23.68	21.06	32.09

difficult to judge from these data the extent to which youths in the sample have fallen behind in their schooling. As a crude estimate of school problems, we assumed that youths of any particular age, call it x, should have completed grade x–6. Of course this is not necessarily true, so this measure of school performance should be viewed as approximate. Using this estimator, almost 10 percent of the sample is three or more years behind in school, 23 percent is at least two years behind, and 57 percent has fallen at least one year behind in schooling (not shown in Table 9.1). PA and COMP had nearly identical percentages for each year behind in schooling, except that PA had a slightly larger percentage of youths exactly one year behind, and a slightly lower percentage that did not score as behind at all.

Finally, participants acknowledged considerable numbers of lifetime arrests for criminal offenses that led to formal charges. Indeed, more than half of PA and COMP youths report two or more such arrests. The distribution of lifetime arrests was comparable for PA and COMP.

DISCUSSION

Youths referred to Phoenix Academy and the comparison group homes exhibit serious behavioral and developmental problems in addition to substance abuse including legal, family, school, and social problems. Phoenix Academy of Los Angeles provides a modified therapeutic community for adolescents designed to facilitate change in each of these domains using developmentally appropriate interventions.

Considerable anecdotal evidence of the effectiveness of the Phoenix Academy approach exists with adolescent probationers. Few rigorous studies have compared outcomes of youths treated in adolescent therapeutic communities such as Phoenix Academy with those receiving other treatments. The ongoing RAND study will provide this important comparative data.

Although comparison group homes were selected because they bore structural similarities to Phoenix Academy, the samples entering Phoenix Academy and these other group homes, differ in several important respects. In particular, youths assigned to Phoenix Academy are more likely to report a need for treatment and symptoms of substance dependence than those assigned to the comparison group homes. Those assigned to the comparison group homes have somewhat more extensive histories of trouble with the law. These differences limit the conclusions that may be drawn from any observed differences in outcomes across conditions. We expect to substantially overcome this limitation by using statistical techniques to identify the subset of youths in the COMP condition that most closely match youths in the PA condition in terms of baseline characteristics (background and recent behavior). This analysis will be the subject of a forthcoming report.

REFERENCES

De Leon, G. (1997). Therapeutic communities: Is there an essential model? In G. De Leon (Ed.), *Community as method: Therapeutic communities for special populations and special settings* (pp. 3-18). Westport, CT: Praeger.

Dennis, M.L. (1999). *Global Appraisal of Individual Needs (GAIN): Administration guide for the GAIN and related measures (Version 1299)*. Bloomington, IL: Lighthouse Publications. Available online at: <www.chestnut.org/li/gain>.

Jainchill, N. (1997). Therapeutic Communities for adolescents: The same and not the same. In G. De Leon (Ed.), *Community as method: Therapeutic communities for special populations and special settings* (pp. 161-178). Westport, CT: Praeger.

Substance Abuse and Mental Health Services Administration (2001). Treatment Episode Data Set (TEDS): 1993-1998. Department of Health and Human Services. <http://wwwdasis.samhsa.gov/teds98/teds98.htm>.

Chapter 10

Dynamic Youth Community, Incorporated: A Multiphase, Step-Down Therapeutic Community for Adolescents and Young Adults

Patricia D. Perry
Tanya L. Hedges
Douglas Carl
William Fusco
Karen Carlini
James Schneider
Nicholas Salerno

INTRODUCTION

Dynamic Youth Community, Inc. (DYC) is the oldest therapeutic community in New York State designed specifically for adolescents. It began in 1970 in response to a New York City initiative to provide services to youths, and grew to include residential, day service, and ambulatory treatment. Located in the heart of Brooklyn, New York, DYC is now a three-year, multiphase therapeutic community serving young men and women ages fourteen to twenty-one, who have severe

This chapter was supported by funding from the U.S. Substance Abuse and Mental Health Services Administration (SAMHSA), Center for Substance Abuse Treatment (CSAT), grant # KD1 TI11423. The opinions expressed herein are solely those of the authors and do not represent official positions of SAMHSA, CSAT, or the New York State Office of Alcoholism and Substance Abuse Services.

Please address correspondence to Patricia D. Perry, NYS Office of Alcoholism and Substance Abuse Services, 1450 Western Ave., Albany, NY 12203.

substance abuse problems. The vast majority of these New York City youth begin the program in a seventy-six-bed residential facility located in a rural community 150 miles north of Brooklyn. After a year of residential treatment, youths return to their homes and attend the Brooklyn facility for one year of intensive day-service treatment; adolescents conclude the program with one year of evening group meetings also held at the Brooklyn facility.[1] These multiple program phases allow an adolescent to be reintroduced gradually into the larger society as he or she transitions out of the therapeutic community setting.

Therapeutic Communities

Therapeutic communities (TCs) are typically drug-free residential programs that derive their approach from the self-help model. TCs are based on the belief that addiction is a symptom of larger socialization problems rather than an independent disorder. Thus, if the underlying reasons for drug use are uncovered and addressed, a need or desire to abuse drugs will no longer exist. More specifically, the TC philosophy is that those people who are addicted to drugs have psychological and social deficits that precipitated their substance use behavior; the goal of treatment then becomes to change the negative thinking, feelings, and circumstances that led to the addictive behavior.

Therapeutic communities are complex, multidimensional programs whose fundamental elements have been described elsewhere (see De Leon, 1988, 1997, 2000; Kooyman, 1993; Yablonsky, 1989). It is well beyond the scope of this chapter to describe all the TC elements that are found within the DYC model. Therefore, readers who are unfamiliar with the TC perspective on substance abuse treatment are encouraged to refer to one of these seminal works for a more complete description of the history, philosophy, and therapeutic interventions found within a typical TC.

Rehabilitation in a therapeutic community involves treating the whole person by changing addictive attitudes, beliefs, and lifestyles. According to TC philosophy, this is accomplished through total immersion in a community that teaches principles of "right living" from peers and staff who have had similar substance use experiences and successfully changed their behavior. Indeed, De Leon suggests that the community itself is the quintessential element of the TC approach in that "what distinguishes the TC from other treatment approaches and other communities is the *purposive use of the peer community to facilitate social and psychological change in individuals*" [author's italics] (De Leon, 1997, p. 5). Basic treatment strategies within a therapeutic community include: (1) group sessions (e.g., encounter groups)—in which individuals learn from their peers and staff the ways in which their behaviors and attitudes contributed to their substance use; (2) work crews[2]—in which members learn self-discipline and basic life skills; and (3) behavior monitoring—in which members learn to accept consequences for their own misbehavior. All of these strategies work together within a network of peers and staff so that no single strategy can be separated from another. Hence, it is the community itself, rather than one specific therapeutic intervention, that fosters change within the individual.

Adolescent TCs and Dynamic Youth Community

To address the specialized needs of adolescents, DYC modified the traditional adult-centered approach to therapeutic communities by creating a multistage, step-down therapeutic community that gradually reintroduces youths into the larger society. Jainchill (1997) suggests that the typical adolescent TC modification to the adult model includes a shorter length of stay; limited use of peers (i.e., increased reliance on staff); use of a horizontal authority structure among members (i.e., staff maintains the majority of the responsibility within the community); and inclusion of parents or other relative sponsors in the therapeutic process. While the DYC model includes parents and relative sponsors in the therapeutic process, it differs from the typical adaptations described by Jainchill such that DYC (1) has a *longer* length of stay compared to adult TCs (e.g., three years in DYC compared to one to two years in a typical adult TC); (2) uses *peer modeling* (positive adolescent peer pressure) to promote change within community members; and (3) in contrast to the typical adolescent TC, uses a *vertical* authority structure among members for the daily operations of the TC.

This chapter describes these adaptations and discusses the ways in which basic therapeutic community elements (e.g., group therapy, work crews, and behavior monitoring) are operationalized within the model to meet the specialized needs of adolescents. In addition, since this project is part of a national initiative to evaluate adolescent drug treatment programs, the chapter concludes with a brief description of the model's current evaluation process, and presents an overview containing selected characteristics of DYC members participating in the evaluation.

Funding for the DYC Program

Funding for the DYC program is derived from several sources. The residential facility is supported by public assistance shelter allowance and food stamps, the New York State Office of Alcoholism and Substance Abuse Services (which includes the Substance Abuse Prevention and treatment block grant and state funding), and private donations. Medical expenses are covered either by Medicaid fee-for-service (clients in residential facilities are exempted from managed care) or private health insurance. The day and ambulatory services are supported primarily through the NYS Office of Alcoholism and Substance Abuse Services.

Clients Served

Dynamic Youth Community accepts into the treatment program adolescents and young adults between the ages of twelve and twenty-two—although the majority of program members fall between ages fourteen and twenty-one upon admission. Approximately three-quarters of the program's members are male, although this trend seems to be changing in recent years. Currently young women account for 28 percent of the program's population. Since DYC is a community-based program, it has evolved over the years to respond to the ethnic distribution in the community itself. Most DYC members are Caucasian; however, slightly less than half of these Caucasian members are from first- or second-generation Russian immigrant families (see Mixed/some other group in Table 10.1). In addition, DYC serves a significant number of African-American and Latino members and families. The result is a program that consists of multiple ethnic and racial identities.

Frequently, adolescents enter DYC with extensive drug abuse histories that include prior treatment episodes at other facilities. DYC members' primary substances of abuse include marijuana, heroin, and cocaine. However, members often report combining two or more drugs in their daily use (e.g., cocaine and marijuana or heroin and marijuana). Thus, while an adolescent might list marijuana as his or her primary substance of abuse, he or she might also be using heroin and/or cocaine concurrently with the marijuana. In addition, the focus of treatment at therapeutic communities in general, and DYC in particular, is on resocialization rather than drug-specific treatment. For these reasons, staff at DYC do not categorize members based on their primary substance of abuse. See Table 10.1 for a more complete description of member demographics.

Admission

Youths are primarily referred to DYC by school counselors, other treatment programs, parents, and the criminal justice system, and are admitted to DYC without regard to racial or ethnic background. Criteria for a youth to be admitted to DYC include (1) history of a severe alcohol and/or substance abuse problem; (2) parental (or other family member, i.e., grandparent or adult sibling) willingness to participate in DYC parent groups for the duration of treatment; and (3) lack of previous violent behavior such as rape or arson. Youths with severe cognitive disabilities are not admitted to DYC; however, youths with mental health concerns or attention deficit disorders (ADD or ADHD) are considered for admission on an individual basis. During the admission interview, the program requirements are explained to both the youth and his or her parent(s), and the adolescent has an opportunity to speak with current program members to learn more about the community's expectations.

DYC THERAPEUTIC COMMUNITY TREATMENT PHASES

Residential Treatment

Once youths enter the residential facility they are gradually introduced into the daily structure of the therapeutic community. For example, the day begins as members rise, shower, and straighten their rooms; new members learn a correct way to make their bed, fold

TABLE 10.1. Responses from Adolescents Admitted to the Residential Component Only (N = 54)

Item	N	%
Gender		
Male	39	72
Female	15	28
Age		
11-12	0	0
13-14	5	9
15-16	12	22
17-18	17	31
19 and over	20	37
Ethnicity		
Black	8	15
White	19	35
Hispanic (Puerto Rican, Mexican, Cuban, other)	9	17
Mixed/some other group[a]	18	33
Living situation[b]		
A house or apartment (yours or parents)	42	78
Jail, detention center, or other correctional institution	5	9
A friend's or relative's house or apartment	<5	5[c]
A nursing home, hospital, inpatient or residential	<5	5
Temporary or emergency shelter	0	0
Vacant buildings	<5	5
Any other housing situation	0	0
A foster home or public housing	0	0
Present work or school situation[d]	N/A	N/A
Substance dependence (meeting criteria)	50	92
Substance treatment needed for		
Any kind of alcohol	6	11
Marijuana, hashish, etc.	19	35
Crack, freebase cocaine, other cocaine	10	18
Inhalants	0	0
Heroin	12	22

Item	N	%
"Acid" or other hallucinogens	<5	5
Other drugs (includes Amphetamine/metham-phetamine)	<5	5
Age when first got drunk or used any drugs		
Below 15	45	83
15-18	9	17
Over 18	0	0
Last grade or year completed in school		
6-8	21	39
9-10-11	24	44
12-12+	9	17

	Mean	SD
Times in life arrested, charged with a crime, and booked	2.8	3.2
Substance use—last 90 days		
Days used alcohol, marijuana, or other drugs	63.2	32.5
Days drunk or high for most of the day	43.5	35.8
Days in a jail (or other place) where you could not use drugs	19.1	29.0
Times in life admitted to drug treatment or counseling	1.9	4.2

[a]Most respondents in this category self-identified as Russian or Russian-American—also includes American Indian and Asian-Pacific Islander.
[b]Living situation prior to entering residential treatment
[c]<5 arbitrarily set to 5%
[d]Education is provided within the therapeutic community; thus, all respondents attend school if they have not completed high school. No members work outside the community while they are in the residential component of the program.

their clothes, and sweep the floor. Next, breakfast is served by members of a kitchen work crew, and new members learn where to sit, where to return dirty dishes and silverware, and how to clean up after themselves. Following breakfast all members prepare for the morning meeting.

In a therapeutic community, house meetings are used to reinforce community goals and responsibilities as well as to relay information. A typical morning meeting, organized and led by members, begins with an inspirational reading followed by members' personal interpretations of the reading. Next, member announcements take place (e.g., a daily weather report, menu for the day). After announcements, several members enact a short skit illustrating one of the traditional therapeutic community sayings or principles such as "guilt kills," or "You get what your hand calls for." The meeting concludes with staff announcements or other issues of interest to the house ("house" refers to all members in the community) and a recitation of the DYC philosophy by all members. As the day continues, members attend the facility's school and work with their assigned work crews.

Advancing members' educational levels is a major component of the DYC program. Many members may have had difficulty in school prior to DYC due to drug use and/or learning disabilities, yet each member is expected to earn a GED (high school equivalency diploma) or a high school diploma before graduating from the program. At the residential facility, a separate school building is staffed by three teachers funded by the local Board of Education who supervise extracurricular activities (such as photography classes in the school's darkroom) in addition to teaching regular classroom lessons. Those members who earned a high school diploma or a GED prior to entering DYC spend their mornings performing various jobs and chores on their assigned work crews.

Work therapy and the work crew structure form an essential therapeutic component of DYC. All members participate on their assigned work crews for scheduled periods throughout each day. In the residential facility nine different crews do the majority of the work necessary for the community to function—e.g., prepare meals, clean and maintain the buildings, landscape the grounds, decorate the facility, etc. These chores are completed almost entirely by the members, thus eliminating the need for professionally employed janitorial, kitchen, landscaping, and maintenance staff.

House cochiefs (members) oversee the facility's nine work crews, and a separate organizational branch of expediters monitors each crew's overall performance. Each work crew has a stratified hierarchy which consists of the department head (crew leader), two "ramrods" who assist the department head, and general crew members as illustrated for two work crews in Figure 10.1.

artment head organizes the work crew, ensures that each doing what he/she has been assigned, and maintains order

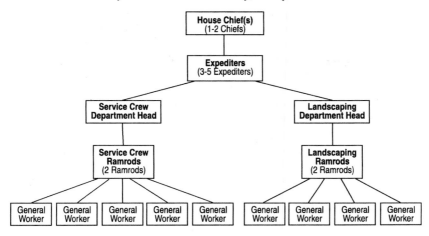

FIGURE 10.1

on the crew. The positions of house chief, expediter, department head, and ramrod connote considerable status and responsibility within the community. The department head and the two ramrods work closely with a staff member to ensure the crew's work is being performed as planned. All members begin their work crew service as general crew members and earn their way to the top of the hierarchy as they begin to understand and become more committed to the program and their own treatment progress.

After lunch, members prepare for their group meetings. DYC utilizes several different types of group therapy—primarily encounter and static groups—in order to fully address all aspects of the adolescents' behavior, thought processes, and emotions. In *encounter* (or indictment) group, members confront one another when they are concerned or angry with one of their peer's behaviors or attitudes. Group membership rotates in each group session so that members may address and be addressed by different peers each day. With the help of peers and staff, members learn how their behavior affects others and why a particular type of behavior may have enabled or contributed to drug use. In contrast, *static* group consists of the same members for three to four months at a time. Static groups enable members to work through important interpersonal issues with the same group of peers over a longer period of time. As members begin to reveal parts of themselves in group, trust, understanding, and bonding occur, creating a supportive and encouraging atmosphere. Currently in the DYC residential treatment center encounter groups are held on Monday and Friday and static groups are held on Wednesday.

A third type of group, *peer* group, is composed of members who are currently at a similar phase in their treatment process. Group discussions in peer groups vary according to members' time in the program. For newer members, peer group discussions might focus on adjusting to the program, or the feelings associated with temporarily living outside of the city. For older members, the discussions might focus on their upcoming transition to day treatment in Brooklyn and the feelings they have about being reunited with their families. Peer groups are occasionally substituted for static groups when therapeutically necessary.

Other types of group, such as *women's* (girls') group, meet on an as needed basis and may also be held in place of or in addition to static group. Periodically, when staff feel that members are in need of extensive group therapy, DYC will convene extended groups or marathon groups which can last from three to thirty-six hours. *Marathon* or *extended* groups focus on the issues and experiences most important to individual members' therapeutic progress. In these cases, topics discussed by the group vary greatly according to the group composition and the members' therapeutic needs.

In general, groups are constructed without regard to member age or phase in the program. For example, an indictment group may contain a cross-section of members ranging from young (fourteen years old) to older (eighteen-plus years), as well as new members and members who have been in the facility for a longer period of time. The cross-section of group membership allows each individual to participate at his or her own level and supports the belief that each member has something unique to contribute to the community as a whole. Since the program usually has more boys than girls, care is taken to ensure that no girl is assigned to a group without at least one or two other girls present.

For members, the day concludes with dinner, an evening meeting (similar to the morning meeting), and time for homework and relaxation. Each weekday follows a similar schedule. On Tuesday and Thursday afternoons, seminars on health-related or other appropriate topics replace group sessions, but the rest of the daily schedule remains the same. Weekends at the residential center are less structured than weekdays, although members are still expected to clean their dorms and perform their assigned tasks. Staff members generally plan weekend outdoor group activities, sports, and occasional field trips on Saturdays. Parents and immediate family members of adolescents who have been in the program for at least one month may visit their children on Sundays.

As members progress through the program, they learn how to conform to the expected behavior within the community and are gradually granted more privileges and responsibilities. After a period of approximately one year, when staff feel the member has made sufficient progress in understanding the individual factors that precipitated his or her drug use, and the member has changed his or her attitudes, beliefs, and behaviors to reflect a more positive drug-free lifestyle, the member is transferred to the Brooklyn site for intensive day treatment.

Day Treatment

Most youths transition to day treatment only after completing the residential component of the program, but on rare occasions youths may be admitted directly to day treatment.[3] Regardless of a member's point of entry, the day treatment program utilizes the same therapeutic community approach as the residential program, but for fewer hours out of the day. The day begins with a morning meeting, followed by school and/or work groups, and concludes with group sessions and a house meeting in the afternoon.[4] Day treatment is provided Monday through Friday, 9 a.m. to 6 p.m. and Wednesday from 9 a.m. to 10:30 p.m.

The critical difference for members in this phase is that they live at home rather than in a community surrounded by peers and staff. In the beginning months of this phase, members are encouraged to strengthen peer relationships with the members who have been in the day treatment program for a longer length of time. To facilitate this process, procedures are in place that aid DYC peer socialization. For example, while the member is at home he or she may not socialize, or receive or make phone calls to anyone who is not a DYC member. If members wish to go out in the evening, they must complete a "trip slip" that states which DYC members they will be going out with, where they are going, and when they will return. Weekend activities are planned by members and staff to include outings with other DYC members only. Gradually, as the adolescents become adjusted to living at home, have established strong relationships among their day treatment peers, and show that they can adhere to the expectations of the community in this environment, they begin to socialize with people who are outside the DYC community; however, DYC members are never allowed to socialize with past friends who might still be involved with drugs.

In addition to expanding socialization circles, after they have spent four to six months in day treatment members begin to seek employment and/or educational activities outside the DYC community. Frequently the DYC counselors, teachers, and vocational staff assist members in obtaining employment or locating an appropriate school outside of the therapeutic community. The combination of increasing one's socialization circle to include people who are not members of DYC, and the experience of applying for employment or reentering school, prepare members for the next phase of the program—reentry.

Reentry

In this phase of treatment, members attend day services treatment three days a week and work (or attend school) three days a week. Specifically, members return to the Brooklyn facility Monday, Wednesday, and Friday and participate in the same program as their peers in the full day treatment phase. Reentry members are not considered a separate group unto themselves, rather they participate in house meetings, work crew, and groups just as if they were in the day treatment phase. On the other days, Tuesday, Thursday, and Saturday or Sunday, members work or attend school outside the therapeutic community.

The combination of work or school and day services provides members with the opportunity to gradually reenter the larger community while retaining the supportive network developed within DYC. It is thought by some members and staff that the work crew experiences gained in the therapeutic community are particularly beneficial, since they prepare members to take pride in their work, to work cooperatively with others, and to follow directions from a supervisor. By this point in their treatment, members should possess the necessary life skills to be productive and functioning members of the larger society. They have been taught how to manage anger and how to express feelings, and have been given the necessary skills to cope with life's adversities. After approximately six months in the reentry phase, members are ready for the final transition to full-time school or employment, and twice weekly meetings at the facility.

Transition

The transition phase is the final component of the program. At this point members have been associated with the program for two years and are functionally living and working in the larger community. They return to DYC for group meetings on Wednesday and Friday evenings each week. During this phase, members work on transition issues such as building and maintaining relationships with people outside the DYC community, but also work on issues common to all young adults such as apprehension over starting college or a new job, and dating issues.

After approximately one year in the transition phase, members are considered ready to complete (or graduate from) the program when they meet the following criteria: they have consistently remained drug-free during treatment and in the transition phase; they have completed a GED or an equivalent degree; they have established a bank account and pay for their housing (this includes paying rent to parents if applicable). Completion of the program is marked by a celebration that includes the entire DYC community and the member's family and friends.

Dynamic Youth Community's multiple phases, beginning with residential treatment and terminating with the transition phase, illustrate the step-down approach for an adolescent therapeutic community. That is, the DYC model begins with a member's complete separation from his or her home community so that new attitudes and beliefs can be instilled within the member. Each phase thereafter gradually reintroduces the member into the larger community while retaining a connection to the therapeutic community. The gradual separation from the therapeutic community and transition into the larger community gives the member time to develop new ways to function outside DYC using the skills, attitudes, and beliefs learned within the TC.

PARENT/RELATIVE SPONSORS

Parents also contribute to the member's gradual reintroduction into the larger community. Indeed, youths are not admitted to the program unless a parent (or other family member such as a grandparent, aunt, or adult sibling) is willing to commit to attending weekly meetings for the duration of the program. Although parent attendance is preferable, other close adult relatives may choose to become the member's primary relative sponsor in the absence of parental support. The critical factor is that the person attending the meetings is a consistent presence in the member's life and will be available to support the member throughout difficult times. Due to the length of the DYC program, parent/relative sponsors must also make a lasting commitment to the program and the adolescent's treatment progress. The adolescent's recovery may become jeopardized should a parent/relative sponsor cease to participate in the program. If this does occur, parents of other adolescents at DYC may step in and serve as "surrogate parents."

Since the parent/close relative component of the program is considered essential in order to adequately treat the adolescent, parents/relative sponsors must participate in groups held each Wednesday evening at the Brooklyn facility from 7 p.m. to 10 p.m. for the duration of the adolescent's association with DYC. These group sessions are intended to assist the family with the issues and emotions surrounding the adolescent's drug or alcohol use and to help the family understand why the adolescent may have turned to drugs. Over time, families learn how they might have contributed to the addictive behavior and learn what family dynamics may need to be changed in order to facilitate the adolescent's recovery. Parent/relative sponsor groups, like the member groups, use a self-help approach wherein families learn from one another under the guidance of DYC staff and parent coleaders.

Some parents/relative sponsors choose to stay affiliated with DYC after their sons/daughters have left the program by serving as coleaders of parent/relative sponsor groups with staff. These coleaders attend monthly meetings with staff to discuss the community concerns (such as parent/relative sponsor retention in the program). Other parents and relative sponsors organize fund raising events to help support program activities. Finally, at a higher DYC organizational level, parents serve on the DYC board of directors and actually constitute the majority of the board membership.

DYC STAFF

Regardless of parental support, the program itself could not exist without the extended staff commitment at both facilities. The therapeutic community method of drug treatment is an all-encompassing approach, so DYC staff must be well versed in TC goals, treatment, and objectives. Current staff come from a variety of social, economic, and drug treatment backgrounds. As is typical in many therapeutic communities, many staff members are graduates of DYC or other therapeutic communities. Other staff members hold degrees in social work, psychology, counseling or related fields. Each counselor is or is in the process of becoming a New York State Credentialed Alcohol and Substance Abuse Counselor. Contrary to the traditional TC model—where all staff members are former members who have completed treatment—DYC directors have combined educationally trained staff with life trained staff. Much of the TC method has been passed down through oral tradition, therefore DYC directors require all new staff members to undergo a year-long orientation period during which they listen to and observe the therapeutic community techniques used at DYC.

Currently the residential facility employees nine clinical staff, eight clerical and administrative staff, and one registered nurse. Three teachers are provided by the local Board of Education. Many residential center clinical staff members and their families reside in staff houses and apartments on the DYC grounds. This proximity enhances the spirit of community and ensures that staff members are always nearby should an emergency arise. Staff members may participate in community events even on their days off, and may occasionally include members in family events such as birthdays and holidays. Thus, the residential staff commitment to DYC occasionally extends beyond the established working hours. Flexibility and willingness to place the community's needs in high regard are key components in residential staff.

Although Brooklyn facility staff do not live on the DYC property, they demonstrate an equal level of dedication to DYC and the adolescents the program serves. As with the residential staff, many of the five clinical staff at the Brooklyn facility are graduates of therapeutic communities; others hold college degrees in social work, counseling, and/or psychology. A certified social worker, family therapist, teacher, and administrative staff also contribute to the Brooklyn facility. A key element to success is staff's ability to reinforce the community structure while conveying compassionate understanding for the adolescents. Staff modify their schedules to accommodate the needs of members and the program, thus their working hours do not always conform to a nine-to-five workday. All Brooklyn center staff members are required to work Wednesday evenings during parent and transition phase group meetings; in addition, individual staff members may occasionally spend a Saturday or Sunday afternoon with a group of members, outside of the context of the center.

Consistent with a therapeutic community approach to treatment, all staff are responsible for contributing to the recovery of each of the members. Thus, while a member is assigned a primary counselor upon admission to each phase, all staff members assume responsibility for the member's therapeutic progress. The primary counselor monitors the member's progress, but one-to-one counseling sessions may be held between the member and the staff member with whom he or she feels most comfortable.

In summary, staff are responsible for conveying and upholding the philosophy and principles of a therapeutic community. They serve as role models for members by living a life consistent with the principles of a therapeutic community. In essence, all staff members must be flexible in their personal schedules, committed to the program, and willing to blend certain aspects of their personal lives with their work lives. This level of personal commitment is necessary for DYC to function as a cohesive therapeutic community.

SUMMARY OF THE DYC MODEL

At DYC, parents/relative sponsors, staff, and peer members work together to form and uphold the therapeutic community values. As members become more attuned to the community standards, they begin to monitor peer behavior, learn how to correct their own misbehavior, participate more freely in group discussions, climb the work crew structure, and learn the skills necessary to live as functioning members outside of the therapeutic community. In addition, members' parents or relative sponsors learn how to change the family dynamics to better support the adolescent/young adult as he or she transitions to and from the residential center, day treatment, reentry, transition, and finally completely out of the therapeutic community.

Although Dynamic Youth Community has always focused on adolescent drug abuse treatment, it is interesting to note that the DYC model illustrates *only one* of the common adaptations of the adult TC model for adolescents as described by Jainchill (1997). That is, DYC includes parents in the therapeutic process and encourages parental involvement in other aspects of the community. In *contrast* to the other common modifications described by Jainchill, DYC *increases* the recommended length of stay, uses a *hierarchical* authority structure in the daily operations of the TC, and uses *peer* modeling and peer feedback to evoke change within the members.

Increasing the length of stay allows continuity of care to be preserved within the model itself so that the program contains all levels of care. The advantage of preserving the least intense level of care within the program, rather than discharging a client to another facility, is that members maintain a connection with the program, peers, and staff that have been supportive throughout their recovery process. Thus, they are able to maximize their prior treatment experiences to facilitate transition into the outside community.

The hierarchical authority structure within the work crews and the general house structure mirrors employment in society, and promotes the development of leadership skills as members learn how to accept positions of responsibility. These skills become particularly helpful when members transition into the broader community and assume work and/or school responsibilities.

Finally, peers are used to facilitate member growth in the community. Given the duration of the program and the multiple opportunities members have to work with one another (e.g., in groups, on work crews, and in maintaining the house structure), members with the greatest amount of experience in the program become adept at helping peers change their behaviors and attitudes to support a drug-free lifestyle. Peers support one another as they transition from one phase to the next, and members who have been in the community the longest, regardless of chronological age, become role models for new members. Thus the DYC model uses a therapeutic community approach to provide a comprehensive treatment model for youths and young adults.

EVALUATION OF THE DYC TREATMENT MODEL

The purpose of the current evaluation of the DYC model is to (1) determine the extent to which youths changed their behavior as a result of exposure to the DYC model (outcome evaluation); (2) determine the factors that members, parents, and staff consider to be important elements of the program (ethnographic study); (3) determine the cost of providing the service (cost study); and (4) produce a treatment manual so the program can be replicated in other settings (see Dennis et al., 2003). Despite the fact that the program has been operating for thirty years, this is the first formal evaluation that has been conducted.

For the outcome evaluation, youths and their parents participated in a structured interview which contained questions about substance use behavior, physical and mental health, risk behaviors, environment and living situation, and legal status. The instrumentation for the structured interview was based on the Global Appraisal of Individual Needs (GAIN) developed by Michael Dennis (see Dennis, 1999). Since DYC is a multistage therapeutic community, youths were recruited into the study as they entered the residential facility and as they transitioned to a new phase of treatment.

Preliminary Findings from the Outcome Evaluation

Given the unusual length of the program, one of the first questions to be addressed is the retention rate. Using data from the New York State Office of Alcoholism and Substance Abuse Service (OASAS), Table 10.2 shows DYC retention rates compared to rates for similar adolescent and young adult treatment programs. DYC is at or above the median retention rates for both short- and long-term retention. (*Note:* the DYC program consists of three separately licensed treatment programs that include the residential, day treatment and reentry, and transition phases. Retention rates are reported for each type of service separately, not the entire course of treatment.)

Staff report that certain periods arise during the course of treatment when members are at greater risk for leaving the program.

TABLE 10.2. DYC Retention Rates Compared to Similar Programs in New York, July 1999-June 2000

Program	OASAS Standard or (Median) Retention Rate(%)[a]	DYC Retention Rate (%)
Residential		
1 month	(79)	79
1 year[b]	(40)	59
% completing program or referred	25	56
Day Services (includes reentry)		
1 month	(81)	78
6 month[b]	40	84
% completing program or referred	25	76
Ambulatory (transition)		
1 month	(88)	100
1 year[b]	25	75
% completing program or referred	25	85

[a]OASAS reports either a standard or (median) retention rate for the comparison programs. The standard retention rate is required by regulation or federal mandate (*Source:* NYS Office of Alcoholism and Substance Abuse Services).
[b]The denominator excludes individuals who left treatment in the first month.

These periods include the first four months of residential treatment, the transition from residential to day treatment, and the transition into the final phase of the program. It is anticipated that information from the ethnographic interviews will contribute to our understanding of why those periods are critical and the factors that contribute to a member's decision to stay in, or leave, the program.

Table 10.1 shows data from initial interviews with DYC youth who were admitted to the residential program (n = 54). A review of Table 10.1 shows that the majority of adolescents in this sample admitted to DYC were male, had substantial involvement with a variety of substances (e.g., marijuana, heroin, and cocaine), and started using substances before they were fifteen years old. Ninety-two percent reported behaviors that were consistent with drug dependence. Youths also self-reported substantial involvement with the criminal justice system and prior treatment experience. Taken together, these data suggest that DYC serves adolescents who are severely involved with substances and who have experienced negative consequences of such use. Additional results of the outcome evaluation, which monitors member changes over a one-year period, will be discussed in subsequent reports. In addition, a cost analysis is being conducted to examine the relationship between program outcomes and the cost of providing the program. The results of the process and cost evaluations will also be described in subsequent reports and publications.

The process evaluation, which includes an ethnographic study of members, their families, and DYC staff, will describe the factors within the DYC experience that contribute to, or impede, recovery. By combining the qualitative and quantitative data from the outcome and process evaluations, findings are expected to touch on several questions of interest in adolescent drug treatment research such as

1. What factors contribute to, or impede engagement and retention in substance abuse treatment programs?
2. What is the effect of using an integrated-age approach in an adolescent TC?
3. How does a TC adapt its program to meet the needs of an ethnically diverse population?
4. What are the stages of change experienced by an adolescent as he or she recovers from addiction and are these changes program dependent?
5. Do gender differences apply in any of the preceding questions?

What is currently known is that DYC is an established adolescent TC that has evolved over time to meet the needs of the adolescent community. DYC has thrived, in part, due to its ability to adapt TC principles to meet the changing demands of adolescents, their parents, and the larger culture. Whether at the residential facility, the day services program, or in the transition phase, members and staff work together to form a community throughout all aspects of treatment. The results of the SAMHSA evaluation of the DYC model and other adolescent drug treatment programs will contribute substantially to our knowledge of the factors that facilitate and impede substance use treatment for youths in today's world.

NOTES

1. The contractual (funded) capacity at DYC for residential, day treatment, and ambulatory services is seventy-six, thirty-five, and twenty clients, respectively; the building capacity for the residential treatment and the Brooklyn center is seventy-six and sixty clients, respectively. Usually DYC serves seventy-six clients in the residential facility, close to sixty clients in day treatment, and fewer in ambulatory services.

2. Clients in DYC are referred to as members to reinforce the concept that they are part of a larger community.

3. Youths are admitted directly to day treatment while awaiting admission to residential treatment, or when residential treatment may not be the appropriate level of care.

4. The Brooklyn facility has an on-site classroom staffed by teachers from the NYC Board of Education.

REFERENCES

Dennis, M. (1999). *Global Appraisal of Individual Needs*. Copyright, Chestnut Health Systems, 720 West Chestnut, Bloomington, IL 61701.

Dennis, M., Dawud-Noursi, S., Muck, R., McDermeit, M. (2003). The need for developing and evaluating adolescent treatment models. In S.J. Stevens and A. Morral (Eds.), *Adolescent Substance Abuse Treatment in the United States: Exemplary Models from a National Evaluation Study* (pp. 3-26). Binghamton, NY: The Haworth Press, Inc.

De Leon. G. (1988). The therapeutic community perspective and approach for adolescent substance abusers. In Sherman C. Feinstein (Ed.), *Adolescent Psychiatry* (pp. 535-556). Chicago, IL: The University of Chicago Press.

De Leon, G. (1997). Therapeutic communities: Is there an essential model? In George De Leon (Ed.), *Community As Method: Therapeutic Communities for Special Population and Special Settings* (pp. 3-18). Westport, CT: Praeger.

De Leon, G. (2000). *The Therapeutic Community: Theory, Model, and Method*. New York: Springer.

Jainchill, N. (1997) Therapeutic communities for adolescents: The same and not the same. In George De Leon (Ed.), *Community As Method: Therapeutic Communities for Special Population and Special Settings* (pp. 161-177). Westport, CT: Praeger.

Kooyman, M. (1993). *The Therapeutic Community for Addicts: Intimacy, Parent Involvement and Treatment Success*. Berwyn, PA: Swets and Zeitlinger.

Yablonsky, L. (1989). *The Therapeutic Community: A Successful Approach for Treating Substance Abusers*. New York: Gardner Press, Inc.

Chapter 11

Thunder Road Adolescent Substance Abuse Treatment Program

Patricia Shane
Linda Cherry
Tom Gerstel

INTRODUCTION

Thunder Road, a fifty-bed residential substance abuse treatment program, serves adolescents thirteen to nineteen years of age. Annual client admissions, with 300 to 340 entering per year, include adolescents who reside in twenty-four counties throughout the state of California, predominately in the northern California region. The treatment facility is owned and operated by Adolescent Treatment Centers, Inc., a nonprofit entity, and is accredited by the Commission on the Accreditation of Rehabilitation Facilities (CARF). It is a self-sustaining affiliate of the Sutter Health East Bay Hospital System. Since the treatment facility opened in 1987, over 3,500 clients have been admitted. The treatment program is housed in a freestanding, two-level

Preparation of this manuscript was supported by funding from the Center for Substance Abuse Treatment, Substance Abuse and Mental Health Services Administration, Department of Health and Human Services through the Adolescent Treatment Models Program (ATM) Grant # TI11432. The content and viewpoints expressed in this publication are those of the authors and do not necessarily reflect the views or policies of the Department of Health and Human Services or those of the funding agency. The authors would like to thank Barbara Delaney, Kimberly Shaw, and Barry Gurdin for assistance in preparing the manuscript.

Correspondence should be sent to Patricia Shane, PhD, MPH, Public Health Institute, 2001 Addison Street, Second Floor, Berkeley, CA 94704 (e-mail: <pshane@phi.org>).

32,000 square foot facility, in Oakland, California. Clients and their families are also served by a county-operated alternative school within the facility and a satellite office that provides assessments, family services, and continuing care support to families living in the San Jose region.

An independent evaluation of this treatment program is being conducted by researchers at the Public Health Institute as part of the Center for Substance Abuse Treatment's Adolescent Treatment Model program. Included in the research are a longitudinal, prospective study of client outcomes as well as manualization of Thunder Road's treatment approach and treatment protocols. Adolescents were recruited into the study on a voluntary basis over a twelve-month period (1999-2000), as they entered treatment. The study cohort are assessed multiple times, at baseline (within seventy-two hours of intake), and at three, six, nine, and twelve months after intake. By agreement, all data gathered from clients are maintained by researchers for evaluation purposes and client-specific data are not made available to the treatment program.

The treatment program operates with dual licensure, as a chemical dependency recovery hospital (CDRH) through the California Department of Health Services, and as a group home (GH) by the California Department of Social Services. Thunder Road's CDRH's hospital-track program, offers an intensive thirty- to fifty-day residential program, serving primarily private-pay clients and those whose treatment is authorized by third-party managed-care payers. Adolescent clients referred and funded by the juvenile justice system or county social services departments generally enter the group home track, with a projected residential stay of six to twelve months. Primary goals in both treatment tracks include reunifying adolescents with families, addressing destabilizing influences within each client's family system, and developing long-term recovery plans.

HISTORY AND ORIGINS OF THE HYBRID THERAPEUTIC COMMUNITY TREATMENT MODEL

Thunder Road was designed in the mid-1980s by a group of five people who synthesized their varying perspectives on treatment and recovery. They incorporated elements of medical and social models, the most dominant approaches at that time. The medical model contributed a management style, individualized treatment plans, focus on individual psychosocial dynamics, psychiatric evaluation upon admission, clinical engagement with clients during and after discharge, medical charting, supervision of weekly treatment planning sessions by a psychiatrist, incorporation of medical and mental health professionals on staff, and use of private third-party reimbursement sources, such as health insurance. Social model elements added an emphasis on client skill building, participation of clients in program operations, use of adolescent peer groups, expansion of treatment to include a focus on family dynamics, imposition of behavioral expectations, reliance on a heterogeneous treatment staff, including blending staff with professional, paraprofessional, and personal recovery backgrounds. Thunder Road was designed to forge a network of youths and adults in a recovering community where the cathartic experience of recovery could be shared (De Leon, 1994; Jainchill, 1997). The original mission was to create a treatment intervention for adolescents that provided a more holistic consideration, identification, and resolution of issues throughout each client's family system. The importance of addressing developmentally appropriate cognitive and behavioral skills while teaching self-monitoring techniques and responsible membership in the community has been pivotal (Kendall and Williams, 1986).

An extended period of residential treatment is intended to create a break in the behavioral patterns of both the adolescent and family members or other significant adults. A majority of adolescents admitted to Thunder Road have become alienated from family, school, and other social resources that help to maintain stability. Treatment planning and interventions are designed to address not only the addictive behaviors of the teenager but family systems issues, as well. Residential treatment provides youths and family members with the opportunity to assess and reformulate more constructive patterns. The transition from drug use to established abstinence requires substantial physical, emotional, cognitive, and behavioral change. Especially for adolescents, change requires a safe and stable environment where they can begin to develop new habits, daily routines, and relationships while drug free.

The twelve steps to recovery have become one of the cornerstones of the program (Alford, Koehler, and Leonard, 1991; Makela, et al.,1996; Wheeler and Malmquist, 1987). The twelve-steps recovery precepts establish an understanding of recovery as a lifelong endeavor, provide a model for sustaining abstinence, and place emphasis on building and strengthening the drug-free peer group network. While in treatment, clients are introduced to the twelve-step language and culture. Adult twelve-step language is modified to provide a symbolic framework for adolescents in treatment. Peer-based twelve-step foci reinforce the importance of peer culture and client governance in the Thunder Road therapeutic community. These aspects of the program

1. encourage clients to rely on peers to help resolve conflicts,
2. provide peer-based community leadership,
3. enhance skills necessary to assume responsible leadership roles,
4. support peer to peer interventions,
5. incorporate behavioral modeling by longer-term residents, and
6. harness aspects of adolescent developmental patterns that are peer focused to promote behavioral change.

Positive peer influence within the residential treatment setting is supported through a system of peer government and leadership. As clients progress in the program, they are required to assume greater responsibility in mentoring others and modeling leadership roles. To sustain recovery after residential treatment, Alcoholics Anonymous and Narcotics Anonymous offer ongoing support opportunities in the wider community and throughout the country.

A unique hybrid treatment model has evolved from these various treatment approaches. The experience-based development of the model combines psychosocial and cognitive-behavioral elements to meet the unique needs of adolescents with problems related to substance abuse and dependence. A highly detailed system of behavioral standards is in place. These behavioral codes address an array of emotional and behavioral difficulties that copresent with adolescent substance abuse and operate in combination with strategies emphasizing family reunification. However, the determination of consequences for misbehavior is not codified or invariant. It is understood that all clients will have different, specific baseline behaviors when they enter treatment. Each person's treatment plan incorporates processes that are designed to decrease the frequency and severity of problem behaviors, even when extinguishing certain behaviors may not be achievable during residential care.

Decisions regarding the program's response to client behaviors are flexible and case-specific. Among factors weighed are: the client's background; his or her contribution to the community prior to the incident or rule violation; the client's ability to discontinue the behavior; the frequency or severity of the client's offense; and the impact of the behavior on all members of the community. Special importance is placed on the welfare of the community. Residents are not permitted to make mistakes that cost other people their chance at becoming clean and sober. For example, smuggling drugs onto the unit and sharing them with other clients is one of the most serious transgressions.

Activities in the treatment setting occur within a structured framework of rules delineating permissible conduct. Rules are designed to reflect standards of the outside community and assist clients to understand and learn to meet these standards. Clients are expected to conduct themselves in a socially acceptable manner, contribute to the recovering community, demonstrate self-respect and respect for others, and exert themselves as active participants in the recovery process for themselves and others. Incentives and privileges are used to encourage clients to abide by rules and to assume leadership roles. Violations of behavioral standards are met with various consequences intended to help adolescents recognize and address negative behaviors and their underlying issues. Peers, as well as staff, are involved in the administration of consequences.

Failure to meet the behavioral expectations, known as cardinal rules, can result in discharge from the program. Cardinal rules are concerned with substance use, violence, threatening behavior, theft, destruction of property, romantic or sexual contact with others, and leaving the facility without authorization (AWOL). In addition, anyone who conceals knowledge of a peer who has violated these rules is also in violation. The goal underlying the system is to engage each client in a course of behavior modification designed to challenge maladaptive behavior within a safe and caring environment. Attitudinal and behavioral factors which mediate or exacerbate alcohol and other drug (AOD) use/abuse are considered integral to all therapeutic interventions.

The local county Office of Education has continuously operated a specialized alternative school within the facility since the treatment program's inception. A collaborative team of county school officials assisted in planning educational services designed to seamlessly interface with treatment services. Educational services for clients are provided throughout the year for clients in the CDRH and GH treatment components. Over the years, the educational staff has formalized participation in the treatment program as collaborating members of the multidisciplinary treatment team. School credits earned at Thunder Road are fully transferable to each client's home school. School staff assume lead responsibility for modifying and integrating the educational curricula with each client's written treatment assignments. Close collaboration between the education and treatment systems has been an ongoing part of the program's design and operation.

COURSE OF TREATMENT

Treatment follows a phased format, consistent with a therapeutic community treatment model. These phases are not strictly linear, since they are intended to reflect a developmental view of the recovery process (De Leon, 1997). Duration of treatment varies as clients progress, and sometimes regress, along the continuum of change. At a conceptual level, the treatment model for both the CDRH and GH treatment tracks is the same and treatment involvement is designed to be, at a minimum, one year in duration for all clients and families. At this level of care, treatment begins with a CDRH inpatient, or GH residential phase of treatment and proceeds through aftercare (continuing care) on an outpatient basis. Adolescents and families in the CDRH treatment track typically participate in the continuing care component of the program longer than clients in the GH track. Both treatment tracks consist of three stages focused sequentially on (1) orientation and education; (2) primary treatment; and (3) reunification and reentry. The inpatient and residential treatment phases merge into the continuing care phase of treatment. These treatment paths are conceived as continuous and fully integrated aspects of the service delivery model. They are not considered separate programs.

Screening/Preadmission

Inquiries for services are referred to an assessment/admissions counselor who schedules an interview appointment for the adolescent and his or her parent or guardian. During the intake assessment, suitability of the adolescent and his or her family for treatment is determined. At this time families are informed about Thunder Road's program philosophy and structure. Information is collected about health or physical problems, family history, educational history, psychological and emotional history, any prior treatment or counseling, legal problems, drug and alcohol related incidents, and social history. Insurance coverage and personal liability issues are also discussed. If a client is referred from juvenile justice, rights and responsibilities of clients and family are explained, including probable consequences for violations of court orders. A counselor meets individually with the adolescent and individually with parents or legal guardians during the session to collect information and to provide an opportunity to share their perspectives. The entire family then reconvenes and the counselor makes recommendations for admission and/or provides referrals to more appropriate services. Final authority for admission to Thunder Road is the responsibility of a staff psychiatrist.

Stage I—Orientation and Education

Entry into Treatment

The beginning steps of treatment at Thunder Road are focused on providing adolescents an understanding of the process and typical treatment milestones and on communicating that it is an environment where they are safe enough to consider and practice newfound recovery lifestyle skills. Simultaneously, a complex assessment process, described in the following, is completed and reviewed, allowing treatment providers to gather essential information necessary to formulate individual treatment plans. During the first twenty-four hours each adolescent remains in his or her room, allowing a brief time for observation, detoxification, initial assessment, and completion of the preliminary treatment plan. Clients also complete basic treatment assignments during this time, prior to formally moving into Stage I of the program. These assignments include completion of a questionnaire on drug use; a brief written autobiography; and a description of the client's "family," its strengths and weaknesses, as well as a history of drug use/abuse within the family system.

Admission/Assessment

A series of interviews and evaluations is conducted, including a health and physical examination by a pediatrician, evaluation by a staff psychiatrist, and interviews with a primary counselor, pastoral counselor, and a member of the nursing staff. All short-term clients receive a psychiatric evaluation during the first week of treatment and long-term clients are evaluated within three weeks of entering the program. The psychiatric evaluation includes: current emotional, behavioral, social, developmental, and family dynamic issues; histories of previous emotional, behavioral, and substance abuse problems and treatment; current functioning; formal mental status exam, appropriate to the age of the client; childhood development; social and peer group pressures; suicidality and psychiatric diagnoses. If psychological testing is indicated, an appropriate referral is made. In addition, the client's attending psychiatrist is responsible for reviewing all psychotropic drug therapies. The psychiatrist makes recommendations to the multidisciplinary team for treatment with special emphasis on issues to be explored in family, group, and individual counseling sessions.

At the time of admission, members of the nursing staff initiate a physical examination, followed by Thunder Road's pediatrician, who completes a medical history and physical examination within the first twenty-four hours of an adolescent's stay. The pediatrician reviews all nonpsychotropic drugs, and orders any medication that is necessary and appropriate. The pediatrician also orders any laboratory and X ray procedures or immunizations needed, prescribes diet or physical activity restrictions, and refers for specialized evaluations, if indicated. The staff pediatrician coordinates treatment referrals for nicotine abuse and recommendations are forwarded to the multidisciplinary team for each client.

Extensive information on the family of each client is collected during the first week in residential treatment. This includes: assessment of environment and home; religion and financial status of family; assessment of family dynamics, e.g., divorce, death, physical or mental illness, physical or sexual abuse in the family, or drug/alcohol use. When an adolescent enters treatment and begins the process of recovery, every change places demands on family members to respond, support, and reciprocate. Often, family members struggle with these changes. In recognition of this, Thunder Road staff simultaneously begin to work with family members in an effort to overcome barriers, strengthen relationships, and ameliorate painful or debilitating experiences.

An ordained minister on staff at Thunder Road interviews each new client to determine whether concepts of spirituality resonate with the adolescent. The assessment establishes baseline information about the extent to which spirituality might become a support in the client's recovery. The minister may also help to explain the disease concept of addiction to families whose religious beliefs may view substance abuse problems differently.

Clients are considered to be in orientation throughout Stage I of their treatment. This lasts for approximately two weeks for short-term CDRH clients and up to three months for long-term GH clients. Stage I includes completion of a number of comprehensive assessments. Substance abuse severity is assessed, as are interrelated consequences, causes, and cooccurring problems that affect the client and the client's family. Collateral information is obtained from a variety of family, referral, school, and legal sources during this process. This information is compiled, entered in the client's chart, and used as the basis for initial treatment and recovery planning. Addiction education and learning assignments on emotional, physical, and intellectual functioning, as well as spiritual development, are integral to Stage I.

All those entering Thunder Road are assigned a peer buddy, whose role is to orient new clients to the program and the therapeutic community. Analogous to twelve-step sponsors, peer buddies carry responsibility for keeping new clients safely in the program for their first week prior to engaging them in the demanding realities of a therapeutic community milieu. Peer buddies can receive consequences if problems arise when new clients assigned to a peer buddy have an inadequate understanding of rules and expectations.

The multidisciplinary team develops the client's individualized treatment plan within seven days, based upon formal and informal assessments. Individualized treatment plans contain emotional, behavioral, social, family, physical, legal, educational, vocational, and other components, in combination with treatment goals specific to AOD use/abuse. Measurable and time limited objectives are written for each goal, problem, or need. These objectives are practical, concrete, and easily understood by the client, family, and staff.

Primary counselors, who usually carry a caseload of four to six clients, are responsible for sharing the treatment plan with their clients and obtaining client input concerning their needs. The philosophy at Thunder Road is that clients will improve most effectively when they are participants in their treatment planning and collaborate with staff. Research points to the importance of involving adolescents in treatment decisions and suggests that it has a positive effect on motivation for engagement in therapy (Adelman, Kaser-Boyd, and Taylor, 1984).

When clients enter the program's regular daily schedule in Stage I, they begin their ongoing participation in individual counseling and multiple group therapy modalities, as well as maintaining regular school attendance and participating in recreation and exercise activities on a daily basis. The focus of groups includes, but is not limited to, therapeutic community concepts, denial, codependency, gender, psychosocial issues, anger management, confrontation, resolution, grief, health, diversity, relapse prevention, twelve-step concepts, multifamily therapy, educational and vocational needs, sexual abuse survivors' support, and reunification issues.

Stage II—Core Issues

Stage II addresses powerlessness, inability to manage age-appropriate skills and tasks, and client's core issues within eight areas:

1. identification with positive role models,
2. responsibility for one's family,
3. development of problem solving skills,
4. skills of self,
5. interpersonal skills,
6. organizational and planning skills,
7. development of judgment, and
8. development of a specific recovery plan for the individual.

With program support, each client seeks to define, identify, and in some cases address, the core emotional or psychological issues that are contributing to his or her substance use/abuse.

This stage has individualized treatment assignments based on the presenting factors for each client. Self-monitoring behavioral techniques facilitate the adolescent's understanding of self, and allow the youth to self-report in accordance with his or her developmental capacities (Kendall and Williams, 1986). Concurrently, effective interpersonal and communication skills training are provided for clients and parents. Clients complete treatment assignments and essays on "What I have learned about my core issues" and "My recovery" in Stage II, "What my goals are" for Stage III, and "Why I deserve Stage III." These assignments serve as intervention strategies, designed to increase the client's awareness of a behavior or set of behaviors, habitual patterns, or antecedents of behavior. The essays require the client to address self-image, while placing a positive value on recovery, and working toward a positive outcome.

The primary task during this phase is to internalize acceptable standards of sober behavior and to function, as fully as possible, within the therapeutic community, developing competencies in primary functional areas of life. Developing age-appropriate self-control and being able to moderate one's own behavior are considered important competencies for each adolescent. These core competencies are seen as particularly useful for adolescents whose families are significantly troubled or are unable to be relied upon as supportive partners in the treatment and recovery process.

When significant progress has been made in the eight specific treatment-planning areas, the clinical multidisciplinary team, the client, and the family begin the process of advancement to Stage III. This stage requires clients to identify how they intend to improve family relationships, handle social situations, use their Higher Power, and take care of themselves emotionally, spiritually, and physically. As appropriate, family members address legal, transportation, and financial issues. Clients also begin negotiating their continuing care contracts with their primary counselor and family members. Clients must present a proposal to advance to Stage III during a multidisciplinary treatment planning meeting. This session focuses on community reentry, relapse triggers, and family reunification or emancipation.

Stage III—Reunification and Community Reentry

During Stage III clients prepare for reentry and family reunification, including preparation of a comprehensive continuing care contract. Based on the assimilation of information in Stage I and the emotional readiness work in Stage II, clients and families participate in building a reentry recovery plan. Group, individual, and multifamily groups continue during Stage III, but the focus shifts to the reentry and reunification process that occurs when clients leave the residential phase of treatment to the outpatient continuing care phase. Clients, families, and primary counselors continue to work on the continuing care contract. It includes a plan to address what clients will be doing when they return to home, school, employment options, recreational and social activities, and meeting the challenges of carrying their recovery into roles and responsibilities in the community. Acceptable forms of behavior between parents and clients are established and contractual understandings are reached, with provisions made to monitor behaviors during the continuing care phase.

Clients in Stage III are expected to demonstrate significant leadership skills. This includes providing support and feedback to peers, confronting inappropriate behaviors among peers, and serving as a peer buddy to new clients. Privileges increase during this period. Clients receive visits from friends, approved by their families and staff, and both supervised and unsupervised passes are granted. During Stage III, clients spend time with parents or guardians, and they may leave the facility to conduct personal business or pursue leisure activities approved by staff.

Treatment assignments continue in Stage III with an increased emphasis on building a solid recovery foundation. Reading and writing assignments continue based on Hazelden's Steps 5, 6, and 7 for Young Adults, and Chapters 6 through 12 in the Alcoholics Anonymous Big Book. Clients complete a daily Narcotics Anonymous Journal, do a Step 1 review, identify and post at least five relapse triggers for themselves, and discuss them in peer groups. They draft and refine reentry plans that address living situations, school, and/or work. They develop relapse prevention plans that are shared in groups. They practice time management by submitting to staff weekly schedules of outside appointments, commitments, passes, and money requests. They plan and complete their Stage III projects that symbolize giving back to the community to demonstrate their appreciation.

Preparation for successful discharge from the facility includes writing and presenting essays on "What I have learned about myself and recovery at Thunder Road" and "What Thunder Road means to me." These are read at a discharge ceremony. Prior to their anticipated discharge date, clients begin saying good-bye to all groups and individuals at Thunder Road. Continuing care contracts are finalized with input from clients, family members, and primary counselors. Residential treatment ends with a discharge ceremony that has symbolic content associated with an adolescent rite of passage.

Discharge

Clients are discharged from residential treatment under one of three conditions: honorable, concerned, and dishonorable. If the multidisciplinary team determines that a client has achieved the goals of his or her treatment plan and the family has developed an awareness and control of family dynamics that can lead to dysfunction, as well as new constructive, behavioral patterns, the client will be honorably discharged. In recent years clients enter treatment with increasingly serious mental health conditions. Although they make progress, they often cannot tolerate the communal treatment program long enough to achieve an honorable discharge. However, staff believe that in the less emotionally intense outpatient setting of continuing care, many can build upon their residential treatment experiences and solidify their recovery. In response, Thunder Road created the status of concerned discharge. This allows these clients to maintain their involvement with the treatment program. Concerned discharge is also often granted to clients whose private insurance coverage for inpatient or residential treatment authorizes only brief stays (less than twenty-eight days), but who still need to complete recommended treatment assignments or twelve-step program work.

Continuing Care

The final stage of treatment is continuing care, an outpatient, aftercare phase. It begins when clients return home after discharge and continues as a complement to residential care. Ideally, the total duration of a client's involvement with the treatment program, from first admission to residential treatment through continuing care, spans an entire year. Thunder Road provides extensive support to clients and family members for this six to twelve month period after completion of the residential phase. Thunder Road clients are not expected to fully resolve their treatment issues during their residential stay. Maintaining behaviors that underlie recovery requires ongoing support. Thunder Road's model assumes that the most challenging phase of treatment occurs after a teenager completes his or her residential stay and returns to school, neighborhood, family, and social networks.

Continuing care services consist of three meetings at the Thunder Road facility each week for clients and family members. At one weekly meeting, groups of youth and parents meet together in a multifamily group. In two additional meetings, youths and their parents/guardians meet in separate group sessions once each week. Groups attempt to have consistent membership and are facilitated by a Thunder Road counselor. A client relapse is viewed as an opportunity for additional learning. A variety of clinical treatment assignments are offered to most clients who have been suspended or terminated, allowing them to reenter and complete treatment. Relapse prevention is considered a core element of recovery planning, as clients make the complex transition back into the community (Spear, Ciesla, and Skala, 1999). Adolescents who participate in Thunder Road's treatment program are expected to develop a sober peer group upon returning to their homes and communities. In addition, twelve-step meetings occur at Thunder Road and off-site throughout the year. Prior to completing residential treatment at Thunder Road, each adolescent is required to establish a relationship with a twelve-step sponsor outside the treatment program.

Adolescents and family members who successfully complete continuing care become "graduates" of Thunder Road. Two or three times each year graduation ceremonies are held for groups of clients and family members. Both adolescents and adult participants receive certificates of program completion. Graduates are invited to become members of the alumni association and to serve as peer counselors.

ELEMENTS OF THE TREATMENT APPROACH

Constructs and Practices

Core constructs are designed to advance the goals of the therapeutic community and treatment model, which are substantially different from a clinical model. Even routine tasks and spontaneous conversations between and among clients and staff are considered to be integral to the therapeutic milieu. Therapeutic interventions are not specific to scheduled sessions, and insight can be found within the routine and mundane aspects of daily life in the community, as well as more highly focused and constructed group or individual sessions. Staff are not the only source of interventions. Interventions frequently occur within peer-to-peer interactions. It is not only credentialed, academically trained staff who are responsible for delivering treatment services. All staff members are valued members of the therapeutic community for whom all interactions with clients are considered therapeutic in nature. All members are viewed as role models, including peers who have been part of the therapeutic community for longer periods of time (De Leon, 1997). This approach offers support and help in restructuring or creating individual behavioral changes, as well as environmentally promoting habilitation, integration, and psychosocial change. The relationship between individual recovery and recovery among many members within the community (including staff and adolescent peers) is reinforcing, mutually dependent, and interactive (Shaw and Borkman, 1990). The focus of treatment is broadly on drug-related problems, not just the use/abuse of alcohol or other drugs. In this model, family systems are viewed as integral to myriad reciprocal relationships.

Overall, Thunder Road advances a family systems approach to dealing with the disease of alcoholism and drug addiction. Since the family's experience with the disease has impacted all its members, the recovery process requires their involvement. The process of recovering from alcohol/drug abuse and dependence requires constant maintenance, since these are chronic diseases (McLellan et al., 2000).

See Table 11.1 for some defining characteristics of the treatment approach at Thunder Road.

Family Involvement

Family involvement is central to Thunder Road's efforts to provide clients with a functional home environment that will support their continued sobriety after residential treatment. Beginning with the admissions process, family members—defined as those with whom the client will live upon discharge—are encouraged to view the Thunder Road experience as essentially family treatment, albeit one that is focused upon the adolescent who has a substance abuse problem. Family involvement is considered integral to improving interpersonal

TABLE 11.1. Elements of Treatment Approach

Elements	Source of Contributing Elements
View of treatment	Hybrid/(S) (12-S) Recovery is a lifelong process but (C) primary treatment requires a residential stay in a licensed medical facility, followed by after care, for relatively time-limited periods.
Relationships	(S) (TC) Those who live and work in the program are to be regarded as family, regardless of position. "Family" becomes a metaphor for accessibility, respect, interdependence, and caring.
Peer orientation	(S) (TC) Peer group processes are rooted in interactions among peers at different stages of recovery.
Orientation to twelve steps	(12-S) Twelve-step programs are foundational, and self-help practices are core aspects of social model recovery.
Authority/knowledge base	Hybrid/(TC) Experiential knowledge of recovery is a major basis of authority. (C) Professionalism and expertise of staff with academic degrees contribute authority.
Staffing	(S) (TC) Multidisciplinary teams, comprised of blended professional and paraprofessional staff, formulate and deliver each client's treatment plan. A predominately horizontal management structure prevails. Recovering staff are in the majority.

Note: S = social model; C = clinical model; TC = therapeutic community; 12-S = twelve-step program.

communication among family members, improving the ability of parents/guardians to consistently provide structure and limit-setting; and addressing addiction patterns in the parents (Windle, Shope, and Bukstein, 1996).

"Family" is defined broadly to include the significant adults in the teenager's life, whether parents, guardians, other relations, or close friends. All those with adolescents in the short-term chemical dependency recovery hospital program are expected to be in the facility for at least nine hours per week. Families in the long-term group home program participate for at least five hours per week. Parental involvement includes attending a series of twelve lectures on addiction, recovery, parenting, and participation in weekly multifamily counseling groups and parent discussion groups, as well as biweekly visits with their children. During the early phases of treatment family system concepts, philosophical underpinnings of recovery, and new vocabulary terms are shared with all family members. Addiction as a family disease, dynamics of chemical dependency, and codependency are explained. Differences between enabling behaviors and nurturing behaviors are discussed. After a client completes the residential phase of treatment, family members must continue to attend twice-weekly meetings at Thunder Road, as part of the continuing care program. This level of involvement often involves an enormous commitment of time and energy, particularly since families often live at a great distance from the treatment facility.

Treatment Planning

Treatment plan development begins within the first twenty-four hours of admission to Thunder Road. After a preliminary plan is devised, a more thorough, individualized treatment plan is completed within seven days, based upon formal and informal assessments. These plans contain emotional, behavioral, social, family, physical, legal, educational, vocational, and other psychosocial components, as well as goals specific to addiction treatment. They include specific objectives that are practical, concrete, and related to presenting problems. Treatment plans are reviewed and updated semi-weekly by members of the multidisciplinary treatment team. During these reviews assessments by multiple members of the staff of each individual client's issues and progress contribute to more comprehensive planning of additional supportive intervention strategies. Clients and parents are occasionally invited to participate in treatment planning to discuss goals and strategies.

Behavior Modification

Thunder Road uses behavior modification to help clients shape their actions and attitudes. Clients are expected to communicate and cooperate with all staff members, to participate in the program by attending all therapy and treatment groups as well as other program activities, and to respect the program, physical facilities, and the surrounding neighborhood. Clients must refrain from destroying property, behave in a socially acceptable manner, and exercise good judgment in relations with their peers. Individualized negotiations take each client's developmental stage into consideration. This blended approach of accountability and clear behavioral rules, combined with an individualized approach to competencies, maturation, and developmentally appropriate expectations, results in an environment of emotional safety for youngsters who may have led chaotic lives and spent little time in safe situations.

Reassessment

Violation of major behavioral expectations results in reassessment, and in extreme cases may lead to dishonorable discharge from the program. Habitual attitudes that run counter to the peer culture of working toward recovery in the community may also lead to reassessment. During reassessment, clinical staff reevaluate the client's status in the program and may require that a client repeat steps or stages in the treatment process, have certain privileges revoked, or again in extreme cases, be dishonorably discharged from the program. During reassessment, a client has no communication with peers and completes written learning experiences, concrete and specific treatment assignments, and/or work assignments given by staff that are designed to guide them through reflective consideration of their behavior(s). Adapted from adult therapeutic community models, reassessment was originally intended to protect the house from disruptions by a particularly disturbed client. Major behavioral rules include:

- In treatment, we are clean and sober, abstaining from all mind-altering substances.
- We are not violent or threatening toward any members of our community.
- We do not steal anyone else's belongings.
- We respect property and do not destroy or deface any of our own, peers', or Thunder Road's property.
- We respect each other's boundaries and do not get involved in any sexual activities with others or become involved in romantic relationships.
- We do not leave treatment without permission (AWOL).

- To keep our community safe, we do not keep secrets or hold contracts of knowledge of any peers who have broken cardinal rules.

Learning Experiences

A "learning experience" (LE) is a treatment intervention tool used in behavioral modification. LEs are used as interventions or consequences in response to inappropriate behavior by a client. Violation of program rules are recorded as "bookings" by staff or peers, while positive "bookings" affirm and acknowledge outstanding behaviors. Positive bookings are accumulated and exchanged by clients for a variety of value-based extra privileges, including special outings or activities. Negative bookings are evaluated on a weekly basis by staff who then assign learning experiences that relate to the infractions, such as essays, work during breaks, dialogues with staff or clients to resolve conflicts or receive feedback, bans on recreational activities, or reflective exercises ("the bench"). Each client has input on corrective measures that need to be undertaken to make personal changes. The client can appeal if he or she feels the bookings are invalid or the assigned discipline is inappropriate or too severe.

The Bench

"The bench" is a simple wooden bench placed against the wall in the hallway. Clients who demonstrate dangerous or inappropriate behaviors or attitudes, and fail to respond to attempts at resolution, are sent to sit on the bench without discussion or complaint. Clients must sit up straight, look straight ahead and maintain silence while on the bench. Staff and peers do not interact with those seated on the bench and clients may not stand up from the bench without permission from a staff member. Most "bench time"(roughly 80 percent) has a duration of five to fifteen minutes. For major rule infractions, in situations where bench time, in combination with other learning assignments, are an agreed upon alternative to discharge from the program, bench time may be required for seven to nine hours. This time would be done in short intervals over a three- to nine-day period, with stretch breaks at least every twenty minutes. Staff members supervise and individualize the use of this intervention technique based upon assessments and standard program protocols. To outside observers, the bench may seem punitive, but it has proven itself to be a vital element in the development of discipline and self-control with clients. The bench contributes to the lack of violent episodes within the program and delimits the need for staff to engage in physical or manual restraints of clients. It is useful in mastering impulsive behaviors and/or assisting in anger management. Once a client learns how to use the bench effectively, he or she is encouraged to use the bench when dealing with overwhelming emotions. This gives clients a place to cope with feelings of anger and frustration without incurring the negative consequences of acting out old behaviors. The development of the capacity for reflection, introspection, and mindfulness of consequences related to behaviors and actions is a critical element.

Staffing

Staff represent diverse approaches within the model. Thunder Road employs a staff of approximately ninety people. Of these, about fifty are usually directly engaged in the provision of therapeutic services, however, all staff are mediators of therapeutic change (De Leon, 1994). They cooperate to develop interventions and individualized treatment plans that maximize the fit with individual needs and issues. Professional treatment staff includes psychiatrists, a pediatrician, nurses, counselors, and interns. Physicians, psychiatrists, and psychologists practicing at Thunder Road are organized into a formal medical staff, which is governed by extensive bylaws and protocols. Professional staff conduct formal programs on quality assurance, utilization review, privileging, and patient care monitoring, as well as staff training and development. Peer counselors are often former clients who return after successful program completion to provide support and serve as role models for clients struggling with the attitude/behavior changes required throughout recovery.

Collaborative Management

During the early 1990s, a collaborative staff management system was introduced. It emphasizes a free flow of program and fiscal information throughout the staff, involvement of staff in decisions that affect their jobs and the status of the program, use of committees and workgroups, and minimization of managerial or professional hierarchies within the staff. In addition to improvement in staff stability and morale, the initiative was perceived to have a positive impact on client satisfaction and outcomes.

The Physical Environment

The program is located in a former medical facility, with a reception area, staff offices, wide corridors and doorways (originally designed to accommodate gurneys), kitchen and dining area, classrooms and activity rooms, and resident bedrooms which open off common hallways have sparse furnishings and institution-style flooring, walls, and lighting. A majority of exit doors are accessible to clients. Most exterior doors are unlocked from the inside but equipped with an alarm system. For security from nonauthorized visitors, all exterior doors are locked from the outside. Room assignments are based on the clients' emotional condition, status in treatment, and ability to appropriately observe privacy. Clients are responsible for cleaning their own living quarters on a daily basis.

PROFILE OF CLIENTS ADMITTED
TO TREATMENT IN 1999

The typical client at Thunder Road is sixteen years old, has been using drugs for about five years, often failing school or chronically truant, has a recent history of involvement with a variety of institutions, including locked facilities, and comes from a family that is struggling with some kind of addiction. Findings suggest that the population served by this residential treatment program have multiple problems with relatively high rates of mental health, physical health, legal, and alcohol and other drug (AOD) problems (Sells and Blum, 1996). The national Adolescent Treatment Model study will yield a much broader understanding of these adolescents, provide information about their social circumstances, schooling, high-risk behaviors, and ultimately provide a clearer picture of their pathways into, through, and after treatment.

In calendar year 1999, Thunder Road admitted a total of 296 adolescent clients from twenty-four counties in the state of California. Of these 119 (40 percent) were female and 177 (60 percent) were male.

By treatment track, 203 (69 percent) entered through the hospital track (CDRH) and 93 (31 percent) entered through the group home track. The average age at admissions for the hospital track was 16.0 and 16.3 for females and males, respectively, and 16.3 and 16.9 for females and males entering the group home track. Ethnicity/race statistics for admissions in calendar year 1999 are reported in Table 11.2; discharge status data are reported in Table 11.3. These data suggest that the composition of the study cohort is comparable and well matched on age, gender, and treatment track to those who entered the treatment program during a calendar year when the study was in process.

TREATMENT CHALLENGES

Thunder Road has always distinguished between adhering to its guiding principles and allowing innovation and change in the specific building blocks of its program. The capacity for change has protected the program in times of fiscal and regulatory turbulence. It has also allowed for modification and adaptation of adolescent treatment approaches. This flexibility has been integral to success during a time when significant changes have occurred throughout the larger system

TABLE 11.2. Ethnicity/Race Statistics for Admissions in Calendar Year 1999[*]

Race/Ethnicity	Group Home Track		Hospital Track	
	N	%	N	%
Native American/Alaska Native	0	0	2	.9
Asian/Pacific Islander	2	2	8	3.9
Black	16	17	11	5.4
White	45	48	132	65.0
Mixed Other	6	7	11	5.4
Hispanic				
White	5	5	11	5.4
Black	1	1	2	.9
Other	18	19	24	11.8

[*]Includes fourteen clients who were discharged or readmitted.

TABLE 11.3. Discharge Status of Clients in Treatment (1999)[a]

Discharge Status (1999)	Group Home TX* Track		Hospital TX Track	
	N	%	N	%
AMA	0	0.00	11	4.89
AMA AWOL	46	48.90	44	19.56
CC	20	21.28	135	60.00
NC	1	1.06	23	10.22
TF	26	27.66	4	1.78
TF 5150	1	1.06	8	3.56

*TX = Treatment
Note: AMA = against medical advice; AMA AWOL = discharged when absent without leave; CC = continuing care; NC = noncompliant; TF = transfer to facility (juvenile hall, hospital, other program); TF 5150 = transfer to a psychiatric hospital.
[a]Includes fourteen clients who were discharged or readmitted.

of care, including shifts in funding mechanisms that are central to the program's capacity to deliver services. Among the most important trends which have impacted treatment and services are (1) the movement toward managed care, cost-containment pressures, and the resultant shift toward shorter lengths of stay; (2) the gradual, sweeping changes in public policy toward incarceration of youth involved in substance abuse, violence, and other criminal behaviors; and (3) rapid and profound changes in the demographic character of California and the Greater Bay Area of San Francisco leading to an increasingly culturally diverse population (see Table 11.4).

Although the adolescents who enter Thunder Road are highly diverse, it is possible to identify characteristics commonly found among those who receive treatment services there. The adolescents are often disadvantaged in multiple ways. In the aggregate, these adolescents demonstrate a more profoundly troubled subpopulation than school-enrolled, community-dwelling teenagers throughout the country. Among residents there are higher rates of psychiatric impairment, higher rates of involvement with the juvenile justice system, and higher rates of teens whose parents use/abuse alcohol or other drugs. Among study participants, 46 percent report alcohol problems in their immediate families and 55 percent report drug use within the family. These patterns are also

TABLE 11.4. Characteristics of ATM Study Cohort (N = 208)

Item	N	%
Gender		
Male	132	63
Female	76	37
Age		
Less than 15 years	27	13
15-18 years	178	86
Greater than 18 years	3	1
Ethnicity		
American Indian/Alaskan Native	5	2
Asian or Pacific Islander	3	1
Black	16	8
White	124	60
Hispanic (Puerto Rican, Mexican, Cuban, other)	23	11
Mixed/some other group	37	18
Current Living Situation		
A house or apartment (yours or parents)	160	77
A foster home or public housing	1	0
A friend's or relative's house or apartment	27	13
A nursing home, hospital, inpatient or residential	0	0
Jail, detention center or other correctional institution	7	3
Temporary or emergency shelter	1	0
Vacant buildings	1	0
Any other housing situation	11	5
Present work or school situation		
Working full time	4	2
Working part time	7	3
Unemployed or laid off	24	12
Have a job, but not working because of treatment, illness, seasonal	9	4
In school or training only (even if not in session now)	159	76
In jail or prison	1	0
Some other work situation	3	1

Item	N	%
Substance dependence (meeting criteria)	183	88
Substance treatment needed for		
Any kind of alcohol	72	35
Marijuana, hashish, etc.	122	59
Crack, freebase cocaine, other cocaine	10	5
Amphetamine/methamphetamine	43	21
Inhalants	0	0
Heroin	0	0
"Acid" or other hallucinogens	12	6
Some other drug	28	13
Age when first got drunk or used any drugs		
Below 15	195	94
15-18	13	6
Over 18	0	0
Last grade or year completed in school		
< 6	1	0
6 - 8	55	26
9 - 10	118	57
11 - 12	34	16
> 12	0	0
Times in life arrested, charged with a crime, and booked		
0	65	31
1-2	77	25
3+	63	30
Times in life admitted to drug treatment or counseling		
0	82	39
1-2	109	52
3+	17	8
	Mean	**SD**
Times in life arrested, charged with a crime, and booked	2.39	3.44
Substance use—last 90 days		
Days used alcohol, marijuana, or other drugs	53.62	28.62
Days drunk or high for most of the day	35.90	29.17

TABLE 11.4 *(continued)*

Item	N	%
Days in a jail (or other place) where you could not use drugs	14.44	22.60
Times in life admitted to drug treatment or counseling	1.07	1.97

evident in their peer group, with 86 percent reporting drug use among peers and 74 percent reporting high levels of alcohol use (got drunk weekly or had five or more drinks in a day) among peers. There is a higher prevalence of social and cognitive deficits. A greater number of youths have educational deficits, school failure, and chronic truancy patterns. Higher prevalence of deviant identity formation, e.g., gang affiliation, earlier onset of drug use (M = 11.7 years), and higher prevalence of poly-substance dependence is found. In a review of adolescent treatment research wherein factors associated with relapse or noncompletion of treatment were identified, very similar factors were found to be most closely associated with poorer treatment outcomes (Catalano et al., 1991; Hubbard et al., 1985; McMenamy, 1996; Winters, Latimer, and Stinchfield, 1999). Hence, Thunder Road is working with adolescents who present with an array of factors that elevate risk and, in the aggregate, contribute a greater likelihood of less successful treatment outcomes (Knapp et al., 1991; NIDA, 1999). In fact, many have previous treatment failures. Among those in the CDRH track, 62 percent report having received previous treatment for their alcohol or drug use, while prior treatment episodes are reported by 55 percent of those in the group home track.

In addition to factors that the identified adolescent brings, his or her family and kin networks are often strained or dysfunctional. Many clients and client families have experienced trauma, loss, and hardship. Identifying an adolescent's substance use will often be one of many complex issues which must be addressed before healthy lifestyles and developmental growth can be reestablished, or in certain cases, established. Working toward rehabilitation and/or habilitation is a considerable challenge. Since each teenager's drug-using behaviors are imbedded in a psychosocial and behavioral constellation that is interconnected with the family, family systems become a key component of all therapeutic interventions.

The national ATM study will provide vital information on treatment needs, increase our understanding of cooccurring symptoms, patterns of drug use, vulnerability to relapse, and document service utilization patterns among these high-risk adolescents. It will yield answers about their involvement with the juvenile justice system and their status regarding education and employment. A more thorough examination of adolescents referred to residential treatment, and the opportunity to follow their progress after treatment, will facilitate our understanding of ways that adolescents differ from adults. Perhaps what is most important, the initiative delves inside the programs that deliver treatment services and provides an opportunity to examine specific treatment modalities while learning which approaches yield more successful outcomes.

REFERENCES

Adelman, H.S., Kaser-Boyd, N., and Taylor, L. (1984). Children's participation in consent for psychotherapy and their subsequent response to treatment. *Journal of Clinical Child Psychology,* 13:170-178.

Alford, G.S., Koehler, R.A., and Leonard, J. (1991). Alcoholics Anonymous-Narcotics Anonymous model inpatient treatment of chemically dependent adolescents: A 2-year outcome study. *Journal of Studies on Alcohol,* 52:111-126.

Catalano, R.F., Hawkins, J.D., Wells, E.A., Miller, J., and Brewer, D. (1991). Evaluation of the effectiveness of adolescent drug abuse treatment, assessment of risks for relapse, and promising approaches for relapse prevention. *International Journal of the Addictions,* 25:1085-1140.

De Leon, G. (1994). The therapeutic community: Toward a general theory and model. In F. Tims, G. De Leon, and N. Jainchill (Eds.), *Therapeutic Community: Advances in Research and Application* (pp. 16-53). NIDA Research Monograph Series, Number 144. DHHS Pub. No. (ADM) 94-3633. Rockville, MD: National Institute on Drug Abuse, 16-53.

De Leon, G. (1997). Therapeutic communities: Is there an essential model? In G. DeLeon (Ed.), *Community as Method: Therapeutic Communities for Special Population and Special Settings* (pp. 1-18). Westport, CT: Praeger Publishers/Greenwood Publishing Group, Inc.

Hubbard, R.L., Cavanaugh, E.R., Craddock, S.G., and Rachel, J.V. (1985). Characteristics, behaviors and outcomes for youth in TOPS. In A.S. Friedman and G.M. Beschner (Eds.), *Treatment Services for Adolescent Substance Abusers* (pp. 49-65). Washington, DC: USDHHS. 49-65.

Jainchill, N. (1997). Therapeutic communities for adolescents: The same and not the same. In G. DeLeon (Ed.), *Community as Method: Therapeutic Communities for Special Population and Special Settings* (pp. 161-177). Westport, CT: Praeger Publishers/Greenwood Publishing Group, Inc.

Kendall, P.C. and Williams, C.L. (1986). Therapy with adolescents: Treating the "marginal man," *Behavior Therapy,* 17:522-537.

Knapp, J., Templer, D., Cannon, W.G., and Dobson, S. (1991). Variables associated with success in an adolescent drug treatment program. *Adolescence,* 26:305-317.

Makela, K., Arminen, I., Bloomfield, K., Eisenbach-Stangl, I., Bergmark, K., Kurube N., Mariolini N., Olafsdottir, H., Peterson, J., Philips, M., Rehm, J., Room, R., Roseneqvist, P., Rosovsky, H., Stenius, K., Swiatkiewicz, G., Woronowica, B., Zielinski, A. (1996). *Alcoholics Anonymous as a Mutual-Help Movement: A Study in Eight Societies.* Madison, WI: University of Wisconsin Press.

McLellan, A.T., Lewis, D.C., O'Brien, C.P., and Kleber, H.D. (2000). Drug dependence, a chronic medical illness: Implications for treatment, insurance, and outcomes evaluation. *Journal of the American Medical Association,* (284)13: 1689-1695.

McMenamy, R.N. (1996). Treatment outcomes in an adolescent chemical dependency program. *Adolescence,* 31(121):91-107.

National Institute on Drug Abuse (NIDA) (1999). *Principles of Drug Addiction Treatment: A Research-Based Guide.* Bethesda, MD: National Institutes of Health, USDHHS. NIH Publication No. 99-4180.

Sells, C.W. and Blum, R.W. (1996). Current trends in adolescent health. In R.J. DiClemente, W.B. Hansen, and L.E. Ponton (Eds.), *Handbook of Adolescent Health Risk Behavior: Issues in Clinical Child Psychology* (pp. 5-34). New York: Plenum Press.

Shaw, S. and Borkman, T. (Eds.) (1990). *Social Model Alcohol Recovery: An Environmental Approach.* Burbank, CA: Bridge Focus, Inc.

Spear, S.F., Ciesla, J.R., and Skala, S.Y. (1999). Relapse patterns among adolescents treated for chemical dependency. *Substance Use Misuse,* 34(13):1795-1815.

Wheeler, K. and Malmquist, J. (1987). Treatment approaches in adolescent chemical dependency. *Pediatric Clinics of North America* (34):437-447.

Windle, M., Shope, J.T., and Bukstein, O. (1996). Alcohol use. In R.J. DiClemente, W.B. Hansen, and L.E. Ponton (Eds.), *Handbook of Adolescent Health Risk Behavior* (pp. 115-154). New York: Plenum Press.

Winters, K.C., Latimer, W.L., and Stinchfield, R.D. (1999). Adolescent treatment. In P.J. Ott, R.E. Tarter, and R.T. Ammerman (Eds.), *Sourcebook on Substance Abuse: Etiology, Epidemiology, Assessment, and Treatment* (pp. 350-361). Boston, MA: Allyn and Bacon.

Index

Page numbers followed by the letter "b" indicate boxed material; those followed by the letter "f" indicate figures; and those followed by the letter "t" indicate tables.

SPECIAL 25%-OFF DISCOUNT!
Order a copy of this book with this form or online at:
http://www.haworthpressinc.com/store/product.asp?sku=4680

ADOLESCENT SUBSTANCE ABUSE TREATMENT IN THE UNITED STATES
Exemplary Models from a National Evaluation Study

_____in hardbound at $44.96 (regularly $59.95) (ISBN: 0-7890-1606-0)
_____in softbound at $29.96 (regularly $39.95) (ISBN: 0-7890-1607-9)

Or order online and use Code HEC25 in the shopping cart.

COST OF BOOKS_____

OUTSIDE US/CANADA/
MEXICO: ADD 20%_____

POSTAGE & HANDLING_____
*(US: $5.00 for first book & $2.00
for each additional book)
Outside US: $6.00 for first book
& $2.00 for each additional book)*

SUBTOTAL_____

IN CANADA: ADD 7% GST_____

STATE TAX_____
*(NY, OH & MN residents, please
add appropriate local sales tax)*

FINAL TOTAL_____
*(If paying in Canadian funds,
convert using the current
exchange rate, UNESCO
coupons welcome)*

☐ **BILL ME LATER:** ($5 service charge will be added)
(Bill-me option is good on US/Canada/Mexico orders only;
not good to jobbers, wholesalers, or subscription agencies.)

☐ Check here if billing address is different from
shipping address and attach purchase order and
billing address information.

Signature_____

☐ **PAYMENT ENCLOSED: $**_____

☐ **PLEASE CHARGE TO MY CREDIT CARD.**

☐ Visa ☐ MasterCard ☐ AmEx ☐ Discover
☐ Diner's Club ☐ Eurocard ☐ JCB

Account # _____

Exp. Date_____

Signature_____

Prices in US dollars and subject to change without notice.

NAME_____

INSTITUTION_____

ADDRESS_____

CITY_____

STATE/ZIP_____

COUNTRY_____ COUNTY (NY residents only)_____

TEL_____ FAX_____

E-MAIL_____

May we use your e-mail address for confirmations and other types of information? ☐ Yes ☐ No
We appreciate receiving your e-mail address and fax number. Haworth would like to e-mail or fax special
discount offers to you, as a preferred customer. **We will never share, rent, or exchange your e-mail address
or fax number.** We regard such actions as an invasion of your privacy.

Order From Your Local Bookstore or Directly From
The Haworth Press, Inc.
10 Alice Street, Binghamton, New York 13904-1580 • USA
TELEPHONE: 1-800-HAWORTH (1-800-429-6784) / Outside US/Canada: (607) 722-5857
FAX: 1-800-895-0582 / Outside US/Canada: (607) 722-6362
E-mailto: getinfo@haworthpressinc.com
PLEASE PHOTOCOPY THIS FORM FOR YOUR PERSONAL USE.
http://www.HaworthPress.com   BOF02